JOURNAL FOR THE STUDY OF THE NEW TESTAMENT SUPPLEMENT SERIES
135

Executive Editor
Stanley E. Porter

Sheffield Academic Press

A Text-Critical Study
of the Epistle of Jude

Charles Landon

Journal for the Study of the New Testament
Supplement Series 135

This book is dedicated to Dr Esbeth van Dyk in recognition
of her friendship and kindness during my stay in Stellenbosch

Copyright © 1996 Sheffield Academic Press

Published by Sheffield Academic Press Ltd
Mansion House
19 Kingfield Road
Sheffield S11 9AS
England

Printed on acid-free paper in Great Britain
by Bookcraft Ltd
Midsomer Norton, Bath

British Library Cataloguing in Publication Data

A catalogue record for this book is available
from the British Library

ISBN 1-85075-636 8

CONTENTS

Preface

The assertion that Jude has been neglected by modern scholars is less valid now than it was when Douglas Rowston described it as 'the most neglected book in the New Testament', but we still lack a comprehensive text-critical analysis of Jude. This work investigates textual variation throughout Jude and is identical in content to my Stellenbosch doctoral dissertation. It is my firm belief that the Greek text of the New Testament should be reconstructed with much greater reliance upon internal evidence than is apparent in modern editions such as GNT4, a belief which is reflected in this experimental attempt to reconstruct the Greek text of Jude.

I am very thankful to have benefited during my doctoral candidature from the wise and thoughtful advice of my tutor Dr Johan Thom on grammar and rhetoric, and from the expert guidance of my co-tutor Dr Kobus Petzer on matters text-critical. My greatest debt of gratitude is to these two scholars, both of whom offered me all of the support and encouragement I needed.

Several helpful improvements were suggested by Dr J.K. Elliott, Reader in New Testament Textual Criticism at the University of Leeds, and I am very thankful for these. As a disciple of Dr Elliott, I was greatly honoured by his positive evaluation of my work.

Fr L. Arnold at the Vatican, Professor R.J. Bauckham of St Andrews, Miss L. Hunt of Oxford, Professor G.J.C. Jordaan of Potchefstroom, Professor G. van W. Kruger of Stellenbosch, Dr E. Wendland of Lusaka and Dr W. Whallon of Michigan are all cordially thanked for helping in the search for secondary literature. Dr J. Botha of Stellenbosch is thanked for his interesting and constructive criticism of my work. Mej. L. Bonthuys of Stellenbosch is thanked for her diligence in processing my two grant applications: financial assistance was generously provided by the University of Stellenbosch and by the HSRC respectively. Finally, I would like to thank Professor S.E. Porter for accepting my work into the JSNT Supplement Series and everyone responsible for evaluating and typesetting the MS.

New Testament quotations are from GNT4 unless otherwise indicated. References to Professor B.M. Metzger's *Textual Commentary* are to the second edition unless otherwise indicated. Abbreviations for MSS, fathers and early versions are identical to those in the introduction to GNT4, except that papyri are cited with unraised numerals.

ABBREVIATIONS

AnBib	Analecta Biblica
ANRW	Aufstieg und Niedergang der römischen Welt
ANTF	Arbeiten zur neutestamentlichen Textforschung
BAGD	Bauer *et al.*, *Lexicon*
BA	*Biblical Archaeology*
BDF	Blass, Debrunner and Funk, *Grammar*
BETL	Bibliotheca ephemeridum theologicarum lovaniensium
BFBS2	Kilpatrick, Η ΚΑΙΝΗ ΔΙΑΘΗΚΗ
Bib	*Biblica*
Bover	Bover, *Novi Testamenti*
BSac	*Bibliotheca Sacra*
BT	*The Bible Translator*
CBQ	*Catholic Biblical Quarterly*
De Zwaan	De Zwaan, *II Petrus en Judas*
Diglot	Kilpatrick, *Greek-English Diglot*
EFN	Estudios de *Filología Neotestamentaria*
ETL	*Ephemerides theologicae lovanienses*
ExpTim	*Expository Times*
GNTMT	Hodges, *Majority Text*
GNT4	Aland *et al.*, *The Greek New Testament*
HTR	*Harvard Theological Review*
IGNTP	The International Greek New Testament Project
Int	*Interpretation*
JB	The Jerusalem Bible
JBL	*Journal of Biblical Literature*
JETS	*Journal of the Evangelical Theological Society*
JSNT	*Journal for the Study of the New Testament*
JSNTSup	*Journal for the Study of the New Testament*, Supplement Series
JTS	*Journal of Theological Studies*
LXX	Rahlfs, *Septuaginta*
LCL	Loeb Classical Library
LN	Louw and Nida, *Lexicon*
LSJ	Liddell, Scott and Jones, *Lexicon*
Merk	Merk, *Novum Testamentum*
MHT	Moulton, Howard and Turner, *Grammar*

NA26	Aland *et al.*, *Novum Testamentum Graece*
NDT	Ferguson *et al.*, *New Dictionary of Theology*
NEB	*The New English Bible*
Neot	*Neotestamentica*
NovT	*Novum Testamentum*
NovTSup	*Novum Testamentum*, Supplement Series
NTS	*New Testament Studies*
NTSSA	The New Testament Society of South Africa
NTTS	New Testament Tools and Studies
RB	*Revue Biblique*
ResQ	*Restoration Quarterly*
RSV	The Holy Bible, *Revised Standard Version*
SBL	The Society of Biblical Literature
SBLDS	SBL Dissertation Series
SBLSP	SBL Seminar Papers
SD	Studies and Documents
SJT	*Scottish Journal of Theology*
SNTS	The Society for New Testament Studies
SNTSMS	SNTS Monograph Series
SPCK	The Society for Promoting Christian Knowledge
TEV	*Today's English Version*
Tischendorf	Tischendorf, *Novum Testamentum Graece*
TR	The Textus Receptus
TZ	*Theologische Zeitschrift*
UBS	The United Bible Societies
Vogels	Vogels, *Novum Testamentum*
von Soden	von Soden, *Neuen Testaments*
WH	Westcott and Hort, *New Testament*
WTJ	*Westminster Theological Journal*
WUNT	Wissenschaftliche Untersuchungen zum Neuen Testament
ZNW	*Zeitschrift für die neutestamentliche Wissenschaft*

Grammatical Abbreviations

A	adjective
AS	adjective or substantive
DA	definite article
PN	pronoun
PR	preposition
QG	qualifying genitive
S	substantive
SP	substantive governed by a preposition
Π	πᾶς

General Abbreviations

hom.	*homoioteleuton*
HSRC	Human Sciences Research Council, South Africa
om.	omit
vid	evidently (word in MS unclear)

Chapter 1

INTRODUCTION

1. *Research Aims*

The present work aims to provide an eclectic text-critical analysis of Jude. Its secondary aim is to evaluate the extent to which the text of Jude in GNT4 can be described as an eclectic text.

2. *Preamble*

Despite the fact that 'considering the brevity of Jude, the textual critical problems are numerous and difficult',[1] thus far few of the 25 verses in Jude have generated text-critical discussions in journals and monographs. As an *eclectic* text-critical study of Jude, the present work attempts to treat all of the major textual problems in a systematic way. The need for an eclectic *text-critical* study of Jude will become apparent as eclecticism is defined and substantiated later in this introduction. The need for an eclectic text-critical study of Jude is evident since neither of the two existing textual studies of Jude can be regarded as complete. C.A. Albin's Swedish exegetical and textual commentary on Jude contains notes on some of the internal aspects relating to 21 variation units.[2] Sakae Kubo's study of the relationship between 𝔓72 and B in

---

1.   R.J. Bauckham, 'The Letter of Jude: An Account of Research', ANRW II.25.5 (1988), p. 3792.
2.   See C.A. Albin, *Judasbrevet. Traditionen, Texten, Tolkningen* (Stockholm: Natur och Kultur, 1962), pp. 590-631. Most of these pages are taken up with an admirably detailed critical apparatus. Whatever the merits of *Judasbrevet* as an exegetical commentary, it falls far short of being a comprehensive internal text-critical study of Jude. The comments which Albin makes at the end of each verse in his text-critical section are for the most part extremely brief, and he has no comment to make on variation at vv. 2, 6, 7, 8, 9, 10, 11, 17, 19, 20 and 24 except: 'Inga textkritiska problem föreligger'. Direct quotations from *Judasbrevet* hereafter will be from the German summary.

Jude and 2 Peter contains notes on 20 variation units in Jude, but like Albin's work it does not aspire to be a complete text-critical study.[3] In addition to these works, there have been several studies on textual problems in individual verses in Jude. These will be cited and commented on as they are encountered.

Three factors can be enumerated in favour of Jude as a suitable text for an eclectic text-critical study: (1) Jude has never been subjected to an exhaustive text-critical analysis; (2) the author has a consistent style; and (3) much pioneering material on exegesis, style and rhetoric of the author has been published since the publication of the works by Albin and Kubo mentioned above.[4] Exegesis, style and rhetoric in particular are vital intrinsic criteria which must be considered in any internal text-critical analysis. The text of Jude is ideally suited to the rigours of an internal study not least because the author is scrupulously consistent in adhering to certain stylistic and rhetorical techniques.[5]

3. Defining and Substantiating an Eclectic Approach

The Definition

The OED provides us with the following definition for the word 'eclectic':

---

3.   See S. Kubo, *𝔓72 and the Codex Vaticanus* (SD, 27; Salt Lake City: Utah University Press, 1965), pp. 58-59; 84-92; and 140-47.

4.   Examples are: E.E. Ellis, 'Prophecy and Hermeneutic in Jude', in E.E. Ellis (ed.), *Prophecy and Hermeneutic in Early Christianity: New Testament Essays* (WUNT, 18; Tübingen: Mohr & Siebeck, 1978); R.J. Bauckham, *Jude, 2 Peter* (Waco: Word, 1983); D.F. Watson, *Invention, Arrangement and Style: Rhetorical Criticism of Jude and 2 Peter* (SBLDS, 104; Atlanta: Scholars Press, 1988); J.D. Charles, 'Literary Artifice in the Epistle of Jude', *ZNW* 82 (1991), pp. 106-24. For a critique of Watson's work, see E.R. Wendland, 'A Comparative Study of "Rhetorical Criticism" Ancient and Modern: With Special Reference to the Larger Structure and Function of the Epistle of Jude', *Neot* 28 (1994), pp. 193-228. As Wendland points out, Jude's overall rhetorical structure is more likely to be Hebrew-Semitic than Graeco-Roman; though, as Watson has shown, Graeco-Roman rhetorical devices are evident at the level of individual phrases and sentences. To avoid confusion, reference will be made henceforth to Jude's midrash structure rather than to its 'Hebrew-Semitic' rhetorical design.

5.   Bauckham, *Jude, 2 Peter*, p. 142, has described Jude 4-18 in particular as 'a piece of writing whose detailed structure and wording has been composed with exquisite care'. The issue of Judan style is explained in more depth later in this introduction.

eclectic, a. and sb. [ad. Gr. ἐκλεκτός, f. ἐκλέγ-ειν to select]. **A.** adj.
1. In ancient use, the distinguishing epithet of a class of philosophers
who neither attached themselves to any recognized school, nor constructed independent systems, but *selected* [italics mine] such doctrines as
pleased them in every school. Diogenes Laertius speaks of an 'eclectic
sect' founded by Potamon of Alexandria in the second century after
Christ. In mod. times this designation has been for similar reasons given
to or assumed by various philosophers, notably V. Cousin, and it is also
applied to those who combine elements derived from diverse systems of
opinion or practice in any science or art. So also eclectic method, system,
etc. **2.** More vaguely: That borrows or is borrowed from diverse sources.
Also, of persons or personal attributes: *Unfettered by narrow system in
matters of opinion or practice* [italics mine]; broad, not exclusive, in matters of taste. **3.** In etymological nonce-uses. a. Made up of 'selections'.
b. That *selects* [italics mine], does not receive indiscriminately. **B.** sb. a.
An adherent of the Eclectic school of philosophy. b. One who follows the
eclectic method; one who finds points of agreement with diverse parties or
schools.

The key words in the definition above are 'selected' and 'selects'. To
this definition it can be added that the word 'eclectic' is understood by
modern New Testament textual critics to refer to the selection of text-
critical criteria which are relevant to a given problem, or to the selection
of a reading from a variety of readings preserved in various MSS.[6] It
should be stated at the outset that eclectic New Testament textual critics
can be divided into two main groups: (1) eclectic generalists; and
(2) thoroughgoing eclectics. Thoroughgoing eclecticism has been developed and practised mainly by George Kilpatrick and Keith Elliott, and
concentrates on internal evidence at points of variation in the New
Testament text. By contrast, eclectic generalism relies upon a combination of internal and external evidence. As J.H. Petzer has pointed out,
eclectic generalists form the majority of textual critics, and constitute
two groups: (1) reasoned eclectics; and (2) local genealogists.[7] Reasoned
eclecticism is espoused by American critics such as Bruce Metzger,

---

6. E.J. Epp and G.D. Fee, *Studies in the Theory and Method of New Testament Textual Criticism* (SD, 45; Grand Rapids: Eerdmans, 1993), pp. 141-73, esp.
p. 142, where Epp reminds the reader that the first person to use the word 'eclectic'
in the context of New Testament textual criticism was the French critic L. Vaganay in
1934.

7. J.H. Petzer, 'Eclecticism and the Text of the New Testament', in
J.H. Petzer and P. J. Hartin (eds.), *Text and Interpretation: New Approaches in the
Criticism of the New Testament* (NTTS, 15; Leiden: Brill, 1991), pp. 50-54.

Gordon Fee and Bart Ehrman. Local genealogy was developed by Kurt Aland and is presently practised by Barbara Aland and by Petzer himself. Of these critics, Ehrman has perhaps shown the greatest willingness to allow internal evidence to override external evidence, and is thus procedurally as close to a thoroughgoing approach as his reasoned ideology will allow.[8] Thoroughgoing eclecticism is the main focus of attention in this introductory chapter.

Eldon Jay Epp asserts that the term thoroughgoing eclecticism is a 'terminological inconsistency' because its adherents are supposedly limited in their eclecticism because of their exclusive concentration on internal evidence. This assertion presupposes that the term 'eclectic' refers to the practice of selecting from a range of text-critical canons, rather than to the practice of selecting readings from MSS. Epp is aware of this presupposition and posits that the term 'thoroughgoing eclecticism' is not a misnomer if it is meant to be understood as a reference to an open choice of readings from any MSS rather than a choice from criteria. Such an eclecticism is thoroughgoing in as much as 'it never swerves from...openness to every extant reading'.[9] Elliott confirms that thoroughgoing eclecticism involves choosing from readings: '[Thoroughgoing eclecticism] is concerned with finding plausible explanations based on internal considerations to justify the choice of one reading as original and the others as secondary'.[10] An important feature of thoroughgoing eclecticism has escaped Epp's attempt at defining it, but is crucially visible in our OED definition: '...of persons or personal attributes: Unfettered by narrow system in matters of opinion or practice'. It could be argued that thoroughgoing eclecticism is unfettered from adherence to the range of external canons which channels our preferences in the narrow direction of a 'best' MS or a 'best' group of MSS. This is what

8.   An example is Ehrman's preference for ὁ μονογενὴς υἱός at Jn 1.18 as outlined later in this introduction.

9.   Epp and Fee, Th*eory and Method*, p. 171.

10.   J.K. Elliott, 'Rational Criticism and the Text of the New Testament', *Theology* 75 (1972), pp. 338-43. The term 'rational criticism' in the title of this essay is slightly misleading since Elliott used it here as a synonym for thoroughgoing eclecticism at a time when his methodology and terminology were both at early stages of development. The distinction is that whereas rational criticism is now used to refer to criticism which involves the internal evaluation of a given *individual* MS, thoroughgoing eclecticism involves restoring the New Testament text from as many extant MSS and readings as possible on the basis of internal evidence. The similarity is that both approaches concentrate on internal evidence.

distinguishes thoroughgoing eclecticism from eclectic generalism: the former does not rely upon the alleged external superiority of MSS to choose from variant readings in the New Testament, whereas the latter often does.

Beyond these distinctions, part of the definition given by Carlo Martini for eclecticism generally sees it as the product of a measure of dissatisfaction with external evidence:

> (1) Dissatisfaction with external evidence. Neither individual manuscripts (as B ℵ D), nor families (as Fam. 13 or Fam. 1) nor local texts (as Alexandrian or Caesarean) can give sufficient support to establish at least the probability of a reading against another. Therefore all the principles accepted so far are seen as no longer valid. Westcott and Hort (1882) gave great value to the concordance of B and ℵ; von Soden generally preferred the reading of H and I against K, except when there was a Tatian reading or a harmonization. All these kinds of procedures are abandoned as unsatisfactory.[11]

Martini differentiates between eclecticism in a broad sense (he does not actually use the term 'thoroughgoing' to describe this broader eclecticism) and what he calls 'an eclectic procedure in the constitution of a critical text'.[12] The latter is possibly comparable with reasoned eclecticism, since it 'acknowledges the importance of historical text types for the decision on variants'.[13] Martini adds of the UBS committee's procedure[14] for analysing variants in Acts that 'in cases of doubt...transcriptional and intrinsic probabilities control the decision'.[15] Thoroughgoing eclectics would maintain that what Martini says of Acts ('that the original text cannot be found exclusively in one single historical text type') is

---

11.   C.M. Martini, 'Eclecticism and Atticism in the Textual Criticism of the Greek New Testament', in M. Black and W.A. Smalley (eds.), *On Language, Culture and Religion in Honour of Eugene A. Nida* (The Hague: Mouton, 1974), p. 150.

12.   Martini, 'Eclecticism and Atticism', p. 150.

13.   Martini, 'Eclecticism and Atticism', p. 151.

14.   The UBS committee which Martini refers to has lost some of its original members in recent years. A new UBS committee was responsible for the publication of GNT4. The companion volume to GNT4 is B.M. Metzger, *A Textual Commentary on the Greek New Testament: A Companion Volume to the United Bible Societies' Greek New Testament (Fourth Revised Edition)* (Stuttgart: Deutsche Bibelgesellschaft, 2nd edn, 1994). This new *Textual Commentary* contains input both from the original UBS committee members and from their superseders.

15.   Martini, 'Eclecticism and Atticism', p. 151.

valid for the entire New Testament text. When I reach Martini's conclusion, I realise that he is not advocating a truly thoroughgoing form of eclecticism:

> ...'eclecticism' should be always connected with a careful study and evaluation of the manuscript tradition. This study may reveal that there is a certain favourable presumption on the trustworthiness of certain manuscripts because they were transmitted in a situation which was not influenced by the trend of stylistic emendation which was felt at other places and times. It may be that after all the basic intuition of Westcott and Hort of the value of the old Alexandrian tradition has much to commend itself even today.[16]

Martini's implication here that some MSS escaped stylistic emendation is misleading: no MS (Alexandrian or otherwise) is free of corruption. Although Martini admits to a 'dissatisfaction with external evidence' in accounting for the rise of eclecticism, I may note here his approval of a 'careful study and evaluation of the manuscript tradition...[based on] the trustworthiness of certain manuscripts'.[17] The idea that certain MSS are more trustworthy than others is problematic for thoroughgoing eclectics for reasons which will be made clear below.

A final feature of thoroughgoing eclecticism is a reluctance to view conjectural emendation as an ideal solution to textual problems in the New Testament.[18] Four main arguments against conjectural emendation emerge from an essay by Kilpatrick on the subject: (1) critics may agree that a given passage is corrupt, but they seldom agree that a given conjecture is satisfactory; (2) the sort of conjectures directed at ironing out awkward expressions may obscure evidence about an author's stylistic peculiarities; (3) conjectures may represent what an author intended to write rather than what he actually wrote; and (4) if one is engaged in the process of identifying and rejecting deliberate scribal improvements, it hardly makes sense to propose one's own improvements.[19]

16.   Martini, 'Eclecticism and Atticism', p. 155.
17.   Martini, 'Eclecticism and Atticism', p. 150.
18.   Conjectural emendation occurs when a critic or an editor feels that the original reading at a given point of variation in an ancient text has been lost and introduces a reading of his own. Emendation among modern critics is sometimes driven by a wish to demonstrate intimate knowledge of an ancient language.
19.   G.D. Kilpatrick, 'Conjectural Emendation in the New Testament', *The Principles and Practice of New Testament Textual Criticism: Collected Essays of G.D. Kilpatrick* (BETL, 96; ed. J.K. Elliott; Leuven: Leuven University, 1990), pp. 98-109. Kilpatrick was responding in this essay to the opposite viewpoint as

The Development of Thoroughgoing Eclecticism
Most handbooks on New Testament textual criticism provide informa-
tion on the stages by which a critical text was developed and on the factors which influenced these stages, so it will suffice here to give a brief
outline of the origin and development of thoroughgoing eclecticism. In a
sense, any critic who devotes attention to internal evidence in the evaluation of a given variant reading can be described as eclectic, though the
focus here is upon individuals whose critical work is most strongly
influenced by considerations such as style, context and theology. In his
account of the development of eclecticism, Bruce Metzger has identified
Bernhard Weiss as the first critical scholar to produce an edition of the
Greek New Testament based mainly upon internal evidence.[20]

In the early twentieth century, scholars realized that the evidence of
mixture in all New Testament MSS meant that an archetype could not be
recovered through a genealogical tree, since the lines of descent are
fragmented and impure. It was the failure of genealogy as a method of
reaching back to the original New Testament text which led Marie-
Joseph Lagrange to adopt a methodology known as rational criticism,
whereby the quality of individual MSS was evaluated according to how
well they stood up to internal evidence at points of variation in the text.
It is very clear from Lagrange's comments on harmonization, correction, omission, addition and mistakes in ℵ and B that he did not advocate
unquestioning loyalty to what Elliott has described as the 'cult' of the
best manuscripts.[21]

In his critical and exegetical notes on Mark, C.H. Turner shifted the
emphasis from MSS to individual readings, replacing Hort's proposition
that 'knowledge of documents should precede final judgment upon

expressed by J. Strugnell, 'A Plea for Conjectural Emendation in the New
Testament, with a Coda on 1 Cor. 4.6', *CBQ* 36 (1974), pp. 543-58.

20.   B.M. Metzger, *The Text of the New Testament: Its Transmission, Corruption and Restoration* (Oxford: Clarendon Press, 2nd edn, 1968), pp. 176; 137-38.

21.   M.-J. Lagrange, *Études Bibliques: Introduction à l'étude du Nouveau Testament: Deuxième Partie. Critique Textuelle II: La Critique Rationelle* (Paris:
Gabalda, 1935), pp. 86-87; 94-95; 101. Other exponents of this sort of textual criticism are J.N. Birdsall, 'Rational Eclecticism and the Oldest Manuscripts: A Comparative Study of the Bodmer and Chester Beatty Papyri of the Gospel of Luke', in
J.K. Elliott (ed.), *Studies in New Testament Language and Text: Essays in Honour
of George D. Kilpatrick on the Occasion of His Sixty-Fifth Birthday* (NovTSup, 44;
Leiden: Brill, 1976), pp. 39-51, and G. Zuntz, *The Text of the Epistles: A Disquisition upon the Corpus Paulinum* (London: Oxford University, 1953).

readings' with the proposition that 'knowledge of an author's usage should precede final judgment alike as to readings, as to exegesis'.[22] The extent and nature of Turner's contribution to the development of an eclectic approach to New Testament textual criticism is explained in some detail by Elliott.[23] Turner's insights into Marcan style 'knocked a big hole in the WH theory of the text'.[24] Although Turner respected the work of WH, he differed with them at points of variation in Mark where 'Western' MSS contained readings which Turner accepted as original on grounds of Marcan style. However, it would appear that Turner was not willing to apply his eclectic approach to readings other than those pre-served in 'Western' or Alexandrian MSS.[25] The challenge which remained for Kilpatrick and Elliott, and which they accepted as a logical extension of Turner's approach to the text of Mark, was to attempt to extend Turner's criteria to all New Testament MSS and to every New Testament author.

Taking his cue from Turner's approach to Mark, Kilpatrick did much to develop eclecticism as an approach which should be used for all New Testament MSS, and for the entire New Testament, and from 1958 to 1962 he released the fascicles of his *Greek-English Diglot for the Use of Translators* for private circulation. Kilpatrick defined and demonstrated the application of a new internal text-critical canon: Atticism.[26] Elliott (one of Kilpatrick's Oxford doctoral students) continued Kilpatrick's work on Atticism and defended the approach of thoroughgoing eclecticism in num-erous contributions to critical seminars and international journals. Elliott's major contribution has been to highlight the many respects in which a truly eclectic text of the New Testament would differ from the Nestle-Aland and UBS editions of the Greek New Testament and to substan-tiate the eclectic approach to textual problems with practical examples.[27]

---

22.   C.H. Turner, 'Marcan Usage: Notes, Critical and Exegetical on the Second Gospel', *JTS* 25 (1924), p. 377, reprinted in J.K. Elliott (ed.), *The Language and Style of the Gospel of Mark: An Edition of C. H. Turner's 'Notes on Marcan Usage' Together with Other Comparable Studies* (NovTSup, 71; Leiden: Brill, 1993), p. 3.

23.   Elliott, *Language and Style of the Gospel of Mark*, pp. xiii-xix.

24.   Elliott, *Language and Style of the Gospel of Mark*, p. xvii.

25.   Elliott, *Language and Style of the Gospel of Mark*, pp. xvii-xviii.

26.   I will look at Atticism in more detail below.

27.   As an example of Elliott's work, I may cite his review of NA26, one of the most detailed theological book reviews ever written: see J. K. Elliott, 'An Examina-tion of the Twenty-Sixth Edition of Nestle-Aland *Novum Testamentum Graece*', *JTS* 32 (1981), pp. 19-49.

Additionally, Elliott was the first scholar to give formal expression to thoroughgoing eclecticism as a text-critical methodology.[28]

The History of the Text and its Implications
Although several attempts have been made to describe the early history of the New Testament text, not enough progress has yet been made to break the deadlock between the position of Elliott and Kilpatrick, on the one hand, and that of eclectic generalists, on the other. To complicate matters further, those who do not accept the position of thoroughgoing eclectics regarding the history of the text are themselves divided into several mutually incompatible groups.

To highlight the diversity of opinion which still exists concerning the early history of the New Testament text: Aland argues that the 'Western' text is an early derivative of the Alexandrian text;[29] Christian-Bernard Amphoux defends the priority of the 'Western' text over against the Alexandrian text;[30] and Zane Hodges argues for the originality of a predominantly Byzantine form of text.[31] Meanwhile, the position of Kilpatrick and Elliott is that many variant readings in the New Testament already existed by 200 AD, and that it is impossible to argue that any single text type has (to use the terminology of H.J.M. Milne and T.C. Skeat) a 'monopoly of the truth'.[32] The mere fact of such lack of

28. See J.K. Elliott, *The Greek Text of the Epistles to Timothy and Titus* (SD, 36; Salt Lake City: Utah University Press, 1968), pp. 1-14.
29. At an international conference held at Notre Dame University in 1988, B. Aland asserted that we have no evidence of the 'Western' text in the second century, an assertion opposed by Helmut Koester who demanded an explanation for numerous 'Western' readings found in Justin Martyr and other writers. The conference papers were subsequently published in W.L. Petersen (ed.), *Gospel Traditions in the Second Century: Origins, Recensions, Text, and Transmission* (Notre Dame: Notre Dame University Press, 1989).
30. L. Vaganay and C.-B. Amphoux, *An Introduction to New Testament Textual Criticism* (trans. J. Heimerdinger; Cambridge: Cambridge University Press, 1986), pp. 91-98.
31. Concerning the latter standpoint, see Epp and Fee, *Theory and Method*, p. 100, where Epp asks: 'Am I being facetious only to a limited extent when I ask, If [a text similar to] the TR can still be defended, albeit in merely a pseudo-scholarly fashion, how much solid progress have we made in textual criticism in the twentieth century?'
32. For further details, see G.D. Kilpatrick, 'The Transmission of the New Testament and Its Reliability', *BT* 9 (1958), pp. 127-36, esp. pp. 128-29; J.K. Elliott, *Essays and Studies in New Testament Textual Criticism* (Estudios de *Filología*

certainty among scholars about the early history of the text underscores the justification for a method which does not place emphasis on external evidence: this, at any rate, will apply at least until the theoretical history of the New Testament text which is being developed at Münster is revealed to us in its entirety.

Epp has criticized those who practise thoroughgoing eclecticism for ignoring the history of the New Testament text. Epp says that thoroughgoing eclectics would not be likely to alter their procedures for establishing the New Testament text even if 'by some miracle' a definitive reconstruction of the history of early New Testament transmission should appear.[33] To this Elliott has responded that there is no denying that there was an early history of the text, but that Epp would be more justified in his criticism if he 'is able to point out what the history of the New Testament text was and how proponents of thoroughgoing eclecticism ignore or reject it'.[34] The charge that thoroughgoing eclecticism ignores the history of the text has been answered thus:

> Now we point out that far from lacking a sense of history the proponents of [thoroughgoing] eclecticism are very much aware of it. In fact, the very practice of the kind of eclecticism which produces reasons how the secondary readings arose positively encourages such an historical approach. It is, however, not the kind of history of documents which tries to explain the rise of alleged major recensions, nor is it an attempt to trace the genealogical pedigree of manuscripts. Rather it tends to be a history of textual variation, which is a different thing altogether.[35]

This refusal to work from the assumption that a given group of MSS is superior or inferior on grounds of either geography or genealogy is a major feature of the approach of Kilpatrick and Elliott. E.C. Colwell has warned that 'the theory of so-called local texts is a snare and a delusion'.[36] To this Elliott has added that 'the New Testament textual tradition is so confused that neither genealogical trees nor even geographically located text types can be established in any detail'.[37] As

Neotestamentaria, 3; Cordoba: Ediciones el Almendro, 1992), pp. 17-37, esp. pp. 26-27 and pp. 36-37; *idem, Timothy and Titus*, pp. 1-3.

33.   Epp and Fee, *Theory and Method*, p. 172.

34.   Elliott, *Essays and Studies*, p. 37.

35.   Elliott, *Essays and Studies*, p. 37.

36.   E.C. Colwell, *Studies in Methodology in Textual Criticism of the New Testament* (NTTS, 9; Leiden: Brill, 1969), p. 83.

37.   Elliott, *Essays and Studies*, p. 27.

Petzer has explained, the earliest period of the transmission of the New Testament text is viewed by Kilpatrick and Elliott as having been 'basically uncontrolled and unstable', with text types not going back far enough to be a norm 'for determining the readings of the original text'.[38] This view of the history of the text has profound implications for an approach to the reconstruction of the New Testament text. If it is accepted that the early history of the text was unstable, without fixed lines of transmission and without geographically located text types, by implication, minimal attention must be devoted to external evidence in the handling of textual variation.[39] An approach based on the rationale of thoroughgoing eclecticism, therefore, implies two broad principles: (1) readings should be considered on internal merit rather than on alleged external strength; and (2) readings can and should be accepted with allegedly weak external attestation if internal considerations support it.

Kilpatrick has been criticized by Metzger for printing readings in the *Greek-English Diglot* with 'the most meagre external support'.[40] But as Elliott has pointed out, the UBS editors have printed readings with weak external support at Jn 3.27; Col. 2.2; Acts 16.12, Acts 4.33 and Heb. 12.3.[41] At other points of variation, Metzger expresses a preference for weakly attested readings but is outvoted by his fellow UBS committee members.[42] The UBS committee is therefore not itself immune

38. J.H. Petzer, 'The History of the New Testament Text: Its Reconstruction, Significance and Use', in B. Aland and J. Delobel (eds.), *New Testament Textual Criticism, Exegesis and Church History: A Discussion of Methods* (Contributions to Biblical Exegesis and Theology, 7; Kampen: Kok Pharos, 1994), p. 30. As Petzer points out in this same chapter, Helmut Koester has also expressed the view that the earliest period of the transmission of the New Testament text was unstable.

39. The phrase '*minimal* attention to external evidence' is used with deliberate precision. See n. 49 for further details.

40. Metzger, *Text*, p. 178. Among the examples of such readings cited by Metzger are ἔκραζον at Mt. 20.30; *om.* εἶπεν at Mt. 22.1; ἀκούσας δὲ ὁ βασιλεὺς ἐκεῖνος at Mt. 22.7; τὰ ὄρη at Mk 5.11; ἀποκριθεὶς αὐτῷ at Mk 9.17; εἰς ἐμέ at Mk 14.6; ἐλάλει μᾶλλον at Mk 14.31; ἐστήριζεν at Lk. 9.51; ἀληθής at Jn 19.35; ἔργων τὴν πίστιν μου at Jas 2.18; ἀπέχεσθαι ὑμᾶς at 1 Pet. 2.11 and πλήρης at 2 Jn 8.

41. J.K. Elliott, 'In Defence of Thoroughgoing Eclecticism in New Testament Textual Criticism', *ResQ* 21 (1978), pp. 104-105.

42. In the same article, Elliott refers to the comments in Metzger's *Textual Commentary* at Mk 10.2; Acts 2.38, 10.16, 25.17, 26.4; 1 Cor. 6.11, 10.2; 2 Cor. 4.6, 4.14; Gal. 1.15; 1 Thess. 2.7; and 1 Pet. 5.10.

from the criticism levelled at thoroughgoing eclecticism that the latter encourages critics to accept readings with allegedly weak attestation.

Quoting Colwell, Fee has taken Kilpatrick and Elliott to task for their reluctance to allow external evidence to shape any given text-critical verdict on the grounds that this reluctance 'relegates the manuscripts to the role of supplier of readings'.[43] Elliott's response to this charge is worth quoting in full, not least because it reinforces the point that the original reading at a given point of variation in the New Testament may occur in any MS, irrespective of the age or text type of that MS:

> Unless one is able to point to one manuscript as the sole possessor of the monopoly of original readings, one is bound to use manuscripts in this way. Unless one is able to reject the peculiar readings of any particular manuscript as untrustworthy (as one is occasionally able to do with certain MSS if it can be demonstrated that its singular and subsingular readings are the aberrations of its particular scribe), then the whole gamut of available manuscripts is at one's disposal. The recent discoveries of papyri whose texts support the previously singular or subsingular readings of, say, a late Byzantine MS make it impossible to reject out of hand, as some editors of Greek New Testaments have done, the peculiar readings of the Byzantine Manuscripts.[44]

This last point of Elliott's reminds me of another dimension to his eclectic approach: a willingness to consider readings in the TR and in GNTMT on intrinsic merit. Kilpatrick and Elliott have both defended individual readings in the TR and in GNTMT, but without ever advocating majoritarianism.[45] Elliott says:

> Often the Textus Receptus does preserve a text which represents the words of the original author where older codices do not. The age of a manuscript should be no guide to the originality of its text. One should not assume that a fourth-century manuscript will be less corrupt than say a twelfth-century one.[46]

43. Epp and Fee, *Theory and Method*, p. 127.
44. Elliott, 'In Defence', pp. 97-98.
45. The term 'majoritarianism' here refers to the belief held by Z. Hodges, W. Pickering and others that the Majority text (the Byzantine text type as reflected in the majority of extant New Testament MSS) represents the original New Testament text. The difference between the Majority text and the TR is explained, for example, by D.B. Wallace, 'The Majority Text and the Original Text: Are They Identical?' *BSac* 148 (1991), pp. 150-69. A noteworthy discussion of the Majority text debate is provided in Epp and Fee, *Theory and Method*, pp. 183-208.
46. J.K. Elliott, 'Can We Recover the Original New Testament?' *Theology* 77 (1974), p. 343.

In his chapter in the MacGregor memorial volume, Kilpatrick supports with practical examples the following assertion: the different sorts of accidental and deliberate changes normally associated with Byzantine MSS (such as harmonization, conflation, stylistic corrections, omission through hom., the deliberate expurgation of Semitic idioms, and the changing of Koine to Attic Greek) can be found in any New Testament MS, not excluding א and B.[47] Kilpatrick credits the three Catholic New Testament text editors—Vogels, Merk and Bover—with accepting some Byzantine readings on intrinsic merit. Metzger has categorized Bover's text in particular as an eclectic one, 'departing frequently from the Alexandrian type of text'.[48]

Conclusion
From my attempt to define and substantiate eclecticism, it should be apparent that the 'eclectic ideal' referred to in the research aims is the ideal of thoroughgoing eclecticism, an approach which I am now in a position formally to define:

> *Thoroughgoing eclecticism is a text-critical methodology which aims to reconstruct the original text of the New Testament from extant New Testament MSS by relying mainly on internal evidence to choose the best reading whenever the MSS divide, which places minimal reliance on external evidence, and which places minimal reliance upon conjectural emendation.*[49]

47. G. D. Kilpatrick, 'The Greek New Testament Text of Today and the Textus Receptus', in H. Anderson and W. Barclay (eds.), *The New Testament in Historical and Contemporary Perspective: Essays in Honour of G.H.C. MacGregor* (Oxford: Blackwell, 1965), pp. 189-206. For examples of Kilpatrick's preference for certain Byzantine readings, see also *idem*, 'Atticism and the Text of the Greek New Testament', *Collected Essays of G.D. Kilpatrick*, pp. 15-32.

48. Metzger, *Text*, p. 144.

49. I have chosen my words with deliberate care here. Since Elliott has advocated that an occasional appeal may be made to rational-critical arguments in the analysis of some variation units, it would be oversimplifying matters to claim that his approach involves an *exclusive* concentration on internal evidence. It would be more accurate to say that he relies much more heavily upon internal evidence than any of his fellow textual critics. The circumstances under which rational-critical arguments may be used in an approach based on thoroughgoing eclecticism are made clear in Elliott, 'In Defence', pp. 97-98. An applicable example in Jude occurs at variation unit 10.3 below, where I have rejected the singular reading διαφθείρονται because of a scribal peculiarity in Ψ. This is *not* an attempt to make any claim about the

The discussion which follows will illustrate a few of the respects in which GNT4 falls short of this eclectic ideal, thereby highlighting the need for a systematic study such as this in which an attempt is made to determine the extent to which the text of a given author as printed in GNT4 can be described as eclectic.

4. *Practising an Eclectic Approach*

The comments on internal evidence which follow are motivated by an imperative to show exactly how the internal canons are viewed by adherents of thoroughgoing eclecticism and to highlight some of the problems which can arise from the handling of internal evidence. Epp has provided a list of internal criteria which will serve as an outline for the discussion:

1. A variant's status as the shorter or shortest reading
2. A variant's status as the harder or hardest reading
3. A variant's fitness to account for the origin, development, or presence of all other readings
4. A variant's conformity to the author's style...vocabulary [and use of rhetoric]
5. A variant's conformity to the author's theology or ideology
6. A variant's conformity to Koine (rather than Attic) Greek
7. A variant's conformity to Semitic forms of expression
8. A variant's lack of conformity to parallel passages or to extraneous items in its context generally
9. A variant's lack of conformity to Old Testament passages
10. A variant's lack of conformity to liturgical forms and usages
11. A variant's lack of conformity to extrinsic doctrinal views.[50]

With the exception of majoritarians such as Hodges who are reluctant to discuss internal evidence, most critics would accept that Epp's list as

superiority or inferiority of a given MS such as Ψ: it is merely to reject a *particular* reading on the grounds of a *specific* scribal peculiarity.

50. Epp and Fee, *Theory and Method*, pp. 163-64. Although for our purposes rhetoric has been subsumed under the fourth canon, if in future years textual critics pay more attention to the interrelationship between rhetoric and textual variation, then rhetoric may become an internal canon in its own right. Ellis ('Prophecy and Hermeneutic', p. 225) has shown that the midrash in Jude 4-19 comprises a series of 'texts' and 'commentaries', and that verbs in the texts are mostly aorist, and verbs in the commentaries are mostly present, a deduction which is important at several variation units. Jude's use of Graeco-Roman rhetorical devices at the level of individual verses as shown by Watson is also an important intrinsic consideration.

cited above is an acceptable and accurate representation of the different sorts of internal evidence one might be expected to discuss. These canons concern transcriptional probability (the accidental or deliberate changes a scribe is likely to have made), and intrinsic probability (what the author is likely to have written).[51]

The Shortest Reading

Exponents of thoroughgoing eclecticism regard this canon as problematic and seldom invoke it. The GNT4 editors appear to have based a decision on this canon at Lk. 24.53, for which they supply the following apparatus:

αινουντες και ευλογουντες   A C² W Δ Θ Ψ *Lect*
ευλογουντες   𝔓75 ℵ B C* L syr^{s,pal} cop^{sa,bo} geo
αινουντες   D it^{a,b,d,e,ff2} Augustine

The longer reading αἰνοῦντες καὶ εὐλογοῦντες is rejected by them as a conflation of the two shorter readings.[52] Against this view, Kilpatrick has argued that the longer reading is original and that the two shorter readings arose through hom. due to the similar endings (ΟΥΝΤΕΣ— ΟΥΝΤΕΣ) of αἰνοῦντες and εὐλογοῦντες.[53] The UBS committee's verdict in favour of εὐλογοῦντες is defended by reference to the older MSS in which εὐλογοῦντες is preserved, a standpoint which ignores the possibility that the longer reading αἰνοῦντες καὶ εὐλογοῦντες could predate MSS such as A. The transcriptional and external arguments in favour of εὐλογοῦντες at Lk. 24.53 are clearly not decisive, and this example illustrates that the canon of the shorter or shortest reading needs, where possible, to be invoked not in isolation, but with supporting intrinsic evidence.[54]

The Hardest Reading

The second of our canons has been defined by J.J. Griesbach as follows:

---

51. This distinction has been made, for example, by R.L. Omanson, 'A Perspective on the Study of the New Testament Text', *BT* 34 (1983), p. 110.
52. Metzger, *Textual Commentary*, pp. 163-64.
53. Kilpatrick, 'Textus Receptus', p. 191.
54. To this discussion I should add that, as Metzger points out in his textbook, there are other situations where a longer reading should be selected in preference to a shorter one if it can be demonstrated (1) that hom. has occurred, or (2) that there has been a deliberate scribal omission.

> The more difficult and more obscure reading is preferable to that in which
> everything is so intelligible and cleared of difficulties that every scribe is
> easily able to understand it.[55]

It is important here that a 'difficult' reading should be difficult, not impossible. But where should the line be drawn?

Perhaps a good example of a difficult reading is ἐποιεῖτε at Jn 8.39 preserved in 𝔓75 א* B² D W and others, accepted by the UBS committee on the grounds that other variants at this variation unit 'arose in an effort to make a more grammatically "correct" condition'.[56] Another example occurs at Jn 8.53, where the original UBS committee would print πατρὸς ἡμῶν as a difficult reading in view of the fact that its exclusion from some MSS appears to have been deliberate.[57]

This canon may perhaps be a good way of expressing a conclusion at a given unit, but I am also required (as Elliott would express it) to explain why and how the variation came about. I would therefore hesitate before invoking this canon mechanically and instead perhaps see it as one among several ways of formally articulating the *results* of a discussion.[58]

The Reading Which Explains All Other Readings
The internal canon whereby we should select the reading which explains the origin or presence of rival readings is very similar to Griesbach's eleventh canon:

> The reading is preferable, among many in the same place, that lies
> midway between the others, that is, the reading that, as it were, holds
> together the threads in such a way that, if this reading is admitted as origi-
> nal, it becomes obvious how or, better stated, by what origin in error all
> the other readings have arisen from it.[59]

---

55.   This canon has been translated from the original Latin in Epp and Fee, *Theory and Method*, p. 151. Epp is reliant upon H. Alford, *The Greek Testament* (4 vols.; Chicago: Moody, 1968 [1875]), where Griesbach's canons are reprinted.

56.   Metzger, *Textual Commentary*, pp. 192-93.

57.   This decision is substantiated in the first edition of Metzger's *Textual Commentary*, p. 226, but although the substantiating comment has been removed from the second edition of the same commentary, the decision is upheld in GNT4.

58.   For more detail on this canon, see, for example, E.A. Nida, 'The "Harder Reading" in Textual Criticism: An Application of the Second Law of Thermodynamics', *BT* 33 (1981), pp. 430-35.

59.   Translated in Epp and Fee, *Theory and Method*, p. 152.

At Heb. 9.10 the UBS committee would print βαπτισμοῖς, δικαιώ-
ματα preserved in 𝔓46 ℵ* A I P 33 and other MSS on the grounds that
this reading best explains the origin of rival readings.[60] At Jn 7.39
πνεῦμα read in 𝔓66ᶜ 𝔓75 ℵ T Θ Ψ and others is regarded by the same
committee members as the reading from which all other readings at the
same unit developed.[61]

The point cannot be overstressed that this canon should never be
invoked as a substitute for a full discussion of the evidence wherein it is
explained why one particular reading is seen as the precursor of its rivals
and why the arguments for rival readings are unconvincing. Like the
second canon, this third canon should be seen as a means of articulating
results rather than as a shortcut to unsubstantiated verdicts.

The Writer's Style
Of paramount importance to thoroughgoing eclecticism is the criterion
relating to an author's style and vocabulary.[62] One of Fee's defences of
reasoned eclecticism is that WH's high opinion of ℵ and B was based not
on genealogy, but on internal evidence. But Elliott's work on style
shows recurrently that WH's internal judgments were sometimes
superficial, and so, as a consequence, where they have followed superficial decisions in WH, the same criticism can be levelled at the GNT4
editors.[63] Eclecticism (whether generalist or thoroughgoing) demands
that I consider the author's style as an important intrinsic factor at points
of variation in the New Testament text, but Elliott's work has shown

60.   This decision is substantiated in the first edition of Metzger's *Textual
Commentary*, p. 668, and upheld in GNT4.
61.   Metzger, *Textual Commentary*, p. 186. A clear case of conflation in B and
other MSS, it seems to me, is πνεῦμα ἅγιον δεδομένον at the same variation unit.
62.   Style is usefully defined by J.E. Botha, 'A Study in Johannine Style:
History, Theory and Practice', (DTh disssertation; Pretoria: University of South
Africa, 1989), p. 59, as a contextually determined phenomenon, implying a consideration of aspects such as phonology, vocabulary, syntax, grammar, semantics, and
social and literary contexts.
63.   See, for example, J. K. Elliott, 'Jerusalem in Acts and the Gospels', *NTS*
23 (1977), pp. 462-69; *idem*, 'Κηφᾶς: Σίμων Πέτρος: ὁ Πέτρος: An Examination
of New Testament Usage', *NovT* 14 (1972), pp. 241-56; *idem*, 'Μαθητής with a
Possessive in the New Testament', *TZ* 35 (1979), pp. 300-304; *idem*, 'An Eclectic
Textual Commentary on the Greek Text of Mark's Gospel', in E.J. Epp and
G.D. Fee (eds.), *New Testament Textual Criticism, Its Significance for Exegesis:
Essays in Honour of Bruce M. Metzger* (Oxford: Clarendon, 1981), pp. 47-60.

that both WH and the GNT4 editors often fail to allow the style of a given New Testament author to shape their judgments.

The example of Mk 12.23 illustrates, simultaneously, the apparent desire of the GNT4 editors to consider the author's style and the presuppositions they hold about 'best' MSS which prevent them from invoking this internal canon in a thoroughgoing fashion. At Mk 12.23 the preferences of Elliott, WH and the GNT4 editors respectively are as follows:

Elliott	ἐν τῇ ἀναστάσει ὅταν ἀναστῶσιν
WH	ἐν τῇ ἀναστάσει
GNT4	ἐν τῇ ἀναστάσει [ὅταν ἀναστῶσιν]

The decision against WH in GNT4 here is made because 'the pleonasm [in the longer reading] is in accord with Mark's style'.[64] This is possibly as close as the GNT4 editors get to invoking the style canon in a thoroughgoing fashion.

At other points of variation in Mark,[65] the GNT4 editors again rely upon the perceived superiority of their 'best' MSS, ignore the matter of the writer's style, and follow WH more often than not:

1.27	Elliott	τίς ἡ διδαχὴ ἡ καινὴ αὕτη
	GNT4, WH	διδαχὴ καινή
1.41	Elliott	ὀργισθείς
	GNT4, WH	σπλαγχνισθείς
5.22	Elliott	*om.* ὀνόματι Ἰάϊρος
	GNT4	ὀνόματι Ἰάϊρος
	WH	ὀνόματι Ἰάειρος
6.3	Elliott	τοῦ τέκτονος υἱός
	GNT4, WH	τέκτων, ὁ υἱός
6.22	Elliott	θυγατρὸς αὐτῆς τῆς Ἡρῳδιάδος
	GNT4, WH	θυγατρὸς αὐτοῦ Ἡρῳδιάδος
6.41	Elliott	μαθηταῖς αὐτοῦ
	GNT4	μαθηταῖς [αὐτοῦ]
	WH	μαθηταῖς
8.13	Elliott	πάλιν ἐμβὰς εἰς τὸ πλοῖον
	GNT4, WH	πάλιν ἐμβὰς ἀπῆλθεν εἰς τὸ πέραν

64. Metzger, *Textual Commentary*, p. 93.
65. Elliott's preferences for Mark are cited from *Essays and Studies*, pp. 159-70.

11.24	Elliott	λαμβάνετε
	GNT4, WH	ἐλάβετε
11.31	Elliott	τί εἴπωμεν
	GNT4, WH	ἐὰν εἴπωμεν

Elliott's preferences as shown above reflect the priority he accords to Marcan style in dealing with variation. The inferences are clear: (1) a truly eclectic text of Mark would differ with WH and GNT4 on grounds of the writer's style at many points of variation; (2) it *cannot* be taken for granted that the GNT4 editors have properly considered the writer's style at points of variation elsewhere in the New Testament text.

Petzer has drawn my attention to the respects in which the style canon is problematic. Focusing on the logion problem at Lk. 23.34, he makes the following important observations: (1) thoroughgoing eclecticism depends for its results partly upon the presupposition that a given author has a consistent style; (2) it is sometimes difficult to prove whether a given word in a variant reading (such as Πάτερ in the logion at Lk. 23.34) authenticates the variant on stylistic grounds, or whether the same given word was introduced by a scribe as an attempt to imitate the style of the author; and (3) the style canon is especially problematic for Paul and Luke-Acts, since Pauline style can vary from book to book, and since stylistic patterns change in Luke-Acts.[66]

With Jude as the focus of an eclectic study, Petzer's first and third observations pose minimal difficulty, (1) because the author has a consistent style; and (2) because the special problems posed by Pauline books and Luke-Acts for an eclectic study are not applicable to Jude. Petzer's second observation (that scribes can imitate an author's style in making changes) poses a serious challenge to any eclectic textual study, the only possible response being that it necessitates that stylistic evidence should be examined with great accuracy and care, and that, where possible, supporting intrinsic and transcriptional evidence should be cited. Although Petzer's concluding remark on style and theology—'on its own, however, this evidence can never be used to solve textual problems'—may appear daunting to critics who rely heavily on intrinsic evidence, I am reassured by the important role assigned to style in his

---

66. Petzer, 'Eclecticism', p. 49; pp. 58-59. See also G. van W. Kruger, *Die skrywers van die Nuwe Testament* (Stellenbosch: Universiteits-Uitgewers, 1981), pp. 36-37, where it is explained that the Pauline letters can be divided into no less than five groups on grounds of style and vocabulary.

rational-critical study of the text of D in Acts 14.7-20.[67] Petzer's general point at Lk. 23.34, meanwhile, is important: the style canon is indeed problematic in different ways, a fact which is taken into consideration in my concluding chapter.

Since style is such a prominent eclectic criterion, those aspects of style and language special to Jude which will be of significance in the resolution of textual problems are here outlined. It is possible to show that Jude does indeed have a consistent and distinctive style. To begin with, Jude contains fourteen words not found elsewhere in the New Testament, and if we include *hapax legomena* which are unique to Jude and 2 Peter, the figure rises to twenty-two.[68] The presence of so many *hapax legomena* in such a short text has implications for my handling of transcriptional evidence at some points of variation in Jude: scribes habitually substituted unfamiliar words with familiar words, and the possibility of such substitution having been effected must always be considered whenever a *hapax legomenon* is not firm in the text in Jude.[69] Meanwhile Daryl Charles has drawn my attention to five other major features of Judan style: (1) triadic illustration; (2) catchwords; (3) synonymous parallelism; (4) paronomasia; (5) contrast or antithesis.[70] Eclectic verdicts on variation units in Jude often rely on one or more of these five aspects of style, each of which will be explained in greater detail as it is encountered.[71] Additionally, the writer's conformity to certain set expressions and word order patterns common in New Testament Greek, together with the distinctive rhetorical structure of his letter, all serve to confirm an impression of stylistic consistency.[72]

67.   J.H. Petzer, 'The Lystre Healing in the Codex Bezae (Acts 14.7-20)', in J.H. Barkhuizen, H.F. Stander and G.J. Swart (eds.), *Hupomnema: Feesbundel opgedra aan Prof. J.P. Louw* (Pretoria: Pretoria University, 1992), pp. 175-87.

68.   Bauckham, *Jude, 2 Peter*, p. 6; J. Gunther, 'The Alexandrian Epistle of Jude', *NTS* 30 (1984), p. 551.

69.   For further detail on *hapax legomena* in Jude, see, for example, variation unit 7.3.

70.   See Charles, 'Literary Artifice', pp. 111-23.

71.   For further detail on textual variation and the major features of Judan style, see, for example, variation units 1.3 (catchwords), 2.2 (triadic illustration), 8.4 (synonymous parallelism), 15.1 (paronomasia) and 19.1 (contrast or antithesis).

72.   Such conformity and consistency is shown, for example, at variation unit 6.5 (word order), variation unit 8.2 (midrash rhetorical structure), and variation unit 13.5 (set expressions).

The Writer's Theology
The principle that we should choose the variant which conforms most closely to the author's theology or ideology is problematic for Petzer, who describes why in his estimation it cannot guide us towards a correct decision at Lk. 23.34, where we have to decide whether ὁ δὲ Ἰησοῦς ἔλεγεν, Πάτερ, ἄφες αὐτοῖς, οὐ γὰρ οἴδασιν τί ποιοῦσιν belongs in the text of Luke or in the apparatus:

> The logion [at Lk. 23.34] seems at first sight also in accord with Lucan theology, since there are parallel occurrences of the ignorance motif in Acts (3.17, 13.27)... Whether the theology of this reading is in accord with Lucan theology is... not so certain and depends upon interpretation. It could just as easily be shown why it is not in accord with Lucan theology if other matters are being emphasized. The fact that Jesus prays for forgiveness, has, for example, no parallel and seems in direct opposition to the way in which Jesus is generally pictured in the Third Gospel, i.e. as having the power to forgive vested in him.[73]

Petzer argues ultimately for the exclusion of the logion at Lk. 23.34 on external grounds. The UBS committee members have printed the logion within double square brackets, indicating a reading of 'evident antiquity and importance' (to borrow the expression from GNT4), but one which is not regarded as original.[74] Against these positions, John Nolland has argued recently that five internal factors justify the inclusion of the logion at Lk. 23.34.[75] Petzer's point is well taken that theological evidence can be handled subjectively, but Nolland's argument is not exclusively reliant upon the theological criterion.

Another instance of the handling of theological evidence is provided by Earle Ellis.[76] The main problem at 1 Cor. 14.34-35 for some scholars is that despite its inclusion (albeit at different places) by all MSS,

---

73. Petzer, 'Eclecticism', pp. 58-59.

74. See Metzger, *Textual Commentary*, p. 154, for further details.

75. See J. Nolland, *Luke 18.35–24.53* (Dallas: Word, 1993) pp. 1141-44, whose arguments can thus be summarized: (1) a parallel exists between the logion at Lk. 23.34 and a similar prayer made by Stephen (cf. Acts 7.60); (2) the logion accords with Lucan style; (3) the logion contains the Lucan motif of ignorance (cf. Acts 3.17, 13.27, 17.30); (4) the logion emphasizes forgiveness (cf. Lk. 1.17; 24.47); and (5) the logion embodies the teaching of Jesus on loving one's enemy (cf. Lk. 6.27-28). Two of these arguments are altogether excluded from Petzer's analysis of variation at Lk. 23.34.

76. E.E. Ellis, 'The Silenced Wives of Corinth (1 Cor. 14.34-5)', *Essays in Honour of Bruce M. Metzger*, pp. 213-20.

1 Cor. 14.34-35 appears to be in conflict with Paul's teaching at 1 Cor. 11.2-16.[77] Against this theory, Ellis advances six theologico-contextual arguments.[78] Ellis ties these strands together by showing that the cultural context makes the inclusion of 1 Cor. 14.34-35 theologically acceptable:

> [1 Cor. 14.34-35] reflects a situation in which the husband is participating in the prophetic ministries of a Christian meeting. In this context the coparticipation of his wife, which may involve her publicly 'testing' (διακρίνειν, 14.29) her husband's message, is considered to be a disgraceful (αἰσχρόν) disregard of him, of accepted proprieties, and of her own wifely role. For these reasons it is prohibited.[79]

This insightful handling of theological evidence by Ellis is the best answer to those who regard the textual problem at 1 Cor. 14.34-35 as intrinsically insoluble.[80] The fact of disagreement among scholars about

77. C. Holsten, *Das Evangelium des Paulus. Teil I* (Berlin: Reimer, 1880), pp. 495-97; and J. Weiss, *Der erste Korintherbrief* (Göttingen: Vandenhoeck & Ruprecht, 1970 [1910]), pp. 342-43, both regard 1 Cor. 14.33b-36 as a non-Pauline interpolation. These works are cited in Ellis, 'Silenced Wives', p. 213.

78. Ellis, 'Silenced Wives', pp. 213-18, defends 1 Cor. 14.34-35 thus: (1) the possible common source for 1 Cor. 14.34-35 and 1 Tim. 2.11-15 need not imply that 1 Cor. 14.34-35 is post-Pauline; (2) theological differences in New Testament documents need not be interpreted 'in terms of chronological distance'; (3) 1 Cor. 14.34-35 'is not a prohibition on the public ministry of women, as has traditionally been supposed, but is an ordering of the ministry of wives to accord with their obligations to their husbands'; (4) 'the marriage role regulates the ministry of women in 1 Cor. 11 and in 1 Cor. 14.34-35'; (5) 1 Cor. 14.26-40 'is concerned to regulate the ministry of pneumatics, in other words, those with gifts of inspired speech and discernment... The "silence" imposed on the wives (14.34) is regulative and is no different from that imposed on the tongue-speaker (14.28) or on the prophet (14.30)'; (6) λαλεῖν in 1 Cor. 14.34 refers to pneumatic gifts.

79. Ellis, 'Silenced Wives', p. 218.

80. Against those who have disputed the originality of 1 Cor. 14.34-35, Frederik Wisse's comment is surely correct: 'It would appear that such passages [as 1 Cor. 14.34-35] do not so much violate Paul's style and theology as offend the sensibilities of the modern reader'. For further discussion on these and other related verses, see F. Wisse, 'The Nature and Purpose of Redactional Changes in Early Christian Texts: The Canonical Gospels', in W.L. Petersen (ed.), *Gospel Traditions in the Second Century*, pp. 39-53 esp. pp. 39-41; J. Murphy-O'Connor, 'The Non-Pauline Character of 1 Corinthians 11.2-16?' *JBL* 95 (1976), pp. 615-21; W.O. Walker, '1 Corinthians 11.2-16 and Paul's Views Regarding Women', *JBL* 94 (1975), pp. 94-110; G.D. Fee, *The First Epistle to the Corinthians* (Grand Rapids: Eerdmans, 1987), pp. 696-710; and J.H. Petzer, 'Reconsidering the Silent Women

Lk. 23.34 and 1 Cor. 14.34-35 illustrates that the theological canon can be interpreted in different ways. However, the solution is surely to examine whether a given theological hypothesis coheres with other factors such as style and context. Whereas Petzer at Lk. 23.34 separates and isolates stylistic and theological evidence to underscore its inconclusivity, Nolland at the same variation unit and Ellis at 1 Cor. 14.34-35 both base their judgments upon a combination of as many overlapping internal factors as possible. It is interesting that the latter approach is adopted by Petzer himself when the demand exists for positive results.[81]

Regarding Jude's theology, the description of Jude as 'early Catholic' is based primarily upon a misinterpretation of v. 3.[82] 'Early Catholicism' had three features: (1) the gradual realization that no hope could be placed in the imminent Parousia; (2) institutionalization; and (3) increasing doctrinal orthodoxy.[83] By contrast, Jude's writing is permeated by explicit references to the imminent Parousia, there are no ecclesiastical terms in Jude which indicate institutionalization typical of 'early Catholicism', and v. 3 refers simply to the gospel itself, not to any formalized rule of faith.[84] Further, Jude's use of apocalyptic prophecy and eschatological typology does not prevent me from locating him before the 'early Catholic' period, since 'apocalyptic was a very considerable influence on the whole Christian movement from the very beginning'.[85] The identity of the opponents in Jude is another factor which makes a second-century 'early Catholic' date for Jude very improbable.[86] It is not likely that Jude was written later than the end of

---

of Corinth: A Note on 1 Corinthians 14.34-35', *Theologia Evangelica* 26.2 (1993), pp. 132-38.

81. See, for example, J.H. Petzer, 'Contextual Evidence in Favour of ΚΑΥΧΗΣΩΜΑΙ in 1 Corinthians 13.3', *NTS* 35 (1989), pp. 229-53; *idem*, 'Style and Text in the Lucan Narrative of the Institution of the Lord's Supper (Luke 22.19b-20)', *NTS* 37 (1991), pp. 113-29.

82. Bauckham, *Jude, 2 Peter*, p. 9; J.D. Charles, *Literary Strategy in the Epistle of Jude* (Scranton: University of Scranton Press, 1993), p. 56.

83. J.D.G. Dunn, *Unity and Diversity in the New Testament* (London: SCM Press, 1977), chap. 14, cited in Bauckham, *Jude, 2 Peter*, pp. 8-9.

84. Bauckham, *Jude, 2 Peter*, p. 9; Charles, *Literary Strategy*, p. 57.

85. Bauckham, *Jude, 2 Peter*, p. 10.

86. I.H. Eybers, 'Aspects of the Background of the Letter of Jude', *Neot* 9 (1975), pp. 118-19, shows that the heretics which are attacked in Jude's letter cannot be associated with second-century gnosticism, not least because the concept of

the first century AD.[87] The evidence suggests that Jude's theology is apocalyptic and eschatological rather than 'early Catholic', an important consideration at variation units 0.1 and 26.1.

The Influence of Atticism

Since scholars are still not agreed about the extent to which this canon may be invoked, it may be helpful to provide a brief overview of the main strands of opinion on Atticism. The link between the theory that most New Testament variants came into being prior to 200 AD and the Atticism theory was explained thus by Kilpatrick:

> But for the century AD 100–200 we have to count on Atticism as an effective force in literary fashion. For a book like John it meant that for the whole of the period during which the Gospel was liable to deliberate change Atticism was operative. On the other hand it was effective probably for only the last two thirds of the period during which the Pauline Epistles were exposed to the free treatment of their text.[88]

Gordon Fee disputed Kilpatrick's assumption that textual corruption derived primarily from the second century, and with it the thinking that 'the original text may be found anywhere in the later witnesses',[89] though Kilpatrick was not alone in asserting that the original text may be found anywhere among New Testament MSS.[90]

Fee's main objection to the Atticism theory was that it does not account for the failure of New Testament copyists to Atticize at every opportunity. The example he provided of this failure was the occurrence of ζῆν in the future middle without variation at Mt. 4.4, 9.18; Lk. 4.4,

---

'knowledge'—γνῶσις—is absent from vv. 2, 10, 19 and 20-21 where one might expect to find it, particularly at v. 10 where Jude uses the verb οἶδα instead of a derivative of γινώσκω. Meanwhile Bauckham has argued in his commentary that Jude's polemic is directed at antinomianism of the sort which existed at Corinth in the 50s, and in Asia in the 90s.

87.   Bauckham, *Jude, 2 Peter*, p. 13.
88.   Kilpatrick, 'Atticism', pp. 24-25.
89.   Epp and Fee, *Theory and Method*, p. 127.
90.   Much the same point is made by K. Aland, 'The Significance of the Papyri for Progress in New Testament Research', in J.P. Hyatt (ed.), *The Bible in Modern Scholarship* (London: Carey Kingsgate, 1966), pp. 339-40. Perhaps the distinction should be made that Aland's reference is to theoretical possibility only, whereas Kilpatrick regarded later witnesses as a practical source of readings which could be defended as original.

10.28; Rom. 1.17, 8.13, 10.5; Gal. 3.11, 3.12; and Heb. 10.38.[91] Fee contended further that scribes tended to refrain from Atticizing non-Greek expressions. Martini asked why, if there is an Atticizing corrector at work in Acts, 'did he not correct...passages [at] Acts 12.7, 22.18, 25.4?'[92] These arguments were countered by the point that 'scribes, even in the period before 200 AD, were not scrupulous in weeding out all unclassical expressions in order to conform the text to Attic standards'.[93]

Elliott's contribution to the advancement of Kilpatrick's work on Atticism was to illustrate the influence of Atticist stylists such as Phrynichus or Moeris in greater relief than was previously attempted.[94] One of Elliott's major criticisms of the UBS committee was that it has tended to invoke the Atticism canon selectively.[95] That the Atticism theory could pose a threat to א and B as 'favourite' MSS if invoked consistently can be inferred from Elliott's work on the implications of Atticism to various aspects of textual variation.[96]

91. Epp and Fee, *Theory and Method*, p. 134.

92. Martini, 'Eclecticism and Atticism', p. 153.

93. Elliott, *Essays and Studies*, pp. 65-66. For a detailed rebuttal of Martini's arguments in particular, see G.D. Kilpatrick, 'Eclecticism and Atticism', *Collected Essays of G.D. Kilpatrick*, pp. 73-79; idem, 'Atticism and the Future of ζῆν', *Collected Essays of G.D. Kilpatrick*, pp. 195-200.

94. See, for example, J.K. Elliott, 'Phrynichus' Influence on the Textual Tradition of the New Testament', *ZNW* 63 (1972), pp. 133-38; idem, 'Moeris and the Textual Tradition of the Greek New Testament', *Essays in Honour of George D. Kilpatrick*, pp. 144-52.

95. Elliott, *Essays and Studies*, pp. 31-32, asked why, if Atticism could be given as a reason by the UBS committee for rejecting the reading ἐκτενής at Acts 12.5, the same argument was deemed inapplicable at Acts 11.5 as an argument for rejecting the reading ἄχρι. Elliott's suggestion was that a majority of the UBS committee tend to invoke the Atticism canon to reject a variant only when the variant does not appear in certain 'favourite' MSS, such as א and B.

96. On Atticism and New Testament textual variation, see J.K. Elliott, 'Nouns With Diminutive Endings in the New Testament', *NovT* 12 (1970), pp. 391-98; idem, 'Temporal Augment in Verbs with Initial Diphthong in the Greek New Testament', *NovT* 22 (1980), pp. 1-11; idem, 'The Two Forms of the Third Declension Comparative Adjectives in the New Testament', *NovT* 19 (1977), pp. 234-39; idem, 'The Use of ἕτερος in the New Testament', *ZNW* 60 (1969), pp. 140-41. That Byzantine MSS are also prone to Atticist interference is underscored by Birdsall, 'Rational Eclecticism', p. 46.

As matters now stand, a situation of stalemate still persists, with Elliott maintaining his position, and Fee conceding that Atticism *may* be a factor at some points of variation, while insisting that scribes also made changes in a direction opposite to Atticism.[97] As a postscript to this debate, I may recall that one argument advanced by Fee against Kilpatrick's chronology for New Testament corruption (and therefore against Kilpatrick's expression of the Atticism theory) was that changes made to 𝔓66 show no reaction to heresy.[98] But against Fee here, I may cite Bart Ehrman's recent argument that the reading μονογενὴς θεός at Jn 1.18 (preserved in 𝔓66 and other MSS) represents an anti-adoptionist corruption of the text 'in which the complete deity of Christ is affirmed'.[99] 𝔓66 also shows a reaction to heresy at Jn 6.44, where the phrase *my* father (πατήρ μου) reinforces the idea that Jesus' real father is not Joseph but God.[100] The view that there is no reaction to heresy in 𝔓66 is plainly open to further question.

The Atticism theory has implications for word order variation, a knowledge and awareness of which can assist in making decisions at points of variation in the New Testament where we are faced with a choice between New Testament Greek and Attic word order, New Testament Greek word order being preferable. G.J.C. Jordaan's study of word order variation in New Testament Greek concentrates on examples from Luke.[101] Two areas of discussion are recalled here: order involving verbs and adjectives.

According to Jordaan, in Attic Greek the verb appears in most instances at the end of a sentence, whereas in New Testament Greek, the verb appears in most instances at the beginning of a sentence.[102] At Lk. 6.1, Jordaan rejects the variant τοὺς στάχυας καὶ ψώχοντες ταῖς

97.   The point that some deliberate changes were *anti-Atticistic* is also made, for example, by Metzger, *Text*, p. 179, who refers to the work of Wilhelm Schmid in this respect. At variation unit 4.1 in the analysis, the possibility is explored that anti-Atticistic corruption accounts for variation.

98.   Epp and Fee, *Theory and Method*, p. 127.

99.   B. D. Ehrman, *The Orthodox Corruption of Scripture: The Effect of Early Christological Controversies on the Text of the New Testament* (New York: Oxford University, 1993) p. 78.

100.   Ehrman, *Orthodox Corruption*, p. 57; p. 104 n. 64.

101.   G.J.C. Jordaan, *Die beoordeling van woordorde-variante in die manuskripte van die Griekse Nuwe Testament met besondere aandag aan die Evangelie van Lukas: 'n Metodologiese studie* (Potchefstroom: Westvalia, 1980).

102.   Jordaan, *Woordorde-variante*, pp. 28-33.

χερσὶν ἤσθιον in D it[d,e,f] arm because Luke never uses an imperfect indicative at the end of a sentence.

The usual position of the adjective in Attic Greek is between the article and the noun. Less common in Attic Greek is the order: article + noun + article + adjective. Also acceptable in Attic Greek is the order: noun + article + adjective.[103] So far as New Testament Greek is concerned, two factors determine adjectival positioning: (1) whether the substantive is articular or anarthrous, and (2) whether the agreeing adjective is qualitative or quantitative.[104] If the substantive is articular, then it may permissibly be positioned before or after the adjective. If the substantive is anarthrous, and if the agreeing adjective describes a *quality*, then the adjective is positioned after the substantive. If the substantive is anarthrous, and if the agreeing adjective describes a *quantity*, then the adjective is positioned before the substantive.[105] Jude's conformity to the New Testament Greek tendency in which qualitative adjectives are placed after anarthrous nouns is evident at vv. 7, 12, 13, 20 and 21, a tendency which will guide my judgment at several variation units.

The Influence of Semitism
The extent to which one can be guided by the principle that 'one [can be encouraged] to accept as original the more Semitic variant whenever this...[is] challenged by a normal Greek reading'[106] depends largely upon a given author's proclivity for expressions which are of Semitic derivation. The issue of Semitic style and New Testament writers has provoked sharp diversity of opinion among scholars, an example being Nigel Turner's claim that the parable of the Prodigal Son is 'full of Semitisms'.[107] It is hard to tell whether Moulton would have agreed with Turner in this respect: Moulton's suggestion that Luke 15 cannot have been translated from a Semitic original could be taken to imply a denial that there is the degree of influence suggested by Turner.[108] Turner cites the following expressions as evidence of Semitic influence

103. Jordaan, *Woordorde-variante*, p. 43.
104. BDF §474.
105. BDF §474.
106. Elliott, *Essays and Studies*, p. 32.
107. N. Turner, 'The Quality of the Greek of Luke-Acts', *Essays in Honour of George D. Kilpatrick*, p. 390.
108. MHT, II, p. 8. We should add here that Moulton does not deny the existence of Semitisms in Luke as a whole: see MHT, I, pp. 16-19 for further details.

in Luke 15: (1) twelve individual examples of Semitic expression including γαμίζειν ἐκ (a variant at v. 16) and ἐσπλαγχνίσθη (v. 20); (2) the Semitic position of the verb in the word order of sentences; and (3) the use of redundant participles such as ἀναστάς (v. 18) and ἀποκριθεὶς εἶπεν (v. 29).[109]

The phenomenon of Semitism as observed by Elliott can help us make choices at the following points of variation in the Gospels:

Mk 1.27	διδαχη καινη ℵ B L
	τις η διδαχη η καινη αυτη C K Δ
	διδαχη καινη αυτη Θ
Jn 8.51	τον εμον λογον 𝔓75 ℵ B C D L W Ψ
	τον λογον τον εμον 𝔓66 Θ f^1.13

At Mk 1.27 where there is variation, Elliott would accept the variant with ἡ διδαχὴ ἡ καινὴ αὕτη (article + substantive + article + adjective + demonstrative) on the grounds that such word order is Semitic and accords with this feature of the writer's style, and that the other variants at this unit are mostly attempts to improve upon such non-Greek word order.[110] Meanwhile at Jn 8.51, Elliott would print τὸν λόγον τὸν ἐμόν in 𝔓66 ℵ f^1.13 as the variant which conforms most closely to the writer's Semitic style.[111]

Turner has noted one or two Semitisms in Jude (at vv. 11, 17 and possibly 24) although their comparative rarity does not rule out Semitic *influence* upon Jude's Greek generally.[112] The distinction has been made that although Jude has a characteristically Hellenistic style, he is no less an exponent of biblical Greek than any canonical writer.[113] Possible additions to the examples noted by Turner are ἐκ γῆς Αἰγύπτου (v. 5);

109. Turner, 'Quality of the Greek of Luke-Acts', pp. 391-93. It should be remembered that Turner's theories on Semitism do not enjoy universal acceptance among modern scholars. For a critique of Turner's approach and results, see G.H.R. Horsley, *New Documents Illustrating Early Christianity: Volume 5, Linguistic Essays* (Macquarie: Macquarie University Press, 1989), pp. 49-65. The issue of possible Semitic influence on New Testament Greek is a complex one and is explored along with other related subjects in a very useful introductory overview by S.E. Porter in S.E. Porter (ed.), *The Language of the New Testament: Classic Essays* (JSNTSup, 60; Sheffield: Sheffield Academic Press, 1991), pp. 11-38.

110. Elliott, *Essays and Studies*, pp. 162-63.

111. Elliott, *Essays and Studies*, p. 32.

112. MHT, IV, pp. 139-40.

113. MHT, IV, p. 139.

ὀπίσω with the genitive (v. 7); θαυμάζοντες πρόσωπα (v. 16); ἐπ᾽ ἐσχάτου χρόνου[114] (v. 18); and ἀγάπη at v. 21 'through the influence of the construct state'.[115] Although this canon can sometimes be invoked with confidence in Jude, if it conflicts with the style canon then it is necessary to consider the way in which Jude reworks Jewish source material for stylistic purposes.[116]

Lack of Conformity to Parallel Passages
To say that a variant's lack of conformity to parallel passages gives it preference over against other variants is to express the idea that a variant is preferable because it is not the product of harmonization. This canon is based upon an argument by silence: namely that because a passage has no New Testament parallel, it must be original. At Mk 7.28 the variant ναί, κύριε read in ℵ B and others is derived from the parallel passage in Mt. 15.27 and is therefore rightly rejected by the UBS committee.[117] At the same unit, κύριε preserved in 𝔓45 D W and other MSS is deemed original because it resists conformity to the parallel in Mt. 15.27.[118] Parallels between Jude and 2 Peter call for careful handling of the evidence, since where there is variation at both of two given parallel phrases or passages, theoretically one could argue in either direction. Wherever possible, decisions based on this canon need to be strengthened by supporting intrinsic evidence.

LXX Quotations
According to this canon, which is a version of the harmonization theory, if a passage is being quoted from the LXX by a New Testament writer, and if the New Testament writer makes slight changes to the quotation, scribal tendencies incline towards 'correcting' the LXX quotation to bring it into harmony with the LXX itself. If there are no complicating factors, where there is variation involving a LXX quotation in the New Testament, one should accept the reading least like the LXX source and reject variants which bring the LXX quotation into harmony with the LXX itself. On the grounds that 'the reading least like the LXX is likely

---

114. I have accepted ἐπ᾽ ἐσχάτου χρόνου against GNT4: see variation unit 18.3 for further details.
115. These examples are cited in Bauckham, *Jude, 2 Peter*, p. 6; p. 104.
116. See variation unit 2.2 for an example of this sort of conflicting evidence.
117. Metzger, *Textual Commentary*, p. 82.
118. Metzger, *Textual Commentary*, p. 82.

to be original, other things being equal', Elliott at 1 Tim. 5.18 would print βοῦν ἀλοῶντα οὐ κημώσεις preserved in D 1739 as original, against GNT4.[119] Elliott argues that βοῦν ἀλοῶντα οὐ κημώσεις in D 1739 was deliberately altered because it does not conform to the LXX quotation from Deut. 25.4 and because κημώσεις was changed to φιμώσεις by Atticising scribes. Whether we side with Elliott or with GNT4, the main point is the unacceptability of οὐ φιμώσεις βοῦν ἀλοῶντα in A C P I 33 442 which reduplicates LXX Deut. 25.4.

At Heb. 1.8 the choice is between τῆς βασιλείας σου in A D Ψ K L P *Lect* and τῆς βασιλείας αὐτοῦ in 𝔓46 ℵ B. Although τῆς βασιλείας αὐτοῦ appears to be the best reading since it differs from LXX Ps. 44.7, to invoke the ninth canon here would be misguided, since, as Metzger shows, the variant αὐτοῦ renders the whole verse a non-sequitur: θεός earlier in the verse is vocative, and is consistent with σου rather than with αὐτοῦ.[120] The GNT4 editors are therefore right to reject τῆς βασιλείας αὐτοῦ in 𝔓46 ℵ B.

Liturgical Changes
This canon states that we should prefer variants which resist liturgical forms and usages. Eclectic generalists incline at times towards over-enthusiastic invocation of this canon. The argument that we should prefer a variant which avoids conformity to liturgical forms is often used by the UBS committee to justify excluding the word ἀμήν from the closing doxology of a given canonical writer. At Mt. 28.20 for example, the UBS committee sees a liturgical hand at work:

> After αἰῶνος most manuscripts, followed by the Textus Receptus, termi-
> nate the Gospel with ἀμήν, reflecting the liturgical usage of the text. If
> the word had been present originally, no good reason can be found to
> account for its absence from the better representatives of the Alexandrian
> and the Western text-types.[121]

This sort of argument against ἀμήν is metronomically repeated at Mk 16.20, Lk. 24.53, 1 Cor. 16.24, 2 Cor. 13.13, Eph. 6.24, Phil. 4.23, Col. 4.18, 2 Thess. 3.18, 1 Tim. 6.21, 2 Tim. 4.22, Tit. 3.15, Phlm 25, Heb. 13.25, Jas 5.20, 1 Pet. 5.14, 1 Jn 5.21, 2 Jn 13, 3 Jn 15, and Rev. 22.21. If there were no examples of ἀμήν in New Testament doxologies

---

119. Elliott, *Timothy and Titus*, 82.
120. Metzger, *Textual Commentary*, pp. 592-93.
121. Metzger, *Textual Commentary*, p. 61.

firm in the tradition, then the perception that αμήν is a liturgical addition at all of these verses would be difficult to oppose. But the inclusion of αμήν in the doxology at Jude 25 is universally attested and is not opposed by the UBS editors. From an eclectic viewpoint it seems unacceptably paradoxical that the UBS editors should exclude αμήν at Mt. 28.20, but include it at Gal. 6.18, arguing accidental omission at the latter, but not at the former.

Doctrinal Changes
This canon can be appealed to in support of a variant which does not conform to extrinsic doctrinal views, and against a rival reading which is explicable as a deliberate doctrinal alteration to the text.[122] Like the fourth, fifth and sixth internal canons, this canon is an integral part of the critical armoury of thoroughgoing eclecticism. Concentrating his attention on orthodox changes, Ehrman has identified four types of doctrinal alterations in the New Testament text: (1) anti-adoptionist orthodox corruption; (2) anti-separationist orthodox corruption; (3) anti-docetic orthodox corruption; and (4) anti-patripassianistic corruption.[123] Of these, the two most widespread would seem to be anti-adoptionist and anti-docetic corruption.

Anti-adoptionist orthodox corruption is explicable as a reaction to adoptionism. According to the adoptionist heresy, Jesus was not divine but was a mere man, born of a physical union between Joseph and

---

122. In addition to Ehrman, *Orthodox Corruption*, other important studies in which doctrinal changes are discussed are: J.K. Elliott, 'When Jesus Was Apart from God: An Examination of Hebrews 2.9', *ExpTim* 83 (1972), pp. 339-41; M.C. Parsons, 'A Christological Tendency in ℘75,' *JBL* 105 (1986), pp. 463-79; M.C. De Boer, 'Jesus the Baptizer: 1 John 5.5-8 and the Gospel of John', *JBL* 107 (1988), pp. 87-106; B.D. Ehrman, '1 John 4.3 and the Orthodox Corruption of Scripture', *ZNW* 79 (1988), pp. 221-43; *idem*, 'The Cup, the Bread, and the Salvic Effect of Jesus' Death in Luke-Acts', *SBLSP* (Atlanta: Scholars, 1991), pp. 576-91; *idem* and M.A. Plunkett, 'The Angel and the Agony: The Textual Problem of Luke 22.43-44', *CBQ* 45 (1983), pp. 401-16; E.J. Epp, *The Theological Tendency of Codex Bezae Cantabrigiensis in Acts* (SNTSMS, 3; Cambridge: Cambridge University Press, 1966); *idem*, 'The Ascension in the Textual Tradition of Luke-Acts', *Essays in Honour of Bruce M. Metzger*, pp. 131-45. As Ehrman has pointed out, these and other studies make it clear that WH were wrong in thinking that New Testament MSS are free from doctrinal corruption.

123. Ehrman, *Orthodox Corruption*, pp. 47-118; pp. 119-80; pp. 181-261; pp. 262-73.

Mary. Some anti-adoptionist changes to the New Testament text under-score that Jesus was born of a virgin; other anti-adoptionist alterations designate Christ as God.[124] Anti-docetic orthodox corruption arose from the urge to combat docetism, a heresy which denied that Christ was a human being, denied that he suffered and died, and which held that Christ was a ghost, only human in outward appearance. Anti-docetic changes to the New Testament text emphasize for example the physical aspect of Christ's passion, and stress Christ's bodily ascension into heaven.[125]

What seems unacceptably paradoxical about Ehrman's thesis is that orthodox alterations point in opposite directions: some orthodox changes amplify Christ's divinity, others emphasize his humanity. Against this Ehrman posits that orthodox changes are not on the whole inclined to combat one heresy by promoting another. In other words, changes which stress Christ's divinity are not docetic, and changes which stress his humanity are not adoptionistic. Instead, virtually all orthodox changes are aimed at promoting a 'middle' Christology which stresses that Christ is both human and divine. Another criticism which could be levelled at Ehrman's thesis is the absence of doctrinal corruption in some passages where one would expect it. Ehrman's defence here is similar to an argument which Elliott uses to defend Kilpatrick's Atticism theory: scribes did not effect their changes with consistency.[126] It may be fruitful to recall Ehrman's results at Jn 1.18 where anti-adoptionistic interference is alleged. Whereas the GNT4 editors have printed μονογενὴς θεός preserved in 𝔓66 ℵ* B C* L syrᵖ·ʰᵐᵍ, Ehrman offers no less than five reasons for preferring ὁ μονογενὴς υἱός preserved in A C³ Δ Ψ f¹·¹³ against GNT4.[127] I would view Ehrman's work on

124. Ehrman, *Orthodox Corruption*, pp. 97-99.

125. Ehrman, *Orthodox Corruption*, pp. 241-42.

126. Ehrman, *Orthodox Corruption*, pp. 277; Elliott, *Essays and Studies*, pp. 65-66.

127. Ehrman, *Orthodox Corruption*, pp. 78-82, argues thus: (1) ὁ μονογενὴς υἱός conforms with established Johannine usage (cf. Jn 3.16, 3.18; 1 Jn 4.9); (2) the rival variant μονογενὴς θεός is impossible to understand within a Johannine context; (3) the variant μονογενὴς θεός construed as two substantives standing in apposition is a near impossible syntactical construction; (4) the variant μονογενὴς θεός construed as an adjective-noun combination does not make sense; (5) the variant μονογενὴς θεός is explicable as an anti-adoptionistic change to the text, motivated by an imperative to portray Christ as the 'unique God,' rather than merely the 'unique Son'.

orthodox corruption as a significant contribution to New Testament textual criticism, and I would attempt to ask the sort of questions he would
ask when invoking this canon.

5. *The Apparatus for Jude*

My apparatus for each variation unit in Jude aims to show as much textual variation as possible but does not claim to be a complete apparatus.
The following MSS will be cited consistently: 𝔓72 ℵ A B K L Ψ 049.
Additionally, frequent citations will be made from 𝔓74 𝔓78 C P.
Although this selection may seem rather narrow, it is wide enough to
allow a comparative evaluation of the internal quality of MSS of different
text types and antiquity.[128] Minuscules, fathers and early versions will
only be cited where they preserve readings not contained in MSS cited
consistently, or where they provide proof that a given Byzantine variant
is older than the MS in which it is contained. Minuscules will sometimes
be cited in pairs to show that the reading they support is not singular.
The apparatus for v. 5 has been drawn from Carroll Osburn's study of
the same verse, and for vv. 22-23 from Kubo's chapter in the first
Metzger Festschrift.[129] For the other verses in Jude, the apparatus provided with E. Massaux's collation of the text of Jude in 𝔓72 proved to
be a valuable reservoir of variants, and Junack and Grunewald were
often consulted for readings in 𝔓74, 𝔓78 and 049.[130] Where necessary I
have used Kurt Aland's handlist to transpose minuscule numbers from
Tischendorf's notation to that of Gregory.[131] Other works consulted in

---

128. The apparatus provided in Albin's *Judasbrevet* has been consulted with
confidence by at least two scholars of note (W. Whallon and C.D. Osburn), and I felt
that the objectives of my own work on Jude could be achieved without duplicating
Albin's noteworthy efforts. The apparatus in the present work attempts to represent
as many internally interesting readings as possible. A comparative evaluation of the
MSS I have cited consistently is provided in appendix B.

129. C.D. Osburn, 'The Text of Jude 5', *Bib* 62 (1981), pp. 107-15; S. Kubo,
'Jude 22-23: Two Division Form or Three?', *Essays in Honour of Bruce M.
Metzger*, pp. 239-53.

130. E. Massaux, 'Le texte de l'épître de Jude du Papyrus Bodmer VII (𝔓72)'
Scrinium Lovaniense. Mélanges historiques Etienne Van Cauwenberg (Louvain:
Duculot & Gembloux, 1961), pp. 108-25; K. Junack and W. Grunewald, *Das Neue
Testament auf Papyrus: 1. Die katholischen Briefe* (ANTF, 6; Berlin: De Gruyter,
1986), pp. 159-71.

131. K. Aland, *Kurzgefasste Liste der griechischen Handschriften des Neuen*

the preparation of my apparatus include Albin's *Judasbrevet*, GNT4, NA26, Tischendorf, von Soden, and the *Vetus Latina*.[132] To avoid the necessity of having to repeat MS support for readings in our commentary, the reading which appears *first* in the apparatus at each variation unit is the reading which I have accepted, for example ιουδα ℵ B appears first in the apparatus at variation unit 0.1.

6. *Decimal Headings*

Each variation unit has a decimal heading.[133] The first number within the decimal heading designates the verse itself, and the second number within the heading designates the individual variation unit. Thus, for example, 'Variation Unit 5.2' refers to the second variation unit at Jude 5; 'Variation Unit 0.1' refers to Jude's *inscriptio*; 'Variation Unit 22-23.1' refers to the entire textual problem at Jude 22-23; and 'Variation Unit 26.1' is used to designate Jude's *subscriptio*.

Testaments. Band 1. Gesamtübersicht (ANTF, 1; Berlin: De Gruyter, 1963), pp. 322-33.

132. W. Thiele, *Vetus Latina: Die Reste der Altlateinischen Bibel. Epistulae Catholicae* (vol. 26.1; fasc. 6; Freiburg: Herder, 1967).

133. The term 'variation unit' has been defined by E.J. Epp, in Epp and Fee, *Theory and Method*, pp. 47-61, esp. pp. 59-61. Whereas Epp defines a variation unit as having at least two variant readings, each of which must have the support of at least two MSS, the definition understood in the present work regards a variation unit as having at least two variant readings, one of which may permissibly be a singular reading.

Chapter 2

DISCUSSION OF VARIANTS

Variation Unit 0.1

ιουδα ℵ B
ιουδα επιστολη   𝔓72 A C K Ψ
επιστολη ιουδα   460 618
επιστολη ιουδα του αποστολου   0142 436
επιστολη του αγιου αποστολου ιουδα   L 625 1523
του αγιου αποστολου ιουδα επιστολη   049 131 451
ιουδα επιστολη καθολικη   69 103
ιουδα καθολικη επιστολη   328 385
ιουδα του αποστολου επιστολη καθολικη   P 102
του αγιου αποστολου ιουδα επιστολη καθολικη   133 491

As explained in the introduction above, the writer's theology is not 'early Catholic'. The theological canon can therefore be invoked against those readings in our apparatus which include the word καθολική: Ἰούδα ἐπιστολὴ καθολική, Ἰούδα καθολικὴ ἐπιστολή, Ἰούδα τοῦ ἀπόστολου ἐπιστολὴ καθολική, and τοῦ ἀγίου ἀπόστολου Ἰούδα ἐπιστολὴ καθολική.

Doubts about Jude's canonical status are recorded by Origen, Eusebius, Didymus and Jerome, and the allusions to apocryphal books in Jude meant that it was not accepted as canonical in some quarters until the sixth century.[1] In view of this, the word ἀπόστολος wherever it appears in our apparatus is explicable as a scribal addition made to underscore Jude's canonical status, thereby enabling us to reject the following readings: ἐπιστολὴ Ἰούδα τοῦ ἀπόστολου, ἐπιστολὴ τοῦ ἀγίου ἀπόστολου Ἰούδα, τοῦ ἀγίου ἀπόστολου Ἰούδα ἐπιστολή, Ἰούδα τοῦ ἀπόστολου ἐπιστολὴ καθολική, and τοῦ ἀγίου ἀπόστολου Ἰούδα ἐπιστολὴ καθολική.

---

1.   Bauckham, *Jude, 2 Peter*, p. 17.

Having eliminated the longer readings, I am left with three possibilities: ᾿Ιούδα, ᾿Ιούδα ἐπιστολή, and ἐπιστολὴ ᾿Ιούδα. That Jude begins his epistle as a letter but develops it into what Bauckham in his commentary calls an epistolary sermon may have proved a paradox sufficiently strong for some copyists to provide clarification that Jude is indeed a letter rather than a sermon or even a prayer. The need for such clarification explains the word ἐπιστολή as a scribal addition, thus enabling us to reject (among others) the readings ᾿Ιούδα ἐπιστολή and ἐπιστολὴ ᾿Ιούδα. Thus far, ᾿Ιούδα is the only reading untarnished by additions which do not conform to the theology of the writer, or which are unacceptable for other reasons.

The readings in the apparatus illustrate the phenomenon of what Metzger calls a 'growing text', where scribes 'could not resist the temptation to embroider the simple and [the] unadorned'.[2] The example cited by Metzger is from Gal. 6.17, where the best attested reading is 'I bear on my body the marks of Jesus'.[3] The word 'Jesus' at Gal. 6.17 was gradually adorned by pious scribes with various natural complements and grew to κυρίου ᾿Ιησοῦ, then to κυρίου ᾿Ιησοῦ Χριστοῦ, and ultimately to κυρίου ἡμῶν ᾿Ιησοῦ Χριστοῦ. In the apparatus, ᾿Ιούδα grows to ᾿Ιούδα ἐπιστολή, which in turn is amplified to the longer readings. In view of the intrinsic and transcriptional evidence discussed, ᾿Ιούδα is the reading that should be printed at this unit.

Variation Unit 1.1

ιησου χριστου   𝔓72 ℵ A B L
χριστου ιησου   K P 049

The intrinsic evidence in favour of ᾿Ιησοῦ Χριστοῦ is at first glance compelling, in view of the writer's preference for this order of words elsewhere:

v. 1   ᾿Ιησοῦ Χριστῷ τετηρημένοις κλητοῖς
v. 4   κύριον ἡμῶν ᾿Ιησοῦν Χριστόν
v. 17 κύριου ἡμῶν ᾿Ιησοῦ Χριστοῦ
v. 21 κύριου ἡμῶν ᾿Ιησοῦ Χριστοῦ
v. 25 ᾿Ιησοῦ Χριστοῦ τοῦ κύριου ἡμῶν

Although all of these examples appear in the GNT4 text, the order ᾿Ιησοῦ Χριστῷ is not firm at v. 1, likewise ᾿Ιησοῦ Χριστοῦ at v. 25.

2.   Metzger, *Text*, p. 199.
3.   Metzger, *Text*, p. 199.

The examples from vv. 4, 17, 21 and 25 are all New Testament set expressions which do not necessarily prove the writer's preference for the order Ἰησοῦ Χριστοῦ outside of a set expression. Elliott has shown that the author of the Pastorals prefers the order Χριστὸς Ἰησοῦς whenever Ἰησοῦς is genitive or dative, but that this order is not adhered to if Ἰησοῦς Χριστός is part of a set expression such as κύριος ἡμῶν Ἰησοῦς Χριστός.[4] It is unfortunately not possible to show Jude's preference regarding word order in *nomina sacra* other than in set expressions, since neither of the two groups of *nomina sacra* at v. 1 is firm in the text. My preference for the variant Ἰησοῦ Χριστοῦ at this unit is therefore based mainly upon an argument by silence: that because the order Χριστοῦ Ἰησοῦ appears nowhere in Jude where all the MSS agree, the author is unlikely to have written Χριστοῦ Ἰησοῦ here. Regarding transcriptional evidence, the order Χριστοῦ Ἰησοῦ seems to be a deliberate change introduced through the influence of the order used elsewhere in the New Testament, for example, Χριστοῦ Ἰησοῦ at 1 Cor. 1.2.

Variation Unit 1.2

τοις εν θεω πατρι   𝔓72 ℵ A B K L P Ψ 049
τοις εθνεσιν εν θεω   322 323

Several commentators have commented that the clause τοῖς ἐν θεῷ πατρὶ ἠγαπημένοις καὶ Ἰησοῦ Χριστῷ τετηρημένοις κλητοῖς is grammatically awkward. Moule describes the clause as 'anomalous', and Metzger writes of a 'difficult and unusual combination'.[5] Central to the difficulty which this clause presents is the position and grammatical function of the preposition ἐν. Before an analysis of the different possible solutions is made, it may be helpful to mention why ἐν θεῷ πατρί has been labelled an anomaly. Some exegetes translate ἐν as 'by', for example Fuchs and Reymond.[6] To do justice to this translation, θεῷ πατρί must be viewed as a dative of agent. For θεῷ πατρί to be viewed as agent, it must either be preceded by ὑπό (in which case the

---

4.   Elliott, *Timothy and Titus*, p. 201.
5.   C.F.D. Moule, *An Idiom Book of New Testament Greek* (Cambridge: Cambridge University Press, 1959), p. 47; Metzger, *Textual Commentary*, p. 723.
6.   E. Fuchs and P. Reymond, *La deuxième épître de saint Pierre. L'épître de Saint Jude* (Geneva: Labor et Fides, 2nd edn, 1988), p. 155.

preposition would take a genitive) as suggested by Bauckham[7]—or it must be viewed as agent with ἠγαπημένοις but without being preceded by ἐν. The conjectural emendations which have been advanced by WH and by Green to remove the alleged anomaly are attempts to make θεῷ πατρί a dative of agent construction in combination with the perfect passive participle ἠγαπημένοις by removing the preposition ἐν from its position in front of θεῷ πατρί.[8] The variation at units 1.2 and 1.4 can be attributed at least in part to an urge among scribes to 'improve' the supposedly difficult phrase ἐν θεῷ πατρί. It is possible by a process of elimination to arrive at a decision in favour of τοῖς ἐν θεῷ πατρί.

Beginning with τοῖς ἔθνεσιν ἐν θεῷ, there is a possible parallel with Eph. 3.1 and Eph. 4.17, where the addressees are referred to as ἔθνη ('gentiles'). However, Jude never refers to his addressees as 'gentiles', and the word τοῖς at v. 1 is a definite reference to Jude's addressees. Since Jude invariably refers to his addressees as ἀγαπητοί ('beloved') as at vv. 3, 17 and 20, the reading τοῖς ἔθνεσιν ἐν θεῷ can be rejected on the grounds that it does not accord with the author's diction. Our remaining options are: (1) WH's conjecture; (2) Green's conjecture; and (3) the possibility that the phrase ἐν θεῷ πατρί may not, after all, be a grammatical inconcinnity.

The difference between the conjecture in WH and the reading κλητοῖς τετηρημένοις ἐν Ἰησοῦ Χριστῷ preserved in cop[sa] (shown in the apparatus at variation unit 1.4) is that although both have ἐν preceding Ἰησοῦ Χριστῷ, WH's conjecture removes ἐν from θεῷ πατρί,[9] whereas the Sahidic reading retains the phrase ἐν θεῷ πατρί. Despite this difference, it would seem that the Sahidic reading is the main insipiration behind WH's conjecture. The classicist A.E. Housman in his famous essay is rather scathing about editors who change a few words in the text to 'see what happens', and WH appear to condone such a change here.[10]

7.   Bauckham, *Jude, 2 Peter*, p. 25.

8.   M. Green, *The Second Epistle General of Peter and the General Epistle of Jude: An Introduction and Commentary* (Leicester: Inter-Varsity Press, 1987), p. 168; WH, II, p. 106.

9.   WH, II, p. 106.

10.   A.E. Housman, 'The Application of Thought to Textual Criticism', in J. Diggle and F.R.D. Goodyear (eds.), *The Classical Papers of A. E. Housman* (Cambridge: Cambridge University Press, 1972), pp. 1058-1069.

Green's idea is that because the text does not locate Jude's letter geographically, the writer 'left a gap after the preposition ἐν in verse 1 for the appropriate place name to be inserted... we could then translate, "to those in ____, beloved by God the Father" '.[11] This conjecture permits θεῷ to be a dative of agent with the perfect passive participle ἠγαπημένοις, thus removing the grammatical incongruity of the clause. The problem with this idea is that Green is unable to explain why Jude should have left such a gap at v. 1, when there is no evidence that similar gaps were left for place names at v. 7, where we have Σόδομα καὶ Γόμορρα. Kilpatrick cautioned that in order to arrive at what an author originally wrote, one should not heal an initial conjecture with a second one.[12]

Bauckham mentions that some published translations reflect the immediate sense of the phrase, and render ἐν θεῷ πατρί as 'in God the Father', an example being RSV.[13] Although this solution is feasible, it is slightly misleading in the sense that an equivalent to the Pauline phrase 'in Christ' is implied. The point here is that nowhere else in the New Testament is there a phrase 'in God' equivalent to the Pauline phrase 'in Christ'.[14]

Moulton and Zerwick have shown that the phrase ἐν θεῷ πατρί at v. 1 is not difficult to the point of impossibility. Moulton says that ἐν can be used with a personal dative, and that at v. 1, a possible meaning which can be attached to ἐν θεῷ is 'in God's judgment', where the dative applies to the person judging. This is echoed by Zerwick, who states that 'ἐν θεῷ = παρὰ θεῷ'.[15] If ἐν is translated as Zerwick clearly intends, then, 'in God's judgment' or 'in God's eyes' is the result. Bauer concords with Moulton and Zerwick that ἐν can mean 'in someone's judgment', and he asserts that the phrase ἐν ἐμοί ('in my judgment') can be paralleled with ἐν θεῷ at v. 1.[16] The translation, 'in God's eyes' definitely fits the context of the clause as a whole. With the grammatical difficulty resolved, there is no reason not to accept τοῖς ἐν θεῷ πατρί at this unit.

11.   Green, *General Epistle of Jude*, p. 168.
12.   Kilpatrick, 'Conjectural Emendation', p. 108.
13.   Bauckham, *Jude, 2 Peter*, p. 25.
14.   E.M. Sidebottom, *James, Jude, 2 Peter* (London: Marshall, Morgan and Scott, 1971), p. 82.
15.   MHT, I, p. 103; M. Zerwick and M. Grosvenor, *A Grammatical Analysis of the Greek New Testament* (4th rev. edn; Rome: Editrice Pontificio Istituto Biblico, 1993), p. 738.
16.   BAGD, s.v. ἐν.

Variation Unit 1.3

ηγαπημενοις   𝔓72 ℵ A B Ψ
ηγιασμενοις   K L P 049

The variant ἡγιασμένοις can be defended on the grounds that it coheres with the eschatological and rhetorical purpose of the verse. Bolkestein has commented upon the eschatological significance of the verse as a whole, and Fuchs and Reymond develop this by explaining that those being addressed are being kept for Jesus Christ in view of the Day of Judgment. Kelly observes similarly that the addressees are being 'kept safe for Jesus Christ' for his coming and for the kingdom which Christ will establish. Watson has identified Jude's first two verses as a quasi-exordium with the rhetorical property of linking Jude with his addressees psychologically by means of identifying a common goal—that of sharing a common salvation.[17] Moreover, ἁγιάζω used of a person means 'consecrate, dedicate, sanctify, i.e. *include in the inner circle* of what is holy, in both relig. and moral uses of the word'.[18] Jude's eschatological and rhetorical purpose in defining his addressees as an exclusive spiritual elite is well served by the variant ἡγιασμένοις, a word which connotes their inclusion in an inner circle of consecrated people.

However, ἡγαπημένοις is intrinsically strong, since, as a catchword, it is consistent with the writer's style. Such catchwords are not the product of an arbitrary impulse on the part of the author, but are 'the hallmark of the midrashic procedure'.[19] Daryl Charles has catalogued most of the occasions on which the writer of Jude's epistle uses catchwords:[20]

ἀσεβεῖς / ἀσέβεια	vv. 4, 15 (×3), 18
ὑμεῖς / ὑμᾶς / ὑμῖν	vv. 3 (×3), 5 (×2), 12, 17, 18, 20 (×2), 24
οὗτοι	vv. 4 (τινες), 8, 10, 11 (αὐτοῖς), 12, 14, 16, 19
κύριος	vv. 4, 5, 9, 14, 17, 21, 25
ἅγιος	vv. 3, 14, 20 (×2), 24 (ἄμωμος)
σάρξ, ἐπιθυμία	vv. 7, 16, 18, 23
ἀγάπη / ἀγαπητοί	vv. 1, 2, 3, 12, 17, 20, 21
ἔλεος / ἐλεεῖν	vv. 2, 21, 22, 23

17.   M.H. Bolkestein, *De brieven van Petrus en Judas* (Nijkerk: Callenbach, 1984), p. 198; Fuchs, *Saint Jude*, p. 155; J.N.D. Kelly, *A Commentary on the Epistles of Peter and of Jude* (London: A. & C. Black, 1969), p. 243; Watson, *Invention*, pp. 40-42.
18.   BAGD, s.v. ἁγιάζω.
19.   Ellis, 'Prophecy and Hermeneutic', p. 225.
20.   Charles, 'Literary Artifice', pp. 111-12.

κρίσις, κρίμα   vv. 4, 6, 9, 15
πλανή   vv. 11, 13 (πλανήτης)
πᾶς   vv. 3, 15 (×4), 25 (×2)

The words ἀγάπη, ἀγαπητοί and derivatives such as the variant ἠγαπημένοις are singled out as conformants to a general tendency of the writer to structure his prose by repeating certain words. Despite the contextual case for ἡγιασμένοις, the intrinsic support which ἠγαπημένοις enjoys as part of a chain of catchwords which characterize an aspect of the writer's style is more conclusive, and added support for ἠγαπημένοις is found in the transcriptional probability that ἡγιασμένοις was an alteration made to harmonize with 1 Cor. 1.2, where we have ἡγιασμένοις ἐν Χριστῷ 'Ἰησοῦ.[21] The probability is strong that ἡγιασμένοις was introduced as a reaction to the difficult phrase ἐν θεῷ πατρί in Jude 1, in order to render a more familiar combination by bringing the text closer to 1 Cor. 1.2. A combination of intrinsic and transcriptional evidence compels me to accept ἠγαπημένοις here.

Variation Unit 1.4

ιησου χριστω   𝔓72 ℵ A B L P 049
ιησου χριστου   K 181 450
χριστου ιησου   Ψ 1835
ιησου χριστω *post* κλητοις   cop[sa]

The argument which was advanced in favour of 'Ἰησοῦ Χριστοῦ at variation unit 1.1 is also applicable here: with no firm evidence in the MS tradition that the writer ever used the order Χριστὸς 'Ἰησοῦς, we should reject the variant Χριστοῦ 'Ἰησοῦ at this unit. This leaves three remaining possibilities as discussed below.

The reading 'Ἰησοῦ Χριστοῦ in K 181 450 can also be dismissed on transcriptional grounds, since it seems to reflect a lack of awareness that 'Ἰησοῦ is dative, not genitive, a misunderstanding which I will assume to have engendered the resultant alteration from Χριστῷ to Χριστοῦ. 'Ἰησοῦ Χριστῷ is indisputably dative, being dative of agent along with τετηρημένοις.[22]

---

21.   J.H. Petzer, *Die teks van die Nuwe Testament: 'n inleiding in die basiese aspekte van die teorie en praktyk van die tekskritiek van die Nuwe Testament* (Her vormde Teologiese Studies Supplement Series, 2; Pretoria: Tydskrifafdeling van die Nederduitsch Hervormde Kerk, 1990), p. 271.

22.   MHT, III, p. 240. Turner writes of an instrumental dative here.

The reading with Ἰησοῦ Χριστῷ after κλητοῖς attempts to convey a more logical sequence of ideas by ensuring that those addressed as τοῖς are called (κλητοῖς) before being kept safe (τετηρημένοις), thus improving on the sequence of ideas in the text, an improvement which points in the direction of deliberate interference.

The remaining reading Ἰησοῦ Χριστῷ is acceptable on intrinsic grounds: it conforms to the writer's word order preference, and it retains Χριστῷ to agree with the correct Koine dative form Ἰησοῦ. My choice here is, therefore, in favour of Ἰησοῦ Χριστῷ.

Variation Unit 2.1

και ειρηνη   𝔓72 ℵ A B L P Ψ 049
και ειρηνη εν κυριω   378 614
ειρηνη   K 103 221

The reading καὶ εἰρήνη ἐν κυρίῳ can be evaluated in the light of Jude's general use of κύριος and of ἔλεος in v. 21. If I examine Jude's general use of κύριος first, I may note that there may be a possible case to be made for καὶ εἰρήνη ἐν κυρίῳ, since Jude uses κύριος in isolation from his usual set expressions[23] on three occasions:

> v. 5   πάντα ὅτι κύριος ἅπαξ[24]
> v. 9   ἐπιτιμήσαι ἐν σοι κύριος[25]
> v. 14   ἰδοὺ ἦλθεν κύριος

I, therefore, cannot reject the variant καὶ εἰρήνη ἐν κυρίῳ purely on the grounds that κυρίῳ does not appear as part of a set expression. However, the link between ἔλεος and κύριος at v. 21 renders καὶ εἰρήνη ἐν κυρίῳ at this unit intrinsically suspect. Because ἔλεος ὑμῖν καὶ εἰρήνη is at v. 2, it would be reasonable to expect that if κυρίῳ is part of the original text of v. 2, it might be expected to appear as part of a formula similar to the one used at v. 21. Transcriptional evidence also weighs against καὶ εἰρήνη ἐν κυρίῳ, since ἐν κυρίῳ is explicable as a deliberate scribal addition made to harmonize with ἐν θεῷ πατρί in v. 1.

Meanwhile the omission of καί is not defensible on intrinsic grounds, since the writer is fond of repeating this conjunction as is evident at

23.   κύριος ἡμῶν Ἰησοῦς Χριστός and Ἰησοῦς Χριστὸς ὁ κύριος ἡμῶν as seen at vv. 4, 17, 21 and 25.
24.   The wording in this example is my choice at variation unit 5.3, where I differ with GNT4.
25.   I have accepted ἐν σοι κύριος against GNT4 at v. 9.

vv. 4 and 25. It is difficult to advance a transcriptional reason for the omission of καί, but if it is deliberate, then it could be a reaction to the perceived pleonasm which is rendered by including καί. The omission could also be accidental. With no intrinsic or transcriptional arguments against our remaining reading καὶ εἰρήνη, the latter should be printed.

Variation Unit 2.2

και αγαπη   𝔓72 ℵ A B K L P Ψ 049
om. και αγαπη   88 181

The general preference of the writer for triadic illustration as a stylistic device and the specific use of triadic illustration in v. 2 as a rhetorical mechanism both favour the inclusion of καὶ ἀγάπη here.[26] Charles provides us with a comprehensive collection of most of the instances of triadic illustration in Jude:

v. 1	Ἰούδας, δοῦλος, ἀδελφός
	(the writer's self-designations)
v. 1	ἠγαπημένοις, τετηρημένοις, κλητοῖς
	(attributes ascribed to the audience)
v. 2	ἔλεος, εἰρήνη, ἀγάπη
	(elements in the greeting)
v. 4	προγεγραμμένοι, μετατιθέντες, ἀρνούμενοι
	(participles modifying the main verb)
vv. 5-7	ὁ λαός, οἱ ἄγγελοι, Σόδομα καὶ Γόμορρα
	(paradigms of judgment)
v. 8	μιαίνειν, ἀθετεῖν, βλασφημεῖν
	(actions of opponents)
v. 9	οὐ τολμᾶν, ἐπιφέρειν, λέγειν
	(actions of Michael)
v. 11	Κάϊν, Βαλαάμ, Κόρε
	(examples of woe)
v. 11	πορεύομαι, ἐκχεῖν, ἀπόλλυμι
	(escalation of rebellious action)
v. 12	σπιλάδες, συνευωχούμενοι, ἀφόβως
	(traits of those at love feasts)
v. 12	φθινοπωρινά, ἄκαρπα, δὶς ἀποθανόντα ἐκριζωθέντα
	(traits of the trees)
v. 13	ἄγρια, θαλάσσης ἐπαφρίζοντα, αἰσχύνη
	(traits of the waves)

26.   Charles, 'Literary Artifice', p. 122.

v. 15   πάντας τοὺς ἀσεβεῖς,²⁷ πάντων τῶν ἔργων, πάντων τῶν
          σκληρῶν
          (all the ungodly, all the deeds, all the hard utterances)
v. 16   γογγυσταί, μεμψίμοιροι, κατὰ τὰς ἐπιθυμίας
          ἑαυτῶν πορευόμενοι
          (traits of the opponents)
v. 19   ἀποδιορίζοντες, ψυχικοί, μὴ πνεῦμα ἔχοντες
          (further traits of the opponents)
vv. 20-21 ἐποικοδομοῦντες, προσευχόμενοι, προσδεχόμενοι
          (participles linked to the imperative)
vv. 20-21 ἐν πνεύματι ἁγίῳ, ἐν ἀγάπῃ θεοῦ, τὸ ἔλεος
          τοῦ... Ἰησοῦ Χριστοῦ
          (presence of the trinity)
v. 25   θεός, σωτήρ, κύριος
          (divine designations)
v. 25   πρὸ πάντος τοῦ αἰῶνος, καὶ νῦν, καὶ εἰς πάντας τοὺς
          αἰῶνας
          (view of time)

The density of triplets occurring in the text of Jude is 'unparalleled any-where else in Scripture'.²⁸ Because 'a threefold concurrence yields com-pleteness',²⁹ the greeting extended by the writer at v. 2 must be deemed incomplete if part of this threefold greeting is excluded. Jude's predilec-tion for triadic illustration is nowhere more obvious than at v. 2 where the word ἀγάπη is one of the three elements ἔλεος, εἰρήνη, and ἀγάπη which make up the writer's extended salutation.³⁰

The omission of the phrase καὶ ἀγάπη at this unit can be explained by looking at the philological background of the phrase ἔλεος...καὶ εἰρήνη καὶ ἀγάπη. The expression 'mercy and peace' is a Jewish greet-ing, and the addition by Jude of 'love' to form the triadic expression 'mercy and peace and love' is not a formula which appears in any Jewish

27. I have accepted πάντας τοὺς ἀσεβεῖς against GNT4.
28. Charles, 'Literary Artifice', p. 122.
29. Charles, 'Literary Artifice', p. 122.
30. As Watson, *Invention*, pp. 26-42, has shown, the use of triadic illustration in Jude is not merely for aesthetic effect, but is one of the writer's favourite rhetorical devices. The threefold grouping of ἔλεος, εἰρήνη and ἀγάπη here is cited by Watson as an example of amplification by accumulation. According to Cicero *De Partitione Oratoriae* 15.52, cited in Watson, the intended effect of amplification is 'a sort of weightier affirmation, designed to win credence in the source of speaking'. Some examples of amplification involve repeating the same word or idea for rhetori-cal reasons; other examples of amplification involve the accumulation of a number of different words or ideas. The triadic equation in v. 2 is an example of the latter.

salutation.[31] The omission of καὶ ἀγάπη in part of the tradition could be a conscious effort by scribes to erase the triadic expression in favour of preserving the dual formula of the Jewish greeting 'mercy and peace'.

The problem with my transcriptional argument against the omission of the phrase καὶ ἀγάπη is that it is possible to argue intrinsically in its favour. Elsewhere in my analysis of variation in Jude, I will be defending readings as original on the grounds that Semitic usage is evident at vv. 5, 7, 11, 16, 17, 18, 21 and possibly 24.[32] I have to walk the extra mile here and explain why such an argument cannot also be used to defend the omission of καὶ ἀγάπη which would give me the Jewish greeting reflected in minuscules 88 181. It has to do with Jude's tendency to *rework* Jewish source material and with the way in which he does this to create specific stylistic patterns. At variation unit 15.1 it is shown that Jude reworks material from 1 Enoch 1.9 and that triadic illustration is the stylistic pattern created by this reworking. Similarly I would argue at this unit that Jude has taken a traditional Jewish greeting, 'mercy and peace', and reworked it into one of his distinctive triadic expressions, 'mercy, peace and love'. If the intrinsic argument *in favour* of the omission of καὶ ἀγάπη is invalid, the original transcriptional argument *against* it can be resurrected. All the evidence at this unit favours the inclusion of καὶ ἀγάπη.

Variation Unit 3.1

ποιουμενος   ℵ A B C K L P 049
ποιησαμενος   𝔓72
ποιουμενοι   Ψ

The reading ποιούμενοι is not a serious contender, since it is obviously an attempt at agreement with ἀγαπητοί. The error is that ἀγαπητοί is not the subject of the sentence and should therefore not be made to agree with the participle. This leaves us with two possibilities: ποιησάμενος and ποιούμενος. It can indeed be shown that ποιούμενος fits the context of the verse as a whole and is not grammatically anomalous.

If I accept ποιούμενος, it could designate a general intention to write about the common salvation which was not carried out. According to this interpretation, ποιούμενος as an adverbial participle of concession

---

31.   Bauckham, *Jude, 2 Peter*, p. 20.
32.   MHT, IV, pp. 139-40; Bauckham, *Jude, 2 Peter*, pp. 6, 104.

is combined with the present infinitive γράφειν to suggest that what the author intended to write had to be abandoned in favour of an appeal to the addressees.[33] The second infinitive is aorist to indicate 'a concrete action carried through'.[34]

Although not all commentators accept this line of thinking, the alternative interpretation which sees τῆς κοινῆς ἡμῶν σωτηρίας... παραδοθείσῃ τοῖς ἁγίοις πίστει as synonymous, and which sees ποιούμενος as causal or temporal rather than concessive, does not weaken the case for the reading ποιούμενος. In this alternative interpretation, 'Jude refers to only one letter, which he was intending to write and then actually wrote'.[35] As Kelly has pointed out, ποιούμενος γράφειν fits the context whichever interpretation we prefer.

Meanwhile the reading ποιησάμενος is explicable as an assimilation to Acts 25.17, where ἀναβολὴν μηδεμίαν ποιησάμενος means 'without losing any time', the parallel being that at v. 3 πᾶσαν σπουδὴν ποιούμενος can literally be translated 'making all haste'. If the copyist of 𝔓72 knew that ποιησάμενος appears at Acts 25.17 in the context of not losing time, ποιούμενος at v. 3 may have provided him with what Gunther Zuntz would call an 'incitement to alteration'.[36] Contextual and transcriptional evidence supports ποιούμενος at this unit.

Variation Unit 3.2

γραφειν   A B C K L P 049
του γραφειν   ℵ Ψ
του γραφιν   𝔓72

The blunder γραφιν being unacceptable, the real choice here is between the anarthrous infinitive γράφειν and the articular infinitive τοῦ γράφειν. In view of Turner's comment that articular infinitives were favoured by the Atticists, the variant τοῦ γράφειν should be rejected as an Atticism.[37] Faced with the choice between the Atticist articular

33.   Bauckham, *Jude, 2 Peter*, pp. 29-30; R. G. Bratcher, *A Translator's Guide to the Letters from James, Peter and Jude* (New York: UBS, 1984), p. 172; Green, *General Epistle of Jude*, p. 170; Kelly, *Peter and Jude*, pp. 245-46; Bolkestein, *Petrus en Judas*, pp. 201-202; Fuchs, *Saint Jude*, p. 156; Sidebottom, *James, Jude, 2 Peter*, p. 83; Watson, *Invention*, p. 48.
34.   Kelly, *Peter and Jude*, pp. 245-46.
35.   Bauckham, *Jude, 2 Peter*, p. 30.
36.   Zuntz, *Text of the Epistles*, p. 125.
37.   MHT, III, p. 140.

infinitive τοῦ γράφειν and the anarthrous infinitive γράφειν, the latter is preferable.

Variation Unit 3.3

ημων   𝔓72 𝔓74 ℵ A B C^vid Ψ
υμων   1850 2298 cop^bo
om.   K L P 049

The reading ἡμῶν can be defended on intrinsic grounds, since it is consistent with an important aspect of the writer's style. The predilection of the writer for triadic illustration has already been catalogued in our discussion of v. 2, although for some reason, Charles has not included the triple appearance of ἡμῶν in vv. 3-4 among the examples of triadic illustration which he provides, nor has he classified as a triad the threefold appearance of ὑμῖν in vv. 2-3.[38] Both of these examples of triadic illustration emerge from my discussion on this third variation unit. The first example of triadic illustration which can be added to the catalogue in Charles is from vv. 3-4 as follows:

ἡμῶν σωτηρίας...τὴν τοῦ θεοῦ ἡμῶν χάριτα...κύριον ἡμῶν
Ἰησοῦν Χριστὸν

The triadic structure is therefore: our salvation; the grace of our God; and our Lord, Jesus Christ. The variant ἡμῶν at v. 3 therefore concords with the author's preference for triadic illustration.

The problem as to whether I should choose ἡμῶν or ὑμῶν only becomes soluble when I realise that Jude does not always confine his triadic formulae to a single verse—they occasionally span two verses, as I can see from the two examples in vv. 20-21 which are listed in the discussion of v. 2 above. In view of this, I can safely categorize the double ὑμῖν in v. 3 as part of a triad which begins in v. 2, and not as a triad within v. 3 which includes the variant ὑμῶν. The two triadic formulae can therefore be delineated as follows:

The First Triad: (ὑμῖν x3)

v. 2   ἔλεος ὑμῖν καὶ εἰρήνη καὶ ἀγάπη πληθυνθείη

v. 3   ἀγαπητοί, πᾶσαν σπουδὴν ποιούμενος γράφειν ὑμῖν περὶ τῆς
        κοινῆς ἡμῶν σωτηρίας ἀνάγκην ἔσχον γράψαι ὑμῖν παρακαλῶν
        ἐπαγωνίζεσθαι...

38.   Charles, 'Literary Artifice', pp. 122-23.

The Second Triad: (ἡμῶν x3)

v. 3   ἀγαπητοί, πᾶσαν σπουδὴν ποιούμενος γράφειν ὑμῖν περὶ τῆς κοινῆς <u>ἡμῶν</u> σωτηρίας ἀνάγκην ἔσχον γράψαι ὑμῖν παρακαλῶν ἐπαγωνίζεσθαι τῇ ἅπαξ παραδοθείσῃ τοῖς ἁγίοις πίστει

v. 4   παρεισέδυσαν γάρ τινες ἄνθρωποι, οἱ πάλαι προγεγραμμένοι εἰς τοῦτο τὸ κρίμα, ἀσεβεῖς, τὴν τοῦ θεοῦ <u>ἡμῶν</u> χάριτα μετατιθέντες εἰς ἀσέλγειαν καὶ τὸν μόνον δεσπότην θεὸν[39] καὶ κύριον <u>ἡμῶν</u> Ἰησοῦν Χριστὸν ἀρνούμενοι

It should be clear from the triadic formulae identified above that the reading ἡμῶν at this unit is preferable on intrinsic grounds to ὑμῶν.

Another intrinsic factor which points towards ἡμῶν as the most preferable of the three variants is the writer's rhetorical purpose in v. 3. Watson has shown that v. 3 functions rhetorically as an exordium and that three aims can be attributed to an exordium: 'to elicit attention, receptivity, and goodwill'.[40] Because the reading ἡμῶν indicates that the writer shares a common salvation with the addressees, it serves the strategic purpose of fulfilling two rhetorical aims simultaneously: (1) the receptivity of the addressees to Jude's message is obtained because the writer places himself on their level by identifying a common salvation for himself and for them; and (2) goodwill is obtained by the esteem in which Jude holds the addressees without resorting to flattery.

Exegetical reasons can also be cited in favour of the variant ἡμῶν. According to Kelly, κοινῆς ἡμῶν σωτηρίας (our common salvation) contrasts with the idea of salvation which existed in Hellenistic piety where mystery cults regarded salvation as an individual experience.[41] Kelly affirms that in v. 3, the expression 'our common salvation' brings out the corporate rather than the individual nature of salvation. The variant ἡμῶν reflects this corporality very well: the writer uses the word 'our' to convey the truth that his salvation is not somehow different to the salvation which is available to his addressees: they both anticipate a shared salvation.

The third variant, in which the possessive pronoun is omitted alto-gether, is viewed by Metzger as a reflection of the desire 'to give the idea a universal character'.[42] This view is indirectly corroborated by

39.   I have argued in favour of the variant δεσπότην θεόν at variation unit 4.4 below.
40.   Watson, *Invention*, p. 39.
41.   Kelly, *Peter and Jude*, p. 246.
42.   Metzger, *Textual Commentary*, p. 656.

Kelly and Bauckham, who both assert that we cannot see Jude as a 'Catholic' letter addressed to all Christians.[43] Assuming that Metzger is correct here, this third variant may therefore be regarded as a deliberate change effected by orthodox scribes. All the evidence at this unit points in favour of the variant ἡμῶν.

Variation Unit 3.4

σωτηριας 𝔓72 A B C K L P 049
σωτηριας και ζωης ℵ Ψ
ζωης 1611 2138

The problem with accepting either ζωῆς or σωτηρίας καὶ ζωῆς is that in the New Testament generally, when the noun ζωή is used in an eschatological sense, it is normally qualified by αἰώνιος.[44] Jude accurately uses the New Testament set expression εἰς ζωὴν αἰώνιον at v. 21, and he uses other New Testament set expressions accurately and without tampering with them at vv. 1, 4, 17, 20, 21 (×2) and 25. For either ζωῆς or σωτηρίας καὶ ζωῆς to be convincing on intrinsic grounds at this unit, I might expect to see the qualification αἰώνιος alongside ζωῆς. The reading σωτηρίας καὶ ζωῆς is suspect on transcriptional grounds, since it appears to be a conflation of the other two readings represented in our apparatus. Having thus eliminated ζωῆς and σωτηρίας καὶ ζωῆς, at this unit σωτηρίας should be printed.

Variation Unit 3.5

γραψαι 𝔓72 𝔓74 A B C K L P 049
γραφειν ℵ Ψ

If Bauckham is correct in saying that 'the distinction will be between the general intention of writing [conveyed by the infinitive γράφειν at variation unit 3.2]...and the concrete action actually carried out [conveyed by the infinitive γράψαι at variation unit 3.5]',[45] then the aorist infinitive γράψαι is contextually plausible. Meanwhile γράφειν here is explicable as an internal harmonization with the first γράφειν in the verse, since this first γράφειν is in the present tense.

---

43.   Kelly, *Peter and Jude*, pp. 242-43; Bauckham, *Jude, 2 Peter*, p. 3.
44.   D. Hill, *Greek Words and Hebrew Meanings: Studies in the Semantics of Soteriological Terms* (Cambridge: Cambridge University Press, 1967), p. 189.
45.   Bauckham, *Jude, 2 Peter*, p. 30.

Variation Unit 4.1

παρεισεδυσαν   𝔓72 ℵ A K L P Ψ 049
παρεισεδυησαν   B C

Intrinsically either of these readings could be original. As Bauckham has mentioned, they have the same meaning,[46] so I cannot give preference to one reading or the other on contextual grounds. Further, Jude only uses the verb παρεισδύω once, so it is impossible to base an argument on patterns or tendencies. My decision must therefore be guided by transcriptional evidence. Kubo would print the active παρεισέδυσαν as a difficult reading on the grounds that the middle and passive verb forms are more common, thus causing the change to a more familiar form.[47] Albin also prefers παρεισέδυσαν, arguing that παρεισέδυησαν is an emendation.[48] Tentatively, following Albin and Kubo here, παρεισέδυσαν should be printed.

Variation Unit 4.2

κριμα   𝔓72 ℵ A B C K L P 049
κηρυγμα   Ψ

The text editors are in agreement that κρίμα is the better of the two readings. However, the phrase τοῦτο τὸ κρίμα does not seem to fit the context of the passage, since the writer has not mentioned any condemnation prior to v. 4.[49] Bauckham suggests that τοῦτο τὸ κρίμα refers

46.   Bauckham, *Jude, 2 Peter*, p. 28.

47.   The verb παρεισδύειν (it can also be written παρεισδύνειν) is a *hapax legomenon*, so the view that the middle and passive forms are more common is based upon extra-canonical usage.

48.   According to Albin, *Judasbrevet*, p. 737: 'In beiden Fällen [variation units 4.1 and 4.3] dürfte die schon von cod 𝔓72 bezeugte Lesung vorzuziehen sein... παρεισεδυσαν (Aor 2 A) ist überlegen bezeugt. Die Annahme, dass die Form der längeren Koine Form παρεισεδυησαν (Aor 2 P = dieselbe intransitive Bedeutung wie Aor 2 A) durch Wegfall von η entstanden sei, ist zwar üblich; aber die längere Form in cod B kann auch eine (in B schwerlich überraschende) Emendation in Analogie zu ähnlichen Aor 2 P-Formen (Bedeutung = Aor 2 A) im NT sein: von den Verben /συμ/φυειν (siehe Lk. 8.6 8.7 8.8) und εκφυειν (siehe Mt. 24.32 = Mk 13:28 nach cod E K)'. The view here expressed that the Koine form in B is an emendation lends support to the argument posited by Metzger, Fee and others that scribes sometimes made changes in a direction opposite to Atticism. Meanwhile our eclectic approach must distance us from comments such as 'παρεισεδυσαν... ist überlegen bezeugt'.

49.   Bratcher, *Translator's Guide*, p. 173.

forward to vv. 5-7, v. 11 and vv. 14-15.[50] The context is that the intruders are destined for condemnation (v. 4); certain sins are ascribed to them (vv. 5-19); and judgment will be meted out to them (vv. 6 and 15).[51] The reading κρίμα in v. 4 is morphologically close enough to κρίσιν in vv. 6 and 15 for them both to be identified as catchwords, and this network is an established feature of the writer's style.[52] The reading κήρυγμα is explicable as a deliberate change introduced to eradicate the contextual difficulty suggested by κρίμα. Print κρίμα here.

Variation Unit 4.3

χαριτα   A B
χαρειτα   𝔓72
χαριν   א C K L P Ψ 049

Transcriptionally χάριτα is the better reading, since χάριν is 'een Atticistische correctie'.[53] De Zwaan's judgment here concords with that of Elliott, who cites the Atticist grammarian Moeris to substantiate the observation that 'the Hellenistic form of the accusative [of χάρις] is χάριτα and the Attic χάριν'.[54] My acceptance of χάριτα as the better variant on this basis presupposes acceptance of Kilpatrick's proposition that Koine variants should be preferred and their Attic equivalents rejected.[55] The reading χάριν is explicable as a deliberate alteration, a reaction to χάριτα as the more rare form, the latter occurring only here and at Acts 24.27. Meanwhile χαρειτα [sic] is the result of itacism.

Variation Unit 4.4

δεσποτην θεον   K L P Ψ 049 syr[ph,h]
δεσποτην   𝔓72 𝔓78 א A B C

If it can be shown conclusively that the word δεσπότην in v. 4 refers unequivocally to Jesus Christ, then δεσπότην θεόν can be rejected on contextual grounds. The first part of my discussion, therefore, attempts to establish whether δεσπότην in v. 4 is indeed a reference to Jesus Christ.

---

50.   Bauckham, *Jude, 2 Peter*, p. 37.
51.   Green, *General Epistle of Jude*, p. 174.
52.   See variation unit 1.3 for the complete list of catchwords.
53.   J. De Zwaan, *II Petrus en Judas* (Leiden: Van Doesburg, 1909), p. 135.
54.   Elliott, *Essays and Studies*, p. 74.
55.   Kilpatrick, 'Atticism', pp. 15-32.

Bigg, Bauckham, Kistemaker and Bolkestein all believe that the word δεσπότην at v. 4 is a reference to Jesus Christ, a view which presupposes that δεσπότην is the better variant.[56] In defence of this view, Bauckham cites Eusebius *HE* 1.7.14, where there is a reference to Jewish people known as δεσπόσυνοι. The background in Eusebius concerns Jewish people whose birth certificates and other family records had been burned by Herod. To preserve the memory of their pure lineage, the members of some Jewish families memorized these records. The term δεσπόσυνοι in Eusebius underscores the point that certain Jews were of good stock because of their family connections with τὸ σωτήριον—the Saviour—a word which appears to be a reference to Jesus; although, Bauckham omits to tell his readers that τὸ σωτήριον could equally well refer to God, as it does in v. 25. Bauckham does not deny here that the chronology of his citation from Eusebius makes his argument one of inference rather than proof.

Kistemaker's view that the word δεσπότης at v. 4 refers to Jesus Christ is underwritten by a grammatical rule mentioned in Dana and Mantey. Kistemaker says that '...in the Greek only one definite article precedes the nouns Sovereign [master] and Lord. The rule states that when one article controls two nouns the writer refers to one person'.[57] The applicability of this rule here is questionable. Bauckham recalls the same rule, but points out that κύριος often appears without an accompanying article.[58] It is quite normal for κύριος to be anarthrous in the New Testament, since like θεός, κύριος is near to being a proper noun.[59]

As has been pointed out by Fuchs and Reymond,[60] elsewhere in his epistle, the writer is careful to make the distinction between Jesus Christ and God, and in v. 25 he specifically uses the adjective μόνος in agreement with θεός. Jude is unlikely to have deviated from the set expressions which appear at vv. 17, 21 and 25 as unequivocal references to Jesus Christ: at none of these verses is δεσπότης extant, thus nowhere

---

56.   C. Bigg, *A Critical and Exegetical Commentary on the Epistles of St. Peter and St. Jude* (Edinburgh: T. & T. Clark, 2nd edn, 1902), p. 327; Bauckham, *Jude, 2 Peter*, p. 39; S. J. Kistemaker, *Exposition of the Epistles of Peter and of the Epistle of Jude* (Grand Rapids: Baker, 1987), p. 375; Bolkestein, *Petrus en Judas*, p. 208.

57.   Kistemaker, *Peter and Jude*, p. 375; H.E. Dana and J.R. Mantey, *A Manual Grammar of the Greek New Testament* (New York: Macmillan, 1967), p. 147.

58.   R.J. Bauckham, *Jude and the Relatives of Jesus in the Early Church* (Edinburgh: T. & T. Clark, 1990), pp. 302-303.

59.   MHT, III, p. 174.

60.   Fuchs, *Saint Jude*, p. 160.

in Jude is the word δεσπότης linked to any of the set expressions which refer to Jesus Christ, so my deduction is that at v. 4, the word δεσπότης is separate from the set expression κύριον ἡμῶν Ἰησοῦν Χριστόν. It would seem that the epithets used of God and of Jesus Christ in vv. 4, 21 and 25 follow the pattern discernible elsewhere in the New Testament, with Jesus Christ being referred to within a set expression as κύριος rather than δεσπότης, and with God as δεσπότης.[61] The reference of δεσπότης to God is unequivocal at Lk. 2.29; Acts 4.24; Rev. 6.10; and 2 Tim. 2.21.

The relationship between Jesus and his disciples need not necessarily be perceived as a 'slave-master' relationship. Voelz has made the suggestion that the way in which Jesus hands over authority to his disciples in Lk. 9.1 signifies that they were in a rabbi-pupil relationship, not in a slave-master relationship.[62] If this view is correct, then it decreases further the likelihood that δεσπότην at v. 4 is a reference to Jesus Christ.

The proposition should be considered that the word δεσπότης is not used of Christ anywhere in the New Testament other than at 2 Pet. 2.1. Bauckham has argued convincingly that 2 Peter is dependent upon Jude on the grounds of Jude's more polished and tightly constructed literary structure, and that the word δεσπότης at 2 Pet. 2.1 is borrowed from Jude.[63] However, this hypothesis need not undermine my theory that δεσπότην θεόν may have been the original reading in v. 4. The author of 2 Peter may have seen δεσπότην θεόν in v. 4, and decided for his own reasons to break with Jude's traditional usage. This would account for the appearance of δεσπότην in 2 Pet. 2.1 as an apparent reference to Jesus Christ.

The evidence considered thus far suggests that the word δεσπότην in v. 4 is no less likely to be a reference to God than to Jesus Christ, and so the contextual argument in favour of the reading δεσπότην is not decisive. Thus far I have shown that the reading δεσπότην θεόν cannot be rejected on intrinsic grounds.

61. Although the views of Kelly, *Peter and Jude*, p. 252; Fuchs, *Saint Jude*, p. 160; Green, *General Epistle of Jude*, p. 175; H. Windisch, *Die katholischen Briefe* (Tübingen: Mohr & Siebeck, 1951), p. 39; and R. Knopf, *Die Briefe Petri und Judä* (Göttingen: Vandenhoeck & Ruprecht, 7th edn, 1912), p. 219, that τὸν μόνον δεσπότην at v. 4 is a reference to God all presuppose that δεσπότην is the better of the two variants, their preferences can be regarded as indirect arguments in favour of δεσπότην θεόν.

62. J.W. Voelz, 'The Problem of Meaning in Texts', *Neot* 23 (1989), p. 34.

63. Bauckham, *Jude, 2 Peter*, pp. 142, 240.

Two positive intrinsic arguments can be cited briefly in defence of δεσπότην θεόν: (1) since Jude's source material derives from extra-canonical and Old Testament authors,[64] it is possible that Jude wrote τὸν μόνον δεσπότην θεόν to re-express slightly a phrase known to writers such as Josephus;[65] (2) the presence of a comparatively high number of *hapax legomena* in Jude should prepare us not only to expect words which occur nowhere else in the New Testament, but also phrases which are equally rare, such as δεσπότην θεόν.

Regarding the transcriptional evidence, commentators who have looked at this problem invariably stress that the reading δεσπότην θεόν has θεόν appended to make the sentence less ambiguous since δεσπότην could refer either to Jesus Christ or to God.[66] However the possibility that θεόν was deliberately removed rather than added must also be considered. The reading δεσπότην θεόν is unlikely to be a doctrinally altered reading, whereas the same cannot be said of δεσπότην without θεόν. Ehrman has noted a tendency towards anti-adoptionist corruptions of the New Testament text in 𝔓72:

> A striking example [of anti-adoptionist corruption] occurs in the salutation of 2 Pet. 1.2: 'May grace and peace be multiplied to you in the knowledge of God and of our Lord Jesus'. 𝔓72 omits the conjunction 'and' (καί), leading to the identification of Jesus as God: 'in the knowledge of God, our Lord Jesus'. That this omission was not an accident is confirmed by similar modifications in the same manuscript.[67]

This example from 2 Pet. 1.2 can be used as a paradigm for the problem at Jude 4. If Ehrman is correct about the direction of corruption away from adoptionist 'heresies', and if the conflict between adoptionism and orthodoxy is the reason for the variation at the unit here, then it is likely that δεσπότην θεόν as the reading at v. 4 which shows God and Jesus as two separate entities was shortened by anti-adoptionist orthodox scribes to remove the word θεόν. Such an alteration is explicable as a

---

64.   See J.D. Charles, '"Those" and "These": The Use of the Old Testament in the Epistle of Jude', *JSNT* 38 (1990), pp. 109-24; *idem*, 'Jude's Use of Pseudepigraphical Source-Material as Part of a Literary Strategy', *NTS* 37 (1991), pp. 130-45.

65.   Josephus *Ant.* 18.23 uses the phrase μόνον ἡγεμόνα καὶ δεσπότην τὸν θεόν.

66.   See, for example, Fuchs, *Saint Jude*, p. 160; Kubo, 𝔓72 *and the Codex Vaticanus*, p. 140; and Metzger, *Textual Commentary*, pp. 656-57.

67.   Ehrman, *Orthodox Corruption of Scripture*, p. 85.

wish to show God and Jesus as the same entity, thereby stressing the divinity of Christ.

My decision to accept δεσπότην θεόν at this unit is based mainly on transcriptional evidence, which suggests that of the two readings, it alone resists orthodox interference.

Variation Unit 4.5

om. ημων 𝔓78 ℵ A B C K L P Ψ 049
ημων (*primum*) 𝔓72

The extra ἡμῶν preserved singularly in 𝔓72 is not contextually or syntactically essential and cannot, therefore, be decisively defended. I become more suspicious when I encounter the word order violation in 𝔓72 that involves the position of the second ἡμῶν as explained in more depth at variation unit 4.7 below.

Variation Unit 4.6

και 𝔓72 ℵ A B C K L P Ψ 049
om. και 𝔓78

I have already posited that the removal of θεόν at the fourth unit is explicable as an anti-adoptionistic alteration to the text. By omitting καί, the reading in 𝔓78 places even greater emphasis on Christ's divinity, thus revealing itself as another orthodox alteration. καί should, therefore, be included at this unit.

Variation Unit 4.7

κυριον ημων ιησουν χριστον 𝔓78 ℵ A B C K L P 049
κυριον ιησουν χριστον ημων 𝔓72

The position of the second ἡμῶν in 𝔓72 after κύριον Ἰησοῦν Χριστόν is cause for concern since, in New Testament Greek, it is usual for a pronoun to separate nouns which belong together (for example, ἔλεος ὑμῖν καὶ εἰρήνη, at Jude 1; χάρις ὑμῖν καὶ εἰρήνη at Gal. 1.3).[68] The position of ἡμῶν after κύριον Ἰησοῦν Χριστόν in 𝔓72 is not in harmony with normal New Testament usage. Since I have no evidence of any word order inconcinnities that are firmly in the tradition in Jude, κύριον ἡμῶν Ἰησοῦν Χριστόν should be printed at this

68. BDF §473.

unit. It is not clear why the reading in 𝔓72 should not accord with Jude's word order preference, but the same sort of deviation in 𝔓72 is evident at variation unit 21.3.

Variation Unit 5.1

δε   𝔓72 𝔓78 ℵ A B K L 049
ουν   C Ψ
om. δε   400 458

According to Louw and Nida the particle δέ can have three possible meanings: 'and', 'and then', 'but'. The same lexicographers offer three possible meanings for οὖν: 'therefore', 'indeed', 'but'.[69] From these definitions it can be inferred that οὖν and δέ are synonymous when a mild contrast is implied. It could be argued that since v. 4 focuses on the opponents, and since v. 5 begins by reminding the addressees of certain facts, the context in v. 5 demands the inclusion of a particle denoting a mild contrast. The omission of δέ is, therefore, not a likely option. My choice here is between the two variants which reflect the reality of a mild contrast between v. 4 and v. 5: οὖν and δέ. This mild contrast is shown in NEB at v. 5 where δέ is rendered 'but'.

In order to choose between the variants οὖν and δέ at v. 5, the surest guide will be to look at other verses in Jude where a particle is used to denote a mild contrast:

v. 10   οὗτοι <u>δὲ</u> ὅσα μὲν οὐκ οἴδασιν βλασφημοῦσιν
v. 17   ὑμεῖς <u>δέ</u>, ἀγαπητοί, μνημονεύετε τῶν ῥημάτων[70]
v. 20   ὑμεῖς <u>δέ</u>, ἀγαπητοί, ἐποικοδομοῦντες ἑαυτοὺς
v. 24   τῷ <u>δὲ</u> δυναμένῳ στηρίξαι ἀσπίλους ἀμώμους ἀγνευομένους[71]

At v. 10 δέ is read in all MSS except 1836, where οὖν appears instead. In the examples from vv. 17, 20 and 24, δέ is firmly in the text. Other than singularly in 1836 at v. 10, nowhere is there any evidence that Jude used οὖν to denote a mild contrast, so my preference is clearly for δέ.

Variation Unit 5.2

βουλομαι ειδοτας   𝔓72 A C Ψ
βουλομαι ειδοτας υμας   ℵ B K L 049
βουλομε αδελφοι ειδοτας υμας   𝔓78

69.   LN §§89.87, 89.94, 89.124; 89.50, 89.127, 91.7.
70.   I have accepted μνημονεύετε against GNT4.
71.   I have accepted στηρίξαι ἀσπίλους ἀμώμους ἀγνευομένους against GNT4.

The singular reading in 𝔓78 may be deemed inadmissable for two reasons: (1) βουλομε is a scribal blunder; and (2) if a direct reference to the addressees really appeared in the original text of Jude, ἀγαπητοί should be found rather than ἀδελφοί. The writer's usual preference for ἀγαπητοί has already been mentioned.[72] This leaves two possibilities: βούλομαι εἰδότας, and βούλομαι εἰδότας ὑμᾶς.

Matthew Black has argued that βούλομαι εἰδότας ὑμᾶς at v. 5 is the better reading on the grounds that it is stylistically more difficult: the second ὑμᾶς is awkward and transcriptional probability would incline towards its removal, thus producing βούλομαι εἰδότας as a scribal improvement.[73] Having argued along these lines, Black then provides a caution as to the certainty of his own preference for βούλομαι εἰδότας ὑμᾶς upon realizing that 𝔓72 omits ὑμᾶς, and he concludes that βούλομαι εἰδότας [ὑμᾶς] should be printed, the bracketing being provided to show his uncertainty.[74]

Allen Wikgren reminds his readers saliently that εἰδότας at v. 5 and other conjugatives of εἰδώς may stand alone without a subject or object.[75] This tells me that the reading βούλομαι εἰδότας at v. 5 is a distinct possibility. Contrariwise, Wikgren does not rule out βούλομαι εἰδότας ὑμᾶς because in his view the second ὑμᾶς may exemplify repetition for emphasis.

When I look more closely at the pertinent intrinsic possibilities, it is surprising that Black and Wikgren should have expressed any inclination in favour of the variant βούλομαι εἰδότας ὑμᾶς since it is extremely unlikely that the author of a text composed with such polished precision as Jude could have produced such an awkward and pleonastic expression as ὑπομνῆσαι δὲ ὑμᾶς βούλομαι εἰδότας ὑμᾶς.[76] Since Jude

72. See the discussion of variation unit 1.2, where the variant τοῖς ἔθνεσιν was deemed inadmissible.

73. M. Black 'Critical and Exegetical Notes on Three New Testament Texts: Hebrews 11.11, Jude 5, James 1.27', in W. Eltester (ed.), *Apophoreta: Festschrift für Ernst Haenchen zu seinem siebzigsten Geburtstag* (Berlin: Töpelmann, 1964), p. 44.

74. 𝔓72 is wrongly printed as '𝔓22' by Black's publishers.

75. A. Wikgren, 'Some Problems in Jude 5', in B.L. Daniels and M.J. Suggs (eds.), *Studies in the History and Text of the New Testament in Honour of Kenneth Willis Clark* (SD, 29; Salt Lake City: Utah University Press, 1967), p. 149.

76. Citing Quintilian *Institutio Oratoria* 8.3.53 and 9.3.46-55, Watson, *Invention*, pp. 65-66, explains that pleonasm in ancient rhetoric can be defined either as a figure of speech, or as a stylistic fault. As a fault, pleonasm refers to unnecessary

vv. 4-19 has been described as 'a piece of writing whose detailed structure and wording has been composed with exquisite care',[77] the stylistically awkward double ὑμᾶς should be rejected as being uncharacteristic
of the author. The idea that the second ὑμᾶς exemplifies repetition for
emphasis would have been an acceptable proposition if there were a
third instance of ὑμᾶς within the radius of vv. 4-6 to triadize the hypothetical double ὑμᾶς, but there is not triadic illustration here.[78] It is perhaps more likely that the second ὑμᾶς originates rather from an attempt
by a scribe to 'improve' the text by manufacturing an example of
emphasis by repetition where the original writer did not intend it.
Against GNT4, the variant which should be printed at this unit is
βούλομαι εἰδότας.

Variation Unit 5.3

παντα οτι κυριος απαξ   ℵ Ψ
απαξ παντα οτι ιησους   A B
απαξ παντα οτι ο κυριος   927 1245
απαξ παντα οτι ο θεος   5 623ᶜ
απαξ παντας οτι θεος χριστος   𝔓72
παντας οτι ο θεος απαξ   syrᵖʰ
παντα οτι ιησους απαξ   copˢᵃ·ᵇᵒ
παντα οτι ο θεος απαξ   442 621
παντα οτι ο κυριος απαξ   C 630
απαξ τουτο οτι ο κυριος   L 049
τουτο απαξ οτι ο κυριος   K 056

The primary issue here is whether the subject of the verb ἀπώλεσεν is
Ἰησοῦς, κύριος, θεός, or θεὸς Χριστός. Once a choice has been
made from among these possibilities, it will remain to decide whether the
word ἅπαξ belongs inside the ὅτι clause or not.

   The first possibility is Ἰησοῦς. Black's problem with Ἰησοῦς is that
if it connotes Joshua, the context renders it impossible, since the
destruction of Israel in the wilderness cannot be ascribed to Joshua.

redundancy with words. As a figure of speech, pleonasm is a form of emphasis by
repetition. Jude's use of pleonasm as a figure of speech appears to be restricted (a) to
threefold repetition, e.g. πάντων (×3) at v. 15; and (b) to the twofold repetition of
words which support triadic structures, e.g. καί (×2) at v. 2. At v. 5, ὑμᾶς is
clearly not a figure of speech, and is therefore pleonastic in the negative sense.
   77.   Bauckham, *Jude, 2 Peter*, p. 142.
   78.   It is worth remembering that the two existing examples of threefold repetition involving pronouns are ὑμῖν (×3) in vv. 2-3, and ἡμῶν (×3) in vv. 3-4.

However, Osburn has argued that 'Iησοῦς at v. 5 is a reference not to Joshua but to Jesus.[79] Osburn's idea is that the variant 'Iησοῦς at this unit could be a reference to the pre-existent activity of Christ in Old Testament history. Osburn cites 1 Cor. 10.4 and 1 Cor. 10.9 as parallels. Both verses are cited as proof of the pre-existent activity of Christ in the Old Testament. Against Kelly's view that Christ cannot be credited with imprisoning the fallen angels as described in v. 6,[80] Osburn provides a reference to 1 Enoch 69.26-29 where the Son of Man 'sits in judgment upon these angels imprisoned in chains'.[81] This is given along with references to 1 Pet. 3.22, 1 Cor. 15.24, Eph. 1.19-21, and Col. 2.15. Perhaps the closest parallel to v. 5 among these four New Testament references is 1 Pet. 3.21-22, where Jesus is depicted at God's right hand 'with angels, authorities, and powers subject to him' (RSV). Wikgren also considers the variant 'Iησοῦς to be a strong contender at v. 5, and mentions that in early Christian literature, 'Exodus, Wilderness and Settlement [are combined] into one act of salvation, and it is quite possible that this is what the author of Jude had in mind...when he wrote, "saved out of Egypt"'.[82] According to Justin *Dialogue with Trypho* 120.3 (cited by Wikgren) Jesus is 'the one who led your fathers out of Egypt'.

The idea that Jude could have anticipated Justin by fifty years and written 'Iησοῦς at v. 5 as a reference to the pre-existent Christ active in Old Testament events is discussed in greater depth by Jarl Fossum. Fossum's basic argument is that the subject of ἀπώλεσεν in v. 5 is Jesus acting as the angel of the Lord, the 'deputy of God possessing the Divine Name [YHWH]'.[83] Fossum traces the concept of the angel of the Lord from Abba Hilfi, a Palestinian amora of the second generation, who identifies the archangel Gabriel as the Yahweh who destroyed Sodom and Gomorrah, to Philo *Somn.* 1.85 where the destruction of Sodom and Gomorrah is attributed to the mediating actions of the divine Logos or angel of the Lord. The strength of Fossum's argument is simply that it does not depend for its validity on accepting 'Iησοῦς,

79.   Black, 'Three New Testament Texts', p. 45; Osburn, 'Text of Jude 5', p. 112.

80.   Kelly, *Peter and Jude*, p. 255.

81.   Osburn, 'Text of Jude 5', p. 112.

82.   Wikgren, 'Some Problems in Jude 5', p. 148.

83.   J. Fossum, 'Kyrios Jesus as the Angel of the Lord in Jude 5-7', *NTS* 33 (1987), pp. 226-43.

and it would be equally plausible were one to argue in favour of κύριος. Fossum acknowledges the objections of rabbinic scholarship to his theory, noting the rabbinic view that the rescue out of Egypt was performed 'not by an angel and not by a messenger'.[84]

Objections to Fossum's view that the subject of ἀπώλεσεν in v. 5 is Jesus acting as the angel of the Lord have been expressed by Bauckham.[85] These objections can be seen indirectly as the first major argument against the variant Ἰησοῦς at v. 5 since it is in the spirit of his angel theory that Fossum expresses preference for Ἰησοῦς over the other variants. The first difficulty with the angel theory arises from Fossum's exegesis of v. 6. Fossum has conceded that the destroyer of Sodom and Gomorrah is identical with the one who 'punished Israel in the desert and imprisoned the fallen angels'.[86] Fossum's exegesis of v. 6 depends upon citations from 1 Enoch 10.4-6 and 1 Enoch 10.11-12, citations in which 'there is not one, but two principal angels, and it is not obvious how Jude's κύριος...could apply to Christ as a substitute for one or both of these angels, rather than to God'.[87] Also, against Fossum, I need an explanation as to why Jesus is considered to be the intermediary angel at v. 5, whereas the role of the angel of the Lord at v. 9 is occupied by Michael: if Fossum is correct, I would surely expect to find Michael replaced by Jesus at v. 9.[88] The third problem with Fossum's angel theory is that the traditional examples of divine judgment (including 3 Macc. 2.4-7 and 2 Pet. 2.4-8) upon which vv. 5-7 are modelled contain no reference to an intermediary agent of God.[89]

The second major argument against the variant Ἰησοῦς at v. 5 is Bauckham's contention that Ἰησοῦς at v. 5 was not written by Jude but was introduced by a scribe who was influenced by 'the Joshua-Jesus typology which became popular in the second century'.[90] Bauckham is arguing implicitly against Fossum's theory here: it must be remembered

---

84.   J. Goldin, 'Not By Means of an Angel and Not By Means of a Messenger', in J. Neusner (ed.), *Religions in Antiquity: Essays in Memory of Erwin Ramsdell Goodenough* (Leiden: Brill, 1968), pp. 412-24, cited in Fossum, 'Kyrios Jesus', p. 241. This rabbinic view is confirmed by a reference in Fossum to N. N. Glatzer (ed.), *The Passover Haggadah* (New York: Schocken, 1953), p. 36.

85.   See Bauckham, *Jude and the Relatives of Jesus*, pp. 310-11.

86.   Fossum, 'Kyrios Jesus', p. 228.

87.   Bauckham, *Jude and the Relatives of Jesus*, p. 310.

88.   Bauckham, *Jude and the Relatives of Jesus*, pp. 310-11.

89.   Bauckham, *Jude and the Relatives of Jesus*, p. 311.

90.   Bauckham, *Jude and the Relatives of Jesus*, p. 309.

that Fossum rejects the theory that Ἰησοῦς is a reference to Joshua.[91] Bauckham's idea is: (1) Ἰησοῦς does not refer to the pre-existent Christ since there is no parallel in New Testament canonical literature; and (2) Ἰησοῦς was inserted by a scribe during the second century when Joshua-Jesus typology became popular. It is not necessary to agree with the first of Bauckham's two points in order to accept the logic of the second.[92] This theory that a second-century scribe interpolated Ἰησοῦς without noticing 'the pitfalls it would encounter as the statement continues [in other words, without looking ahead at vv. 6-7]'[93] is all the more plausible when we remember that Bauckham's chronology for Joshua-Jesus typology makes it contempraneous with the period when most New Testament textual corruption occurred, namely, the second century.[94]

The third major argument against Ἰησοῦς at v. 5 is that it is intrinsically improbable on grounds of the writer's style. Whenever Jude mentions Jesus by name, Ἰησοῦς is accompanied by Χριστός. This occurs on six occasions:

v. 1	Ἰησοῦ Χριστοῦ
v. 1	Ἰησοῦ Χριστῷ
v. 4	Ἰησοῦν Χριστὸν
v. 17	Ἰησοῦ Χριστοῦ
v. 21	Ἰησοῦ Χριστοῦ
v. 25	Ἰησοῦ Χριστοῦ

Although there is word order variation at v. 1, such variation does not invalidate the two examples from v. 1. Only the example at v. 25 is in

91. Fossum, 'Kyrios Jesus', p. 226.

92. Although Osburn, 'Text of Jude 5', p. 112, concedes that the name Ἰησοῦς does not have a New Testament parallel as a reference to the pre-existent Christ, he claims that 1 Cor. 10.4 evidences the name Χριστός as proof of the activity of the pre-existent Christ in Old Testament history, where Paul writes ἡ πέτρα δὲ ἦν ὁ Χριστός 'with reference to the rabbinic tradition of the following rock'. However Ehrman, *Orthodox Corruption*, p. 89, views the omission of ὁ θεός in some MSS at 1 Cor. 10.5 as a doctrinal alteration to the text, which, because it makes ὁ Χριστός from the previous verse the subject of the verb in 1 Cor. 10.5, aims to attribute to Christ instead of to God the 'execution of divine wrath'. Ehrman goes on to show that the variant Χριστός at 1 Cor. 10.9 is another doctrinal alteration: it was God, not Christ, who destroyed the Israelites after they had put him to the test. The pattern with both of these alterations is that they attribute divine prerogatives to Jesus Christ.

93. Bauckham, *Jude and the Relatives of Jesus*, p. 309.

94. Kilpatrick, 'Atticism', p. 24.

doubt since some MSS omit Ἰησοῦ Χριστοῦ altogether. Jesus was a common name during Jude's lifetime, and Jude obliges Christians 'who would have needed a way of distinguishing Jesus from others who bore this very common name'[95] by supplying the double name Ἰησοῦς Χριστός whenever referring to Jesus in his epistle. The variant Ἰησοῦς at v. 5 is therefore uncharacteristic of the author since it appears without Χριστός.

In view of the three major arguments against Ἰησοῦς at v. 5, I am left with only κύριος, θεός and θεὸς Χριστός as possible contenders. A theory has been advanced about the tetragram which could be advanced in favour of κύριος or θεός, and which I will now consider.

George Howard sees the variation at this unit in v. 5 to be typical of a situation where the text originally contained the tetragram, a position which favours either κύριος or θεός but not Ἰησοῦς.[96] Howard approvingly reiterates Paap's theory that Gentile Christian scribes considered the word θεός to have the same sacred value as the tetragram and therefore first applied the contraction to θεός and later to other sacred words, but in practice the position Howard adopts seems closer to that of Traube, who has argued that *nomina sacra* were of Jewish origin, since (for example) the tetragram could have been translated as θεός and contracted to ΘΣ without vowels after the Hebrew manner.[97] According to Traube, Hellenistic Jews were the first people to contract not only the word θεός, but also κύριος, πνεῦμα, πατήρ, οὐρανός, ἄνθρωπος, Δαυίδ, Ἰσραήλ, and Ἰερουσαλήμ. Against Traube, Paap argues that (1) Jews wrote the holy name of God as a tetragram and avoided its pronunciation but did not regard the word 'Adonai' (lord) as a word to be avoided, and, therefore, they would not have rendered 'Adonai' as a sacred contraction in Greek in the same manner as ΘΣ; (2) since the Jews were strict monotheists, they would not have used sacred contractions for any word other than θεός.[98] Paap's conclusion after an analysis of the earliest relevant papyral evidence is that, for the

95. Bauckham, *Jude and the Relatives of Jesus*, p. 285.

96. G. Howard, 'The Tetragram and the New Testament', *JBL* 96 (1977), pp. 63-83.

97. A.H.R.E. Paap, *Nomina Sacra in the Greek Papyri of the First Five Centuries AD: The Sources and Some Deductions* (Leiden: Brill, 1959), pp. 119-27; L. Traube, *Nomina Sacra: Versuch einer Geschichte der christlichen Kürzung* (Munich: Beck, 1907).

98. Paap, *Nomina Sacra*, pp. 1-2.

earliest Christian communities, the word θεός (and no other) had the same sacred value as the tetragram and was contracted to ΘΣ based on the borrowed Hebrew convention of consonantal writing, but that this original principle was gradually lost with the spread of Christianity. Other words considered sacred by later generations of Christians were contracted. The first to follow θεός were κύριος, Ἰησοῦς and Χριστός. From this it does not follow that the word κύριος in the New Testament is necessarily a surrogate for the tetragram: Paap's results point in the opposite direction. I am on much safer ground if I restrict my speculations on the tetragram to direct quotations from the LXX which appear in the New Testament and which involve the word θεός either unopposed or as a variant. From all this I can deduce that Osburn is right to regard Howard's comments on v. 5 as improbable and speculative.[99]

It has already been seen that there is considerable doubt among critics as to whether the subject of ἀπώλεσεν at v. 5 is God or the deputy of God possessing the divine name Yahweh. The variant which best accounts for this doubt and ambiguity is κύριος. It is κύριος which best explains the origin of the other variants, since Ἰησοῦς and θεός can both be seen as attempts at resolving the ambiguity surrounding the subject of the verb ἀπώλεσεν.[100] Meanwhile, although Metzger has suggested that the singular reading θεὸς Χριστός in 𝔓72 is a probable scribal error, where possibly θεοῦ Χριστός ('God's annointed one') was the intention, it is surprising that he has not considered an obvious doctrinal factor here. The anti-adoptionist tendency in 𝔓72 has already been mentioned, and the addition of Χριστός to θεός in 𝔓72 seems highly likely to have been motivated by the anti-adoptionist orthodox desire to stress the divinity of Christ.[101] The crucial point is that κύριος is the only variant which is acceptable irrespective of both Fossum's hypothesis that the subject of the verb ἀπώλεσεν at v. 5 is the angel of the Lord—God's deputy bearing the name Yahweh—or Bauckham's conclusion that the subject of the verb ἀπώλεσεν is God.[102]

In view of my preference for κύριος as the subject of ἀπώλεσεν, I am left with five possibilities at this variation unit:

99. Osburn, 'Text of Jude 5', p. 107.

100. Alternatively, see Metzger, *Textual Commentary*, p. 724, where Ἰησοῦς is explained 'in terms of transcriptional oversight (KC being taken for IC)'.

101. Ehrman, *Orthodox Corruption*, pp. 85-86.

102. Fossum, 'Kyrios Jesus', p. 231; Bauckham, *Jude and the Relatives of Jesus*, p. 312.

ἅπαξ παντα οτι ο κυριος   927 1245
παντα οτι κυριος απαξ   ℵ Ψ
παντα οτι ο κυριος απαξ   C 630
απαξ τουτο οτι ο κυριος   L 049
τουτο απαξ οτι ο κυριος   K 056

Although there is word order variation here, it is difficult to base a solution on the grounds of the writer's word order preferences. The writer usually positions πᾶς before its agreeing substantive, as can be seen at vv. 3, 15 and 25. However, the word πᾶς at v. 5 is itself used substantively and does not agree with εἰδότας, so I cannot use the position of πᾶς to defend one particular order of words. BDF point out moreover that word order involving πᾶς in the New Testament as a whole is flexible.[103] The position of ἅπαξ is also doubtful. Wikgren sees ἅπαξ as having two possible meanings: 'once and for all' and 'first'. If 'once and for all' is the original meaning, then scribes who thought that it meant 'first' would have moved ἅπαξ to within the ὅτι clause (τὸ δεύτερον being taken by them to mean 'in the second place') 'by attraction to τὸ δεύτερον'.[104] Despite Wikgren's argument, the following four English translations still reflect doubt about the exact position of ἅπαξ:

> I should like to remind you—though you have already learnt it once and for all—how the Lord rescued the nation from Egypt... (JB)

> Now I desire to remind you, though you were once and for all fully informed, that he who saved a people out of the land of Egypt... (RSV)

> You already know it all, but let me remind you how the Lord, having once delivered the people of Israel out of Egypt... (NEB)

> For even though you know all this, I want to remind you of how the Lord once rescued the people of Egypt... (TEV)

From these translations it is clear that modern scholarship is undecided as to whether ἅπαξ originated outside the ὅτι clause (JB, RSV) or within the ὅτι clause (NEB, TEV). The movement of ἅπαξ may have been in one of two possible directions. It would indeed seem precarious to build an argument around ἅπαξ or πᾶς at v. 5.

A solution to this problem may perhaps lie in deciding whether κύριος should be articular or anarthrous.[105] When κύριος is an unambiguous

103. BDF §292.
104. Wikgren, 'Some Problems in Jude 5', p. 150.
105. Our thinking here is influenced by G.D. Kilpatrick, 'KYRIOS in the Gospels', *Collected Essays of G.D. Kilpatrick*, pp. 213-15; *idem*, 'ΚΥΡΙΟΣ

reference to Jesus Christ as at vv. 4, 17, 21 and 25, it can be either articular as at vv. 17, 21 and 25, or anarthrous as at v. 4. However, when κύριος is not accompanied by a reference to Jesus Christ, as at vv. 9 and 14, κύριος is anarthrous and could be a reference to God. At v. 9 κύριος is anarthrous in all MSS cited except ℵ² and two cursives. At v. 14 anarthrous κύριος is preserved in all of the witnesses cited except ℵ and two cursives. Anarthrous κύριος as a perceived reference to God alone could have been taken by some scribes to imply a denial of the divinity of Christ, and the addition of the article to κύριος in ℵ at vv. 9 and 14 is viewed as a reaction to this implied denial. The effect of the addition of the definite article to κύριος in ℵ at vv. 9 and 14 is to loosen the semantic reference of the word κύριος thus extending the reference either to God or to Christ. If this explanation is correct, then articular κύριος at vv. 9 and 14 is a typical anti-adoptionistic doctrinal alteration to the text in which the divinity of Christ is stressed. At v. 5 the same argument applies: anarthrous κύριος is the uncorrupted reading, and articular κύριος is explicable as a doctrinal alteration. That doctrinal changes were not effected in a consistent manner explains why the doctrinal alteration is preserved in ℵ at vv. 9 and 14 but not at v. 5 in the same MS. In the light of my discussion, πάντα ὅτι κύριος ἅπαξ should be printed here and the four variants with articular κύριος rejected. I might add that the translations of v. 5 which best reflect my chosen reading are those in NEB and TEV.

Variation Unit 5.4

γης αιγυπτου   ℵ A B C K L 049
γης εγυπτου   𝔓 72
της αιγυπτου   Ψ 429 431

Since εγυπτου in 𝔓72 is a scribal error, I have to choose between γῆς Αἰγύπτου and τῆς Αἰγύπτου. In New Testament Greek, names of towns and cities (and by extension those of countries) are anarthrous, unless the reference to them is anaphoric.[106] With regard to Αἴγυπτος in particular, the anarthrous usage in the New Testament is almost universal, as corroborated at Mt. 2.13, 2.14, 2.15, 2.19; Acts 2.10, 7.9, 7.10 (×2), 7.12, 7.15, 7.17, 7.18, 7.34, 7.39; Heb. 3.16, 11.26, 11.27, and

Again', *Collected Essays of G.D. Kilpatrick*, pp. 216-22, esp. 222, where it is shown that anarthrous κύριος in the Gospels denotes God, and that articular κύριος in the Gospels could denote God or Jesus.

106. MHT, III, p. 171.

Rev. 11.8. The only appearance of an articular Αἴγυπτος in the New Testament is apparently τὴν Αἴγυπτον at Acts 7.11, which is anaphoric in the sense that it could refer back to Αἰγύπτου at Acts 7.10. The expression 'the land of Egypt' is also anarthrous, as at Acts 7.36, 7.40, 13.17, and Heb. 8.9. Since 'Egypt' at v. 5 is not anaphoric, the only acceptable variant here is γῆς Αἰγύπτου. The change from γῆς to τῆς is explicable as an accidental transcriptional error, Γ being taken for T.

Variation Unit 6.1

δε A 625 638
τε 𝔓72 ℵ B C K L Ψ 049

Probably for external reasons, the GNT4 editors have printed τέ and have relegated δέ from text and apparatus to oblivion. By contrast, Kilpatrick, *Diglot*, has printed δέ. Kilpatrick's decision can certainly be justified on grounds of style. Unlike at vv. 5, 9, 10, 17 and 20, where δέ denotes a mild contrast, at v. 6 the variants τέ and δέ both carry the semantic force of 'and' or 'and then'.[107] In situations where τέ or δέ would be optional, Jude always prefers δέ:

v. 1	ἀδελφὸς δὲ Ἰακώβου
v. 14	ἐπροφήτευσεν δὲ[108]
v. 24	τῷ δὲ δυναμένῳ στηρίξαι ἀσπίλους ἀμώμους ἀγνευομένους[109]

All three instances of δέ in the citations above are accepted by the editors of GNT4. Two instances of δέ occur without variation: δέ at v. 1, and δέ at v. 24. Were it not for a singular reading, δέ at v. 14 would also be firmly in the tradition.

Kilpatrick has the following to say about τέ elsewhere in the New Testament:

> Pursuit of consistency [in style] produces some borderline instances. τε is a word going out of use in the first century AD, but had a high style value. Mark and John do not use it and Luke has it rarely. The only example of τε in Matthew without a Greek variant, as far as I know, is at 22.10.[110]

---

107. LN §§89.87, 89.94, 89.88, 89.95.
108. I have accepted ἐπροφήτευσεν against GNT4.
109. I have accepted στηρίξαι ἀσπίλους ἀμώμους ἀγνευομένους against GNT4.
110. Kilpatrick, 'Conjectural Emendation', p. 103.

It does not require a great leap of the imagination to view τέ as a stylistic improvement originally introduced at this verse by second-century scribes, later being reflected in MSS such as 𝔓72 ℵ B C K L Ψ 049. On intrinsic and transcriptional grounds, then, print δέ here.

Variation Unit 6.2

αλλα   𝔓72 ℵ A B K L 049
αλλ   C Ψ

To decide whether Jude is likely to have used elision and written ἀλλ᾽ (a possibility in view of ἀπολιπόντας beginning with a vowel), or whether ἀλλά was written in full, I will review the trends and preferences for elision in Hellenistic Greek generally, and then determine whether these trends and preferences are characteristic of Jude.

The general tendency during the Hellenistic period was towards writing out words in full rather than using elision in situations where elision might theoretically be expected, and spoken Greek is more likely to have been elided than written Greek.[111] Elision in New Testament Greek is commonest before words beginning with ε, and rarest before those that begin with α and is more likely to occur before articles, pronouns and particles than before nouns and verbs.[112]

Two examples of elision in Jude are: (1) κατ᾽ αὐτοῦ in v. 15; and (2) ἐπ᾽ ἐσχάτου in v. 18. Since these are not nouns or verbs, both of the examples conform to the general Hellenistic tendency mentioned above. Because there is no evidence firm in the MS tradition of the writer using elision where other New Testament writers would have avoided using it, ἀλλά should be accepted at this variation unit and at unit 9.4, and ὑπὸ ἀνέμων at unit 12.6. Elliott reaches a similar conclusion about the elision of ἀλλά in the Pastorals, noting that 'Atticists would prefer to institute elision wherever possible and to avoid ἀλλά where it occurs before a vowel'.[113]

Variation Unit 6.3

απολιποντας   ℵ A B C K Ψ
απολειποντας 𝔓72 L 049

---

111. BDF §17; MHT, II, p. 61.
112. BDF §17; MHT, II, p. 61.
113. Elliott, *Timothy and Titus*, p. 26.

If Porter's distinction that the aorist conveys a 'perfective' view of a complete process, whereas the present conveys an 'imperfective' view of an ongoing process is accepted,[114] then I can choose between the readings ἀπολείποντας (present) and ἀπολιπόντας (aorist) by determining whether the verb ἀπολείπω as it is used in v. 6 is perfective or imperfective. This can be done by examining the context of v. 6 as a whole. In v. 6, there are two processes which can be regarded as complete: (1) the angels did not keep (μὴ τηρήσαντες) their own position; and (2) the angels abandoned (ἀπολιπόντας) their proper home. These two complete processes resulted in God keeping the angels in eternal chains, God being the presumed subject of τετήρηκεν. Contextual considerations, therefore, favour the perfective variant ἀπολιπόντας. The imperfective variant ἀπολείποντας is likely to have arisen through itacism caused by the similar sounds of the diphthong ει and the vowel ι (cf. αειδιοις [sic] at variation unit 6.5).

Variation Unit 6.4

οικητηριον   𝔓72 ℵ A B C K L 049
κατοικητηριον   Ψ

Both of the variants at this unit are acceptable words in New Testament Greek: οἰκητήριον occurs without variation at 2 Cor. 5.2, and κατοικητήριον can be found firm in the manuscript tradition at Rev. 18.2 and Eph. 2.22. It could be argued that since the word κατά often conveys the meaning 'down' when used in compounds,[115] if the sense intended by the variant κατοικητήριον is an abode in a 'downward' region (as at Rev. 18.2 where κατοικητήριον is a region inhabited by devils) then κατοικητήριον might be an inappropriate word to describe a region inhabited by angels as at v. 6. Against this hypothesis, Louw might object that it rests upon the supposition that the constituents which make up a compound word normally retain their original constituent meanings, a supposition which cannot always be relied upon, and which cannot be guaranteed here.[116] However, altering words by

114. S.E. Porter, *Verbal Aspect in the Greek of the New Testament, with Reference to Tense and Mood* (New York: Lang, 1989), pp. 88-105, cited in J.W. Voelz, 'Present and Aorist Verbal Aspect: A New Proposal', *Neot* 27 (1993), p. 157.

115. MHT, II, p. 316.

116. J.P. Louw, *Semantics of New Testament Greek* (Philadelphia: Fortress Press, 1982), pp. 27-29.

adding prepositions to form compounds seems to be a peculiarity of the copyist of Ψ: other examples are (1) at v. 10, Ψ reads διαφθείρονται where all other MSS read φθείρονται; and (2) at v. 18, Ψ has ἀναστή-σονται where all other witnesses have ἔσονται. The addition of κατά in Ψ may have been effected to place greater emphasis on the downward movement of the angels. Print οἰκητήριον here.

Variation Unit 6.5

δεσμοις αιδιοις   ℵ A B C K L 049
δεσμοις αειδιοις   𝔓72
αλυτοις και αιδιοις δεσμοις   33 2344

Since αειδιοις [sic] is an error resulting from itacism, the main choice to be made at this unit is between δεσμοῖς ἀϊδίοις and ἀλύτοις καὶ ἀϊδίοις δεσμοῖς. The word ἀλύτοις has no reference in BAGD or LN, but it can be traced in LSJ.

That ἀϊδίοις δεσμοῖς in 33 2344 runs contrary to word order tendencies in Jude can be shown by examining adjectival word order tendencies both in Koine Greek generally and in Jude in particular. Two factors affect adjectival positioning in Koine Greek: (1) whether the agreeing noun is anarthrous or articular; and (2) whether the adjective refers to quantity or quality. If the agreeing noun is anarthrous, and if the adjective describes a quality, then the adjective is positioned *after* the agreeing noun.[117] Both of the variants involve an anarthrous agreeing noun (δεσμοῖς) and both involve a qualitative adjective (ἀϊδίοις), so the preference should be for δεσμοῖς ἀϊδίοις, the variant which positions the adjective after the agreeing noun. The validity of my preference for δεσμοῖς ἀϊδίοις is confirmed by Jude's conformity to Koine word order tendencies involving adjectives, a pattern of conformity which is visible in the following examples, each of which shows qualitative adjectives positioned *after* anarthrous nouns:

v. 7	πυρὸς αἰωνίου
v. 12	νεφελαι ἄνυδροι
v. 12	δένδρα φθινοπωρινὰ ἄκαρπα
v. 13	κύματα ἄγρια
v. 21	ζωὴν αἰώνιον

All of the examples above are printed in GNT4. The first three examples are firm in the tradition, and, were it not for a singular reading, the

117. BDF §474.

example from v. 13 would also be firm. Only at v. 21 is there a major variation. To the examples above, I could add v. 16 γογγυσταὶ μεμψί-μοιροι, though, despite Bauer's adjectival entry for μεμψίμοιροι,[118] Moulton classifies μεμψίμοιροι as an action-noun.[119]

The longer reading ἀλύτοις καὶ ἀϊδίοις δεσμοῖς at this unit is explicable as an explanatory supplement, ἀλύτοις being the sort of synonym one might expect in such a deliberate scribal gloss. Print δεσμοῖς ἀϊδίοις here.

Variation Unit 6.6

υπο ζοφον αγιων αγγελων   conjecture from Lucifer Speculum
sanctorum angelorum sub tenebras   Lucifer Speculum
υπο ζοφον   𝔓72 ℵ A B C K L Ψ 049
υπο ζοφον αγριων αγγελων   Clement

The reading *sanctorum angelorum sub tenebras* allows the inference that the original Greek text may have included the words ἀγίων ἀγγέλων. My hypothesis is that ἀγίων ἀγγέλων was known to Clement, who saw it as awkward and changed it to ἀγρίων ἀγγέλων. Other scribes reacted more strongly against ἀγίων ἀγγέλων and omitted it altogether. With this hypothesis in mind, I would like to challenge the view of Mees that ἀγίων ἀγγέλων is an explanatory gloss.[120]

When I read the source material alluded to in v. 6, it becomes clear why J.T. Milik regards the reading *sanctorum angelorum sub tenebras* as original.[121] Central to Milik's view, and to my understanding of it, is the perception that whereas ἀγγελους in v. 6 refers collectively to the angels Asael, Semîhazah and the companions of Semîhazah mentioned in 1 Enoch 10.4-13, ἀγίων ἀγγέλων, reflected in our Latin variant, alludes to the archangels Raphael and Michael who acted 'as executors of the punishments ordered by God'.[122] Milik sees v. 6 essentially as a summary of 1 Enoch 10.4-8 and 1 Enoch 10.11-13, the texts of which are as follows:

118. BAGD, s.v. μεμψίμοιρος.
119. MHT, II, p. 289.
120. M. Mees, 'Papyrus Bodmer VII (𝔓72) und die Zitate aus dem Judasbrief bei Clemens von Alexandrien', *Ciudad de Dios* 181 (1968), pp. 551-59.
121. J.T. Milik (ed.), *The Books of Enoch: Aramaic Fragments of Qumran Cave 4* (Oxford: Clarendon Press, 1976), p. 117.
122. Milik, *Books of Enoch*, p. 117.

And secondly the Lord said to Raphael, 'Bind Azazel [= Asael] hand and foot (and) throw him into the darkness!' And he made a hole in the desert which was in Dudael and cast him there; he threw on top of him rugged and sharp rocks. And he covered his face in order that he may not see light; and in order that he may be sent into the fire on the great day of judgment. And give life to the earth which the angels have corrupted... And to Michael God said, 'Make known to Semyaza [Semîhazah] and the others who are with him, who fornicated with the women, that they will die together with them in all their defilement. And when they and all their children have battled with each other, and when they have seen the destruction of their beloved ones, bind them for seventy generations underneath the rocks of the ground until the day of their judgment and of their consummation, until the eternal judgment is concluded'.[123]

Against Mees, then, ἁγίων ἀγγέλων need not be seen as an interpolation if Milik is correct that ἀγγέλων alludes to the archangels Raphael and Michael. An acceptance of the variant ἁγίων ἀγγέλων here would certainly provide the reason for the use of the definite article at v. 9 with Μιχαήλ, since Μιχαήλ at v. 9 would then be anaphoric—referring back to v. 6.[124]

Milik's preference for the reading *sanctorum angelorum sub tenebras* is certainly corroborated by a consideration of the use of rhetoric in v. 6. As Watson has observed, one of the rhetorical devices which is employed in v. 6 is *reflexio*, a figure of thought '...where the same word is used in two different meanings'.[125] Watson's focus is upon the repeated occurrence in v. 6 of τηρέω: μὴ τηρήσαντας and τετήρηκεν, which exemplify *reflexio*. Watson's thinking here can be applied to the variant. The words ἁγίων ἀγγέλων echo ἀγγέλους, but with a changed meaning; ἀγγέλους being the punished angels, and ἀγγέλων being the archangels authorised to exact punishment; thus giving us another example of *reflexio*. ἁγίων ἀγγέλων can, therefore, be printed at v. 6 in the knowledge that it is entirely consistent with the author's rhetorical inclinations.

In the introduction to *Timothy and Titus*, Elliott states that when a reading with weak attestation is accepted as original, 'it must be shown why and how the variant came about and why it was so widely

---

123.   J.H. Charlesworth (ed.), *The Old Testament Pseudepigrapha, Volume 1: Apocalyptic Literature and Testaments* (New York: Doubleday, 1983), pp. 17-18.

124.   For more detail, see the discussion on Μιχαήλ at variation unit 9.1 below.

125.   Quintilian, *Institutio Oratoria* 9.3.68, cited in Watson, *Invention*, p. 52.

accepted'.[126] Such a statement applies at this unit and obliges me to explain the omission of ἁγίων ἀγγέλων from most MSS. Since there is no explicit reference to Raphael and Michael at v. 6, and since the reference at v. 9 is to Michael alone, it is unlikely that scribes who were confronted by the reading ἁγίων ἀγγέλων would have realised that it was a reference to Raphael and Michael. In view of this, the reading ἁγίων ἀγγέλων must have appeared contradictory. The omission of ἁγίων ἀγγέλων from most MSS can be explained as the result of the deliberate omission of the phrase very early in the transmission of the New Testament text. The variant ἀγρίων ἀγγέλων in Clement also appears to be a reaction to the difficulty posed by ἁγίων ἀγγέλων. Print ὑπὸ ζόφον ἁγίων ἀγγέλων here.

Variation Unit 7.1

ως σοδομα και γομορρα   ℵ A B K L Ψ 049
ως σοδομα και γομορα   𝔓72
ως σοδομα και ως γομορρα   378 547
om. σοδομα και γομορρα και   C*vid

By a process of elimination, it can be adduced that ὡς Σόδομα καὶ Γόμορρα is the correct reading here. To start with, γομορα [sic] is an orthographical error. Meanwhile, it is probable that the omission of Σόδομα καὶ Γόμορρα καὶ is motivated by doctrinal reasons, in this case a prudish avoidance of the mention of two such notorious towns, or, indeed, a wish to avoid linking the angels mentioned in the previous verse with the immorality described in v. 7. Perhaps less easy to dismiss is the reading ὡς Σόδομα καὶ ὡς Γόμορρα. Tentatively it could be argued that the word ὡς should be explicit before Σόδομα and implicitly understood before Γόμορρα and αἱ περὶ αὐτὰς πόλεις: this sequence is logically followed in the sentence introduced by our variant ὡς Σόδομα καὶ Γόμορρα. An alternative possibility is that Jude could have used ὡς explicitly on all occasions. At first glance I could accept the latter possibility as a reason for preferring ὡς Σόδομα καὶ ὡς Γόμορρα, but upon closer examination it is clear that the copyists of 378 547 somewhat illogically supply an explicit ὡς twice but wish the word ὡς to be implicitly understood before the phrase αἱ περὶ αὐτὰς πόλεις. If Jude uses the word ὡς explicitly at all times, then at v. 7 I should expect an explicit ὡς three times in 378 547 and not twice. The extra ὡς in 378 547 appears to have been added to make explicit a meaning which is already implicit before the word Γόμορρα.

Variation Unit 7.2

τροπον τουτοις	𝔓72 ℵ A B C
τροπον αυτοις	Ψ 38
τουτοις τροπον	K L 049
αυτοις τροπον	0142 466

The two matters to be resolved here are: (1) the position of τρόπον; and (2) whether τούτοις or αὐτοῖς should be read. To begin with, it is important to note the agreement between τρόπον and ὅμοιον, τὸν ὅμοιον τρόπον meaning, 'in the same way'.[127] It has already been mentioned that no general word order rule exists in New Testament Greek for adjectives with agreeing articular substantives.[128] However, it is possible to discern a distinctive word order pattern in Jude for adjectives with articular substantives:

v. 4	τὸν μόνον δεσπότην θεὸν[129]
v. 6	τὸ ἴδιον οἰκητήριον
v. 10	τὰ ἄλογα ζῷα

In the examples above, the pattern is: definite article + adjective + agreeing substantive (DA + A + S). The same pattern can be observed in all four of the readings; although, it should be noted that only the third and fourth readings allow a pronoun (PN) to come between A and S:

τὸν ὅμοιον τρόπον τούτοις	=	DA + A + S + PN
τὸν ὅμοιον τρόπον αὐτοῖς	=	DA + A + S + PN
τὸν ὅμοιον τούτοις τρόπον	=	DA + A + PN + S
τὸν ὅμοιον αὐτοῖς τρόπον	=	DA + A + PN + S

In the examples from vv. 4, 6 and 10, no words are allowed to come between DA + A + S, nor is there any evidence elsewhere in Jude that the writer would have allowed PN to come between DA + A + S. Upon this argument by silence I can narrow my choice to those two readings which preserve DA + A + S intact: τρόπον τούτοις and τρόπον αὐτοῖς.

---

127. Bauckham, *Jude, 2 Peter*, p. 43.
128. BDF §474.
129. Against GNT4.

Although Bauckham translates τὸν ὅμοιον τρόπον τούτοις with τούτοις as a reference to ἀγγέλους at v. 6, it is not certain that scribes would have seen the matter in such a clear cut way. Against Bauckham's translation, Kruger has argued persuasively that τούτοις at v. 7 refers not to ἀγγέλους at v. 6, but to οὗτοι (the opponents) at v. 8.[130] Jude always uses the term οὗτοι in the midrash commentaries to introduce the opponents (as at vv. 8, 10, 12, 16 and 19).[131] In addition, τούτοις (the dative of οὗτοι) refers to the opponents at v. 14, which Ellis classifies as a midrash text. If modern commentators cannot agree on the reference of τούτοις at v. 7, then it is equally probable that scribes saw τούτοις as an ambiguous word. Unfortunately I cannot use this ambiguity as an argument to explain the presence of αὐτοῖς in some MSS since at v. 11 αὐτοῖς also occurs (without variation) as a reference to the opponents. This means that the variant τρόπον αὐτοῖς at v. 7 is just as ambiguous as the rival variant τρόπον τούτοις: either reading could connote ἀγγέλους at v. 6 or οὗτοι at v. 8.

Kruger's analysis can help me further. He reminds me that vv. 7 and 8 are linked by catchwords, σαρκός at v. 7 and σάρκα at v. 8. His suggestion is that τούτοις (v. 7) and οὗτοι (v. 8) are also catchwords, both connoting the opponents. It is therefore possible for me to accept τρόπον τούτοις on grounds of style.

Variation Unit 7.3

υπεχουσαι   𝔓72 B C K L Ψ 049
επεχουσαι   𝔓78 378
υπερεχουσαι   A
ουκ εχουσιν   ℵ*
υπεχουσιν   ℵ²
υπαρχουσαι   1845 1846

When I look at the part of v. 7 to which this variation unit belongs, the sense is that 'those practising immorality...are set forth as an example by undergoing punishment of eternal fire'. It is clear from this that the variant ὑπέχουσαι ('undergoing') fits the context of the verse while ἐπέχουσαι ('being alert for, holding firmly to, watching, staying on') does not fit the context of undergoing or experiencing punishment. Also unsuitable for contextual or syntactical reasons are ὑπερέχουσαι

130. Bauckham, *Jude, 2 Peter*, p. 54; M.A. Kruger, 'ΤΟΥΤΟΙΣ in Jude 7', *Neot* 27 (1993), pp. 119-32.
131. Ellis, 'Prophecy and Hermeneutic', p. 225.

('surpassing in value, controlling'), οὐκ ἔχουσιν (they don't have), and ὑπάρχουσαι ('being, being identical to, existing, belonging to').[132]

The variant ὑπέχουσιν (they undergo) is a possibility, though there is already a main verb in πρόκεινται: does the corrector ℵ[2] realise this, or has he (as it seems) mistakenly identified πρόκεινται as a participle, consequently using the indicative for ὑπέχω to give it the impetus of a main verb? Since πρόκεινται is the main verb, there is no doubt that ὑπέχουσαι is the most acceptable variant here.

As Daryl Charles has shown,[133] the following *hapax legomena* occur in Jude:

v. 3	ἐπαγωνίζεσθαι
v. 4	παρεισέδυσαν
v. 7	ὑπέχουσαι
v. 7	ἐκπορνεύσασαι
v. 7	δεῖγμα
v. 10	φυσικῶς
v. 12	σπιλάδες
v. 12	φθινοπωρινά
v. 13	πλανῆται
v. 13	ἐπαφρίζοντα
v. 16	γογγυσταὶ
v. 16	μεμψίμοιροι
v. 19	ἀποδιορίζοντες

My proposition is that ὑπέχουσαι as a *hapax legomenon* would have been unfamiliar to some scribes and explains all of the variation at this unit except ὑπέχουσιν. Print ὑπέχουσαι here.

Variation Unit 8.1

ομοιως 𝔓72 𝔓78 ℵ B C K L Ψ 049
ομως A

The slight difference in meaning between ὁμοίως ('likewise, so, similarly, in the same way') and ὅμως ('all the same, nevertheless, yet')[134] renders ὁμοίως my preferred reading on contextual grounds. Although it could be argued that ὅμως as a difficult reading contextually may have provided a scribal incentive for alteration to ὁμοίως, it has to be remembered that awkward Greek is not a characteristic of the writer.

132. LN §§24.33, 27.59, 31.47, 85.59; 37.17, 65.4; 13.4, 13.5, 13.77, 57.2.
133. Charles, 'Literary Artifice', p. 111.
134. BAGD, s.vv. ὁμοίως; ὅμως.

The contextual suitability of ὁμοίως is apparent when one considers v. 8 in the broader context of vv. 5-8 as a section of Jude's midrash design. Verse 8 is a midrash commentary, identifiable as such by the writer's use of the present tense, whereas vv. 5-7 comprises three paradigms or texts, distinguishable as such by the writer's use of the past tense.[135] The link between v. 8 and vv. 5-7 is simply that the three paradigms in vv. 5-7 (the destruction of those who did not believe; the sin and fate of the fallen angels; and the destruction of the sinful inhabitants of Sodom and Gomorrah) serve as analogies for the immorality and blasphemy of the opponents described in v. 8.[136] It follows that ὁμοίως as the variant better suited for linking vv. 5-7 with v. 8 is contextually preferable to ὅμως. The change from ὁμοίως to ὅμως is explicable through the accidental omission of the omicron and the iota.

Variation Unit 8.2

ουτοι   𝔓72 ℵ A B C K L Ψ 049
αυτοι   𝔓78 92 1885

At this unit, the midrash structure of the text is the overarching consideration. All of the references to the opponents which are made in the midrash commentaries are to the opponents as οὗτοι:

v. 8	οὗτοι ἐνυπνιαζόμενοι σάρκα μὲν μιαίνουσιν
v. 10	οὗτοι δὲ ὅσα μὲν οὐκ οἴδασιν βλασφημοῦσιν
v. 12	οὗτοί εἰσιν οἱ ἐν ταῖς ἀγάπαις ὑμῶν σπιλάδες
v. 16	οὗτοί εἰσιν γογγυσταὶ μεμψίμοιροι
v. 19	οὗτοί εἰσιν οἱ ἀποδιορίζοντες

Apart from οὗτοι at v. 8, all the other instances of οὗτοι cited above are firm in the tradition. In each of the citations above, the writer uses the present tense to signify that he is in commentary mode and that it is the opponents (οὗτοι) whose actions he is describing.[137] In addition to these references from the midrash commentaries, there are two references to the opponents in the midrash texts. Among other verses, Ellis has identified vv. 11 and 14 as midrash texts. In the midrash text at v. 14, Jude refers to the opponents as τούτοις, and in the midrash text at v. 11, Jude uses the word αὐτοῖς to refer to the opponents. It is therefore not impossible that αὐτοί preserved in 𝔓78 92 1885 could be

135. Ellis, 'Prophecy and Hermeneutic', p. 225.
136. Green, *General Epistle of Jude*, pp. 176-81.
137. Ellis, 'Prophecy and Hermeneutic', p. 225.

original at this unit. However, in view of the invariable preference of the writer for οὗτοι (= opponents) in the midrash commentaries, and in view of the fact that Jude is in commentary mode at v. 8, I accept οὗτοι and reject αὐτοί here.[138]

Variation Unit 8.3

σαρκα μεν   𝔓78 ℵ A B C K L Ψ 049
σαρκα   𝔓72 2344

Watson sees σάρκα μέν (the reading normally printed by editors) as part of a rhetorical device used in v. 8, and cites μέν...δέ...δέ in v. 8 as an example of polysyndeton.[139] The three conjunctions and the triple expression which they introduce are intended to effect amplification by accumulation.[140] Although polysyndeton as such occurs nowhere else in Jude, there are many instances of amplification by accumulation in the text: most of the triple expressions listed in the analysis of variation unit 2.2 can be regarded as examples of amplification. In view of this, I can accept the reading σάρκα μέν on grounds of style. However, no arguments can be advanced in favour of σάρκα, and the omission of μέν from 𝔓72 is probably accidental.

Variation Unit 8.4

κυριοτητα   𝔓72 A B C K L 049
κυριοτητας   ℵ Ψ
κυρειοτητα   𝔓78

The reading κυρειοτητα [sic] is the result of itacism, so the choice here is between κυριότητα and κυριότητας. The noun κυριότης is a derivative of κύριος. If I accept κυριότητα, then it could mean either the authority of God or the authority of the Lord.[141] If, on the other

---

138. For more detail on the opponents, see M. Desjardins, 'The Portrayal of the Dissidents in 2 Peter and Jude: Does It Tell Us More about the "Godly" than the "Ungodly"?' *JSNT* 30 (1987), pp. 89-102; F. Wisse, 'The Epistle of Jude in the History of Heresiology', in M. Krause (ed.), *Essays on the Nag Hammadi Texts in Honour of Alexander Böhlig* (Leiden: Brill, 1972), pp. 133-43; G. Sellin, 'Die Häretiker des Judasbriefes', *ZNW* 77 (1986), pp. 206-25; Kelly, *Peter and Jude*, pp. 248-53; Bauckham, *Jude, 2 Peter*, pp. 11-13; Eybers, 'Aspects', pp. 118-19.

139. Watson, *Invention*, p. 55.

140. Watson, *Invention*, pp. 55-56.

141. Bolkestein, *Petrus en Judas*, pp. 220-21.

hand, I accept κυριότητας, then I could read angels or a class of angelic powers.[142] As most commentators have pointed out, the only occurrences of κυριότης in the New Testament other than in Jude are at 2 Pet. 2.10, Eph. 1.21 and Col. 1.16. Of these occurrences, that at 2 Pet. 2.10 is dependent on Jude, while κυριότητος at Eph. 1.21 and κυριότητες at Col. 1.16 both refer to a class of angelic powers.[143] In view of this, it is easy to see why Bauckham has argued that the variant κυριότητα at v. 8 should be accepted, since κυριότητα would have provided the scribes of ℵ and Ψ with an incentive to 'eliminate the difficulty'[144] presented by the singular. This said, Bauckham's argument is not entirely watertight, since κυριότητος at Eph. 1.21 is singular and not plural. To prove that Bauckham's preference for κυριότητα is valid, further evidence must be examined, namely style and context.

It is difficult to be guided by style at this unit. Bauckham sees κυριότητα as a catchword which can be linked with κύριον in v. 4 and κύριος in v. 5. Charles, on the other hand, does not include κυριότητα in his list of catchwords, but sees it instead as part of an example of synonymous parallelism,[145] one among many here reproduced from his list:

v. 3	σπουδὴν ποιούμενος = ἀνάγκην ἔσχον
v. 5	ὑπομνῆσαι = εἰδότας
v. 6	ἀρχή = οἰκητήριον
v. 6	κρίσις = ζόφος
v. 7	ἐκπορνεύειν = ἀπελθοῦσαι ὀπίσω σαρκὸς ἑτέρας
v. 7	πρόκειμαι = ὑπέχειν
v. 7	πῦρ = δίκη
v. 8	μιαίνειν = ἀθετεῖν, βλασφημεῖν
v. 8	κυριότῆς = δόξα
v. 9	διακρίνειν = διαλογίζομαι
v. 9	κρίσιν ἐπιφέρειν = βλασφημία
v. 10	ὅσα οὐκ οἴδασιν = ἄλογα
v. 10	οἴδασιν = ἐπίστανται
v. 12	ἄκαρπα = ἀποθανόντα
v. 13	ἄγρια = ἐπαφρίζοντα
v. 13	ζόφος = σκότος
v. 14	προφητεύειν = λέγειν
v. 15	ποιῆσαι κρίσιν = ἐλέγξαι

142. Kelly, *Peter and Jude*, p. 262.
143. Kelly, *Peter and Jude*, p. 262.
144. Bauckham, *Jude, 2 Peter*, p. 56.
145. See Charles, 'Literary Artifice', p. 113.

v. 16   γογγυσταί = μεμψίμοιροι
v. 19   ψυχικοί = ἀποδιορίζοντες, πνεῦμα μὴ ἔχοντες
v. 20   ἁγιότης = ἅγιος
v. 21   ἀγάπη = ἔλεος
v. 23   σῴζειν = ἁρπάζειν
vv. 20, 24   ἄμωμος = ἅγιος

As shown above, the parallel Charles identifies at v. 8 is κυριότης = δόξα. The alleged synonymy between κυριότης and δόξα at v. 8 implies two possibilities: (1) I should accept κυριότητα and δόξαν since both variants are singular and synonyms of 'lord', or (2) I should accept κυριότητας and δόξας since both variants are plural and both connote angels or angelic powers. Otherwise I must agree with Bauckham and accept κυριότητα as a catchword.

Contextual evidence may take me nearer to a solution. Two of the three sins mentioned in v. 8 have clear parallels in vv. 4-7: σάρκα μιαίνουσιν in v. 8 can be linked with ἀπελθοῦσαι ὀπίσω σαρκὸς ἑτέρας in v. 7; and, as Bauckham notes, κυριότητα δὲ ἀθετοῦσιν in v. 8 mirrors κύριον ἡμῶν Ἰησοῦν Χριστὸν ἀρνούμενοι in v. 4.[146] The third parallel which links vv. 4-7 to v. 8 is more tenuous: δόξας (meaning 'glorious ones') in v. 8 is a reference to ἁγίων ἀγγέλων, which we have argued is original at v. 6. On contextual grounds, then, κυριότητα may be accepted as the best reading here.

Variation Unit 8.5

δοξας   𝔓72 ℵ A B C K L Ψ 049
δοξαν   𝔓78 1799 1831

Either variant could be original here. The case for δόξαν is that it could be synonymous with κυριότητα as explained above. Since they have not accepted ἁγίων ἀγγέλων at v. 6, the GNT4 editors might be expected to accept δόξαν rather than δόξας here, although it would seem that they have been guided by external evidence. Since I have accepted ἁγίων ἀγγέλων at v. 6, I can accept δόξας here as a reference to glorious ones or to angels, the parallel between v. 6 and v. 8 being that in both verses, the authority of the archangels or glorious ones is challenged. The argument for δόξας is not weakened by Bauckham's reminder that the term δόξαι as a reference to angelic beings is attested in the Dead Sea Scrolls and in apocryphal and Gnostic

146. Bauckham, *Jude, 2 Peter*, p. 59.

literature.[147] The reading δόξαν is explicable as a deliberate substitution for δόξας by scribes who could not see the connection between δόξας and ἁγίων ἀγγέλων, the latter reading having been lost early in the transmission process as I have suggested at variation unit 6.6. Thus δόξας is the better reading at this unit.

Variation Unit 9.1

ο δε μιχαηλ ο αρχαγγελος οτε   ℵ A C K L Ψ 049
ο δε μιχαης ο αρχαγγελος οτε   𝔓72
οτε μιχαηλ ο αρχαγγελος τοτε   B vg

The reading μιχαης [sic] is 'probablement faute du copiste'.[148] Thus I have to choose between ὅτε (or ὁ τὲ) Μιχαὴλ ὁ ἀρχάγγελος τότε and ὁ δὲ Μιχαὴλ ὁ ἀρχάγγελος ὅτε. It is not clear whether the scribes of B vg have copied ὅτε or ὁ τέ. It is unlikely that ὅτε is what the author wrote, since this would render Μιχαήλ anarthrous, and I can demonstrate that Μιχαήλ is articular. As Turner has mentioned, the article in Hellenistic Greek is normally used 'after the person has normally been pointed out (anaphoric, or pointing back) or when he is often referred to'.[149] In the case of v. 9, the articular Μιχαήλ can certainly be justified if it is recalled that ἁγίων ἀγγέλων as accepted at v. 6 is an allusion to the archangels Raphael and Michael. If Μιχαήλ at v. 9 refers back to Michael as one of the archangels alluded to in v. 6, then the articular usage for Μιχαήλ can be verified on the grounds that Μιχαήλ is anaphoric. Another argument which can be ranged against the reading in B vg with ὅτε understood is the absence of a verb between ὅτε and τότε. Thus I am left with two possibilities: (1) ὁ τὲ Μιχαὴλ ὁ ἀρχάγγελος τότε (i.e. the reading in B vg with ὁ τὲ understood); and (2) ὁ δὲ Μιχαὴλ ὁ ἀρχάγγελος ὅτε.

As I explained at variation unit 6.1: (1) in situations where δέ or τέ would be optional, Jude always prefers δέ (as at vv. 1, 6, 8, 14 and 24); (2) the high style value attributed to τέ distinguishes it as a scribal improvement. The best reading here is, therefore, ὁ δὲ Μιχαὴλ ὁ ἀρχάγγελος ὅτε.

147. See Bauckham, *Jude, 2 Peter*, p. 57.
148. Massaux, 'Papyrus Bodmer VII (𝔓72)', p. 114.
149. MHT, III, pp. 165-66.

Variation Unit 9.2

σωματος μωυσεως   378 632
μουσεως σωματος   𝔓72
μωυσεως σωματος   ℵ B C L
μωσεως σωματος   A K Ψ 049

The reading μουσεως [*sic*] is an error, ascribed by Massaux to a tendency of the copyist to confuse certain vowels, including ο and ω.[150] Two problems remain: (1) whether I should accept Μωϋσέως or Μωσέως; and (2) whether σώματος should precede or follow the accepted Greek word for Moses. Regarding the first problem, I cannot simply dismiss Μωσέως as an error: there are two ways of spelling Moses in Greek (Μωϋσῆς and Μωσῆς). BDF argue that Μωϋσῆς is the correct form since it is preserved in older MSS and state that Μωϋσῆς is 'an attempt to reproduce Egyptian pronunciation'.[151] If I accept tentatively the preference of BDF for Μωϋσῆς then I can eliminate Μωσέως σώματος. This leaves me with a choice between Μωϋσέως σώματος and σώματος Μωϋσέως.

Effectively my remaining choice is between the order: preposition + definite article + qualifying genitive + substantive governed by preposition (PR + DA + QG + SP) and the order: preposition + definite article + substantive governed by preposition + qualifying genitive (PR + DA + SP + QG):

περὶ τοῦ Μωϋσέως σώματος = PR + DA + QG + SP
περὶ τοῦ σώματος Μωϋσέως = PR + DA + SP + QG

We have no precisely analogous phrases in Jude and must therefore examine tendencies in other canonical writers for appropriate paradigms. What needs to be looked at are the positions in New Testament Greek of QG and SP when the substantive σῶμα is articular and is governed by PR:

Mt. 26.12   ἐπὶ τοῦ σώματος μου
Rom. 7.4   διὰ τοῦ σώματος τοῦ Χριστοῦ
Rom. 7.24   ἐκ τοῦ σώματος τοῦ θανάτου τούτου

150. Massaux, 'Papyrus Bodmer VII (𝔓72)', p. 109.

151. BDF §38, cited in Elliott, *Timothy and Titus*, p. 150. Elliott is noncommital, saying 'either μωσει or μωυσει [at 2 Tim. 3.8] is original'. I doubt whether Elliott would accept the argument in BDF that Μωϋσῆς is preserved in older and 'better' MSS. It is my argument in favour of the reading σώματος Μωϋσέως at this unit which enables me to eliminate all of the other readings.

1 Cor. 6.20	ἐν τῷ σώματι ὑμῶν
2 Cor. 4.10	ἐν τῷ σώματι ἡμῶν
Gal. 6.17	ἐν τῷ σώματι μου
Phil. 1.20	ἐν τῷ σώματι μου
Col. 1.24	ὑπὲρ τοῦ σώματος αὐτοῦ
1 Pet. 2.24	ἐν τῷ σώματι αὐτοῦ

It should be clear from the citations above that New Testament writers have an invariable preference for the order: PR + DA + SP + QG in all cases where σῶμα = SP. Similarly, at this unit, περὶ τοῦ σώματος Μωϋσέως should be accepted, since it adheres to the order: PR + DA + SP + QG.[152] The reading which I have rejected—περὶ τοῦ Μωϋσέως σώματος—is explicable through harmony with the word order used at Mt. 23.2, which reads ἐπὶ τῆς Μωϋσέως καθέδρας.

Variation Unit 9.3

επενεγκειν   𝔓72 ℵ A B C K L 049
υπενεγκεν   Ψ 241 250

The correct reading here is ἐπενεγκεῖν, the context at v. 9 being οὐκ ἐτόλμησεν κρίσιν ἐπενεγκεῖν βλασφημίας—'he did not dare to bring a charge of slander'. Even if I make allowances for the fact that υπενεγκεν [*sic*] might be acceptable as ὑπενεγκεῖν (given that υπενεγκεν is an orthographical error), I must still reject this derivative of ὑποφέρω on the grounds that ὑπενεγκεῖν (to endure) carries a meaning which is directly opposite to the context of the verse. The reading υπενεγκεν reflects uncertainty about the subject of the verb οὐκ ἐτόλμησεν, and is therefore explicable as a deliberate change. The iota, meanwhile, is omitted accidentally in Ψ 241 250.

Variation Unit 9.4

αλλα   𝔓72 A B Ψ
αλλ   ℵ C K L 049

152.   There are a few phrases in New Testament Greek which violate the order PR + DA + SP + QG, one or two of them involving Μωϋσέως, e.g. 1 Cor. 9.9 ἐν...τῷ Μωϋσέως νόμῳ. However I should stress that none of these phrases involves the substantive σῶμα where σῶμα = SP, and it is upon the positioning of the latter that the argument is based. Expressed differently, I would need evidence for σῶμα = SP occupying a position different to that which it occupies in PR + DA + SP + QG for the argument to be invalidated. Without such evidence, the argument stands.

With no evidence that the writer would have used elision in instances where other New Testament writers would have avoided using it, ἀλλά should be printed here in preference to ἀλλ'. The issue of elision is examined in more depth at variation unit 6.2 above.

Variation Unit 9.5

εν σοι B* Ψ
σοι 𝔓72 ℵ A C K L 049

Evidence can be cited in favour of either of these variants: σοι could be correct because it is least like the LXX quotation which the writer uses in this verse (Zech. 3.2 ἐπιτιμήσαι κύριος ἐν σοί, διάβολε). On the other hand, ἐν σοι could be original because it preserves the Hebraic ἐν which may have been removed by Atticising scribes. All of the editors consulted (Tischendorf, von Soden, WH, De Zwaan, Vogels, Merk, Kilpatrick, *Diglot* and the editors of BFBS2 and GNT4) prefer σοί: Kubo by contrast opts for ἐν σοι.[153]

Concerning LXX quotations, Elliott writes: 'the reading least like the LXX is likely to be original, other things being equal. The New Testament author may be quoting from memory, or from an edition of the Old Testament which has not survived'.[154] The reasoning by which the internal canon concerning LXX quotations might be applied can now be given, though it must be borne in mind that Elliott's condition ('other things being equal') may deprive me of a decisive verdict. At v. 9 the LXX quotation from Zech. 3.2 is probably sourced from a text which has not survived: the allusion is to the lost ending of the *Testament of Moses*, though various Christian sources have been consulted and analysed to reconstruct the account of the dispute between Satan and the angel of the Lord which Jude is likely to have known.[155] What concerns me here is whether or not Jude is likely to have reproduced the quotation from LXX Zech. 3.2 in the order preserved in B* Ψ, or whether those MSS which have omitted ἐν reflect more accurately what Jude is likely to have written. There does not seem to be any doubt that Jude is indeed quoting from LXX Zech. 3.2.[156] If I compare the variants with

153. Kubo, *𝔓72 and the Codex Vaticanus*, pp. 58-59.
154. Elliott, *Timothy and Titus*, p. 82.
155. Bauckham, *Jude, 2 Peter*, pp. 67-74.
156. Bauckham, *Jude, 2 Peter*, p. 65; Kelly, *Peter and Jude*, p. 265; Green, *General Epistle of Jude*, p. 184; Bolkestein, *Petrus en Judas*, p. 223; Sidebottom,

LXX Zech. 3.2, it is clear that the reading in B* Ψ is closest to LXX
Zech. 3.2 (ἐπιτιμήσαι κύριος ἐν σοί, διάβολη):

    επιτιμησαι σοι κυριος   𝔓72 A C K L P 049
    επιτιμησαι εν σοι κυριος   B* Ψ
    επιτιμησαι σοι ο κυριος   ℵ² 309 378
    επιτιμησαι σοι ο θεος   ℵ* 322 323

According to the internal canon which concerns LXX quotations, the
reading ἐπιτιμήσαι ἐν σοι κύριος should be rejected on the grounds
that 'scribes would tend to "correct" an Old Testament quotation to the
normal LXX reading'.[157] Kubo claims that the copyist of B did not have
a tendency to 'correct' Old Testament quotations to accommodate LXX
readings and so rejects the argument that ἐπιτιμήσαι ἐν σοι κύριος in
B* Ψ is an improvement made to conform to the LXX.[158] It is difficult
to fathom why WH do not print the reading in B* Ψ unless it is because
of its proximity to the LXX quotation. If I discount for the moment the
two readings in ℵ² 309 378 and ℵ* 322 323, then the possibility cannot
be ruled out that the unanimous preference of text editors for
ἐπιτιμήσαι σοι κύριος is justifiable on the grounds that ἐπιτιμήσαι
σοι κύριος is the reading least like the LXX quotation.

Thus far, the transcriptional evidence favours ἐπιτιμήσαι σοι
κύριος. The alternative possibility that the Hebraic ἐν was deliberately
removed must also be considered. It is possible that the presence of ἐν
in B* Ψ can be traced to Origen and to the lost *Testament of Moses*.[159]
The validity of Kubo's argument depends ultimately on how much trust
we place in Origen, Kubo's assumption being that Origen's source here
is the *Testament of Moses*. A supporting argument which Kubo himself
only hints at is that Atticising scribes may have sought to remove the
Hebraic ἐν, thus rendering ἐπιτιμήσαι ἐν σοι κύριος the best reading
because it resists the Atticism.

Intrinsic evidence can be invoked to resolve the conflicting transcriptional possibilities. As I noted in my introduction, Jude uses Semitic
expressions at vv. 5, 7, 11, 16, 17, 18, 21 and arguably at v. 24. The
Hebraic ἐν should, therefore, be included here on intrinsic grounds.
Print ἐν σοι at this unit.

James, Jude, 2 Peter, p. 88; Watson, *Invention*, p. 56; Bratcher, *Translator's Guide*,
p. 177; Fuchs, *Saint Jude*, p. 168.
    157. Elliott, *Timothy and Titus*, p. 82.
    158. Kubo, *𝔓72 and the Codex Vaticanus*, p. 58.
    159. Kubo, *𝔓72 and the Codex Vaticanus*, p. 58.

Variation Unit 9.6

κυριος   𝔓72 A B C K L Ψ 049
ο κυριος   ℵ² 309 378
ο θεος   ℵ* 322 323

The word κύριος in Zech. 3.2 and the *Testament of Moses* refers to God, but at v. 9 I have to decide whether the reference is to God or to Jesus.[160] Against Bauckham's view that Jude may have intended κύριος as a reference to Jesus at v. 9 are two considerations: (1) whenever the writer intends κύριος to designate Jesus, κύριος appears in conjunction with Ἰησοῦς Χριστός as at vv. 4, 17, 21 and 25; and (2) the deduction that 'anarthrous κύριος [in the Gospels] which derives from the LXX is only used of God' could be applicable at v. 9.[161] Two articular readings are possible contenders at this unit.

The first is ὁ κύριος. When κύριος refers unambiguously to Jesus it can be either anarthrous (as at v. 4) or articular (as at vv. 17, 21 and 25). However, since I have argued that anarthrous κύριος at vv. 9 and 14 may have been interpreted as a reference to God alone, the article may have been added in ℵ² 309 378 to allow the word κύριος to embrace the notion of God and Jesus simultaneously. The addition of the article here may, therefore, have been effected as an anti-adoptionistic orthodox change, as I have argued at v. 5. The definite article has been added deliberately in ℵ at vv. 3 and 14, and this appears to be a similar deliberate change here.

Meanwhile, the reading ὁ θεός is most plausibly explained as an attempt to make the reading κύριος less ambiguous and to 'interpret' κύριος as a reference to God. With no decisive case either for ὁ κύριος or for ὁ θεός, κύριος should be printed at this unit.

Variation Unit 10.1

δε (*primum*)   𝔓72 ℵ A B C K L Ψ 049
ουν   1836

The mild contrast, conveyed here by the word δέ, demarcates the transition from the paradigm of the archangel Michael in v. 9 to the behaviour of the opponents in v. 10: the contrast is that whereas Michael avoids using slander as a means of winning the dispute with the devil, the opponents in v. 10 use slander on an indiscriminate basis. As I have

160. Bauckham, *Jude, 2 Peter*, p. 62.
161. Kilpatrick, 'ΚΥΡΙΟΣ Again', p. 222.

explained at the first variation unit at v. 5, where the writer wishes to convey the word 'but', he invariably prefers δέ to οὖν, as at vv. 5, 17, 20 and 24.

Variation Unit 10.2

τα αλογα ζωα   𝔓72 ℵ A B C K L Ψ 049
τα αλογα   43 1518
αλογα ζωα   618 1898

There is no reason not to accept τὰ ἄλογα ζῷα at this unit. The omission of ζῷα from 43 1518 and of τά from 618 1898 may each be the result of accidental omission due to hom., caused by each of the three words ending in alpha. It is impossible to advance a decisive reason for accepting either of the readings preserved in cursives here.

Variation Unit 10.3

φθειρονται   ℵ A B C K L 049
φθιρονται   𝔓72
διαφθειρονται   Ψ

Firstly, φθιρονται [*sic*] is an error caused by itacism. In 𝔓72, ει is often written where ι belongs, and ι is often copied where ει belongs.[162] My remaining choice is between φθείρονται and διαφθείρονται, the latter reading preserved singularly in Ψ. The copyist of Ψ likes to alter words to form compounds such as διαφθείρονται. At v. 6 οἰκητήριον in all other MSS has been altered in Ψ to κατοικητήριον, and at v. 18 ἔσονται has been altered singularly in Ψ to ἀναστήσονται.[163] In view of this peculiarity in Ψ, I must reject διαφθείρονται and print φθείρονται here.

Variation Unit 11.1

τη οδω   𝔓72 ℵ A B C K L Ψ 049
εν τη οδω   1319

Whether one accepts Bauckham's translation of this clause—'they walked in the way of Cain'—or Boobyer's rendition—'they go to death in the path of Cain', there seems no reason not to accept Boobyer's judgment that τῇ ὁδῷ is one of three instances of the dative of instrument in

---

162.   Massaux, 'Papyrus Bodmer VII (P72)', p. 109.
163.   See variation units 6.4 and 18.4 for further details.

this verse.[164] In New Testament Greek, instrumental datives appear with or without the preposition ἐv.[165] Two of the three instrumental datives at v. 11 are firm in the text without ἐv: τῇ πλάνῃ and τῇ ἀντιλογίᾳ. The three instrumental datives at v. 11 form part of a wider triadic structure in which the writer juxtaposes three Old Testament paradigms:

τῇ ὁδῷ τοῦ Κάϊν ἐπορεύθησαν...
τῇ πλάνῃ τοῦ βαλαὰμ μισθοῦ ἐξεχύθησαν...
τῇ ἀντιλογίᾳ τοῦ Κόρε ἀπώλοντο.

The function of this triadic structure[166] is rhetorical and exemplifies amplification by accumulation, 'the amassing of words and sentences identical in meaning'.[167] In this case, as Watson points out, the writer's purpose is to amplify the sinfulness of the opponents, and (I might add) the condemnation which awaits them.

The similarity in appearance of these datives is not arbitrary, but it is part of the stylistic symmetry of the triadic structure, a symmetry which exists as a rhetorical support structure. In view of this, one should expect either (1) all three datives to be preceded by ἐv; or (2) none of the three datives to be preceded by ἐv. The reading ἐv τῇ ὁδῷ is thus unacceptable because it upsets the symmetry of the triadic structure in the verse. It is probable that the scribe of 1319 was more familiar with the inclusion of ἐv before an instrumental dative and decided to supply the preposition himself because, in New Testament Greek, the inclusion of ἐv with an instrumental dative is more common than the exclusion of ἐv with such a dative.[168] In view of the evidence discussed, the GNT4 editors are right to accept τῇ ὁδῷ here.

Variation Unit 11.2

βαλααμ ℵ A B C K L Ψ 049
βαλαακ 𝔓 7 2

The reference to Balaam at this unit is the second of three Old Testament motifs illustrating ungodly behaviour and divine condemnation.[169]

---

164. Bauckham, *Jude, 2 Peter*, p. 79; G.H. Boobyer, 'The Verbs in Jude 11', *NTS* 5 (1958), pp. 45-47.
165. MHT, III, p. 240.
166. Identified as such by Charles, 'Literary Artifice', p. 122.
167. Watson, *Invention*, p. 27.
168. MHT, III, p. 240.
169. Charles, 'Those and These', pp. 116-17.

Whereas βαλαάμ is correctly spelt, βαλαακ should (if it refers to Balak) have a single alpha. We still have to explore whether Jude is likely to have written Balaam or Balak.

The GNT4 text for our second Old Testament motif reads: τῇ πλάνῃ τοῦ βαλαὰμ μισθοῦ ἐξεχύθησαν. Boobyer translates: 'they are themselves cast away in the error of Balaam'.[170] Kelly translates the same text: 'they have abandoned themselves for profit to Balaam's error'.[171] It is debatable whether the error referred to in this verse should be ascribed to Balaam or to Balak. Citing Num. 22.18, 24.13, Deut. 23.4; and Neh. 13.2, Watson states that Balaam refrained from cursing Israel for financial gain but that these references are contradicted by a post-biblical Jewish tradition, for example, Philo *Vit. Mos.* 1.266-268 which provides the opposite impression.[172] According to Philo *Vit. Mos.* 1.295-300; Josephus *Ant.* 4.126-130; *Targum Pseudo-Jonathan* Num. 24.14, 25; the Jerusalem Talmud *y. Sanh.* 10.28d; the Babylonian Talmud *b. Sanh.* 106a; and Rev. 2.14, Balaam persuaded Balak to lead Israel into idolatry and sins of a sexual nature.[173] If I apply this line of thinking to this unit, then it could be argued that the error mentioned in Jude 11 may have been interpreted by some copyists as Balak's, since Balak allowed himself to be misled by Balaam, hence a deliberate change from βαλαάμ to βαλάκ is effected for contextual reasons and reflected in 𝔓72.

Kelly's summary of the later tradition indicates that Balak was the man offering bribes to Balaam, from which I can infer that the 'error' may plausibly be ascribed to Balaam for yielding to these bribes. Balaam became the 'prototype of unprincipled people who will not shrink from any enormity for monetary gain'.[174] Further, it is Balaam (and not Balak) whom Jude uses to illustrate the fate which is to be meted out to false teachers such as the opponents. This perception of Balaam as a false teacher is a leitmotif which reappears at Rev. 2.14:

> ἀλλ᾽ ἔχω κατὰ σοῦ ὀλίγα ὅτι ἔχεις ἐκεῖ κρατοῦντας τὴν διδαχὴν Βαλαάμ ὅς ἐδίδασκεν τῷ Βαλὰκ βαλεῖν σκάνδαλον ἐνώπιον τῶν υἱῶν Ἰσραὴλ φαγεῖν εἰδωλόθυτα καὶ πορνεῦσαι.

---

170. Boobyer, 'Verbs in Jude 11', p. 47.
171. Kelly, *Peter and Jude*, p. 267.
172. Watson, *Invention*, p. 59.
173. All references here are cited from Watson, *Invention*, p. 59.
174. Kelly, *Peter and Jude*, p. 267.

But I have a few matters to bring against you: you have in Pergamum some that hold to the teaching of Balaam, who taught Balak to put temptation in the way of the Israelites. He encouraged them to eat food sacrificed to idols and to commit fornication (NEB).

The main point at v. 11 seems to be that Balaam is used by Jude as a paradigm for the false teaching which the opponents are promoting.[175] Thus far I have advanced contextual arguments against Balak and in favour of Balaam.

When I look in more detail at the transcriptional evidence, it would seem that the reading βαλαακ arose by accident, with the copyist of 𝔓72 inheriting Βαλάκ written with a single alpha. Βαλάκ in turn originated as an improvement introduced for contextual reasons as I have explained. The alternative and more remote transcriptional possibility is that the copyist of 𝔓72 inherited Βαλαάμ and accidentally copied βαλαακ, M being taken for K. Without a decisive case in favour of βαλαακ [*sic*], I must accept Βαλαάμ at this unit.

Variation Unit 11.3

τη αντιλογια   𝔓74 ℵ A B C K L Ψ 049
τη αντιλογεια   𝔓72
αντιλογια   1834 1874

The reading αντιλογεια is another example of orthographical variation where the scribe has written ει where ι belongs. The main issue here is whether ἀντιλογίᾳ should be articular or anarthrous.

Jude's carefully constructed juxtaposition of the three Old Testament motifs is afforded stylistic balance and symmetry by the equal weight given to each of the three instrumental datives: τῇ ὁδῷ; τῇ πλάνῃ; and τῇ ἀντιλογίᾳ. In view of this balance, either (1) all three datives should be anarthrous; or (2) all three datives should be articular. Since two of the three datives are articular (τῇ ὁδῷ and τῇ πλάνῃ), it is highly probable that the third dative (τῇ ἀντιλογίᾳ) should also be articular. The reading ἀντιλογίᾳ in 1834 1874 is explicable as an error of omission, the article having been omitted by accident.

Variation Unit 12.1

ουτοι εισιν   𝔓72 ℵᶜ A B K L Ψ 049
ουτοι εισιν γογγυσται μεμψιμοιροι κατα (ℵ* κα) τας (+ ιδιας C²) επιθυμιας
  αυτων πορευομενοι   ℵ* C²

175. Watson, *Invention*, p. 58.

The reading οὗτοί εἰσιν γογγυσταὶ μεμψίμοιροι κατὰ τὰς ἰδίας ἐπιθυμίας αὐτῶν πορευόμενοι is a straightforward case of dittography caused by homoioarchon. Verses 12 and 16 in Jude both begin with the phrase οὗτοί εἰσιν. Instead of copying the remaining words in v. 12, the copyists of ℵ* and C² have accidentally copied the first few words of v. 16. The only acceptable reading here is thus οὗτοί εἰσιν.

Variation Unit 12.2

οι   𝔓72 ℵ^c A B L Ψ
om. οι   ℵ* C^{vid} K 049

William Whallon is not happy with the inclusion of οἱ at v. 12. He has argued that the word οἱ does not belong with σπιλάδες since σπιλάδες is feminine.[176] He is also not convinced of the originality of ἀγάπαις, which appears among our variants at unit 12.3 below, saying that Jude cannot have used the word ἀγάπαις to refer to love-feasts. In Whallon's conjecture, two definite articles have been transposed to resolve the gender problem and ἀγάπαις is replaced by the conjectured noun ἀχάταις: οὗτοί εἰσιν <u>αἱ</u> ἐν <u>τοῖς ἀχάταις</u> ὑμῶν σπιλάδες συνευωχούμενοι—'these are the spots in your agates when they share a banquet'.[177] The result is that αἱ now agrees with σπιλάδες, and τοῖς agrees with the conjectured noun ἀχάταις. As well as resolving the gender difficulty, this conjecture (as a metaphor) fits the context of the verse as a whole very well since the writer uses a series of images with which to describe the opponents.

However, Bauckham sees no difficulty with οἱ at v. 12, saying that the agreement is with συνευωχούμενοι, with σπιλάδες in apposition.[178] The omission of οἱ by the copyists of ℵ* C K 049 here appears to be deliberate, motivated by an attempt to avoid the perceived difficulty created by the juxtaposition of οἱ with σπιλάδες. My verdict at this unit is to print οἱ. I can now turn my attention to ἀγάπαις, and see whether I still need Whallon's conjecture.

176. W. Whallon, 'Should We Keep, Omit or Alter the οἱ in Jude 12?' *NTS* 34 (1988), pp. 156-159.
177. Whallon, 'Jude 12', p. 158.
178. Bauckham, *Jude, 2 Peter*, p. 77.

Variation Unit 12.3

απαταις υμων   𝔓72 ℵ B K L 049
απαταις υμων   A C^vid
απαταις αυτων   A^c syr^ph
ευωχιαις υμων   6 424

Similar variation exists in the parallel verse at 2 Pet. 2.13, where the options are ἀπάταις, ἀγάπαις and ἀγνοίαις. The editors of GNT4 have accepted ἀπάταις at 2 Pet. 2.13 and ἀγάπαις at Jude 12, being persuaded mainly, although not entirely, by external attestation.[179] Kilpatrick has argued that since 2 Peter is inspired by Jude, and since it has not been explained why the author of 2 Peter would have wished to change ἀγάπαις to ἀπάταις, the same variant should be accepted at both units, rather than ἀγάπαις at one unit and ἀπάταις at the other.[180] One need only look to the previous verse (2 Pet. 2.12) to see an example of the author of 2 Peter altering material derived from Jude to such an extent that Sidebottom has commented that 'the language [in 2 Pet. 2.12 sourced from Jude 10] is rearranged until the verse becomes virtually unintelligible'.[181] In view of this, I cannot discount the possibility that ἀγάπαις at Jude 12 may have been changed at 2 Pet. 2.1 to read ἀπάταις. It is certainly true (and not disputed by Kilpatrick) that the presence of αὐτῶν at 2 Pet. 2.13 renders ἀπάταις the most plausible choice at 2 Pet. 2.13.[182] Meanwhile the variant εὐωχίαις at Jude 12 is contextually possible, but I become suspicious when I do not find εὐωχίαις among the variants at 2 Pet. 2.13. I will return to εὐωχίαις later. The main choice to be made at this unit in v. 12 is between ἀγάπαις and ἀπάταις.

The first difficulty posed by the eclectic approach here is that even though Atticism may be a factor, I cannot use the Atticism criterion to make a judgment at this unit, since ἀγάπη as a noun may have been rejected by Atticizing scribes, and since where ἀπάτη meant τέρψις it too may have been rejected by Atticizing scribes.[183] Criteria other than Atticism may help me to make a choice at this unit.

Whallon has omitted to mention the possibility, first considered by

179. Metzger, *Textual Commentary*, pp. 634, 658.
180. G.D. Kilpatrick, 'ΑΓΑΠΗ As Love-Feast in the New Testament', *Collected Essays of G.D. Kilpatrick*, p. 179.
181. Sidebottom, *James, Jude, 2 Peter*, p. 115.
182. Metzger, *Textual Commentary*, p. 634.
183. Kilpatrick, 'ΑΓΑΠΗ', p. 178.

Kilpatrick, that the change from ἀπάταις to ἀγάπαις (or vice versa) could be an accidental rather than a deliberate one. Whallon asks: 'If ἀγάπαις is correct, why has it been changed—even in A for Jude, as well as in A and ℵ for 2 Peter—to a word seemingly so imperfect?'[184] I could indeed ask a similar question about Whallon's conjecture: Why is it that the factor of accidental change, which he gives to account for the alleged disappearance of ἀχάταις from the tradition, does not also enter his thinking when it comes to the evidence in the MSS? Kilpatrick is surely correct in suggesting that the variation between ἀπάταις and ἀγάπαις 'is the product of a mistake in copying'.[185] Evidence for this possibility is that ἀπάτη can be misread as ἀγάπη, as at Mk 4.19 απατη] αγαπη Δ.[186] To this I can add that an accidental change from ἀγάπη to ἀπάτη is also a possibility.[187] What remains for me to determine is the direction of the change.

Contextual arguments can be advanced for each of the rival variants. I shall first examine ἀπάταις as a possibility. If ἀπάταις at 2 Pet. 2.13 can be interpreted to mean 'pleasures', then such an interpretation could also apply at v. 12:

> Windisch had the merit of seeing that ἀπάταις in 2 Pet. had the meaning of 'pleasures' (Lüste)... We suggest... that in both passages [Jude 12 and 2 Pet. 2.13] the original reading was ἀπάταις with the meaning 'pleasures, revels' or the like... Jude 12 may be rendered 'These are the hidden rocks in your pleasures as they fearlessly join in carousing, shepherding themselves...'[188]

184. Whallon, 'Jude 12', p. 157.

185. Kilpatrick, 'ΑΓΑΠΗ', p. 178.

186. Kilpatrick, 'ΑΓΑΠΗ', p. 178.

187. For the time being, I will accept Kilpatrick's view at this unit that the change from ἀγάπαις to ἀπάταις (or vice versa) was accidental, but we may also note here that the word ἀγάπη may have connoted immoral activity to contemporaries of Clement of Alexandria, and that such a connotation if understood by scribes may have caused them to react with a deliberate change. This I can infer from R.M. Grant, 'Charges of "Immorality" against Various Religious Groups in Antiquity', in R. Van Den Broek and M.J. Vermaseren (eds.), *Studies in Gnosticism and Hellenistic Religions Presented to Gilles Quispel on the Occasion of His Sixty-Fifth Birthday* (Leiden: Brill, 1981), p. 166, who comments: 'Gnostics in the second century, according to Clement of Alexandria, advocated treating women as common property and in what they called an "agape" practised what they preached'.

188. Kilpatrick, 'ΑΓΑΠΗ', p. 179.

Kilpatrick's translation of part of v. 12 here reveals that he prefers ἀπάταις ὑμῶν to ἀπάταις αὐτῶν. The difference between these two readings at v. 12 is crucial, yet it is not reflected in Kilpatrick's apparatus for this unit. Had Kilpatrick accounted for the presence of ἀπάταις αὐτῶν preserved in A^c syr^ph, he may have had second thoughts altogether about ἀπάταις. I would regard the reading ἀπάταις αὐτῶν as a deliberate change which entered the tradition because of a realization by some scribes that ἀπάταις ὑμῶν preserved in A C^vid does not fit the context. The problem with ἀπάταις ὑμῶν at Jude 12 is that when ἀπάτη connotes pleasure in Hellenistic Greek, the sense is usually pleasure of a sinful nature.[189] Bauer indeed translates ἀπάταις at 2 Pet. 2.13 not as 'pleasures', but as 'lusts'. Clearly, if there is a sinful or immoral aspect to the definition of ἀπάτη as pleasure, then I cannot defend ἀπάταις ὑμῶν on contextual grounds at Jude 12 since it suggests that Jude's addressees are engaged in immoral pleasures. This contextual invalidity seems to be the most logical explanation for the change to ἀπάταις αὐτῶν, a change which affects the context even more adversely since σπιλάδες then becomes inexplicable. Thus far I have explained why the variant ἀπάταις is unacceptable at this unit. It remains for me to state the case in favour of its rival, ἀγάπαις.

Part of the difficulty which I have to overcome in defending ἀγάπαις arises from the fact that, as Spicq and others have pointed out, the word ἀγάπαι to denote love-feasts occurs nowhere else in the New Testament, although, it is a variant at 2 Pet. 2.13. Spicq's definition for ἀγάπαις as it is used at Jude 12 is as follows:

> ...le contexte est celui d'un repas pris en commun, et il faut certainement comprendre ce terme au sens traditionnel d'*agapes*... On comprendra donc les *agapes* de l'église comme une annexe ou un complément de l'eucharistie, et surtout comme un repas de fraternité où s'exprime la joie de se retrouver ensemble et la gratitude que l'on en chante à Dieu.[190]

The idea of a love-feast is, therefore, of a communal meal at which praise and thanksgiving to God are expressed and a common Christian comradeship is experienced. The danger posed by the opponents to the love-feasts held by Jude's addressees is expressed metaphorically, with the opponents being compared to sunken reefs, 'waiting to shipwreck

---

189. BAGD, s.v. ἀπάτη.
190. C. Spicq, *Agapè dans le Nouveau Testament: analyses des textes* (2 vols.; Paris: Gabalda, 3rd edn, 1966), pp. 347-49.

the unwary', as Green expresses it.[191] The parallel noted by Green is the reference given by Clement *Stromata* 3.2 to the immoral behaviour of the Carpocratians at love-feasts. That the word σπιλάδες is used metaphorically to suggest that the opponents pose a moral threat at love-feasts need not present a hermeneutic problem: σπιλάδες is the first in a series of metaphorical references to the opponents in v. 12 which (as Watson shows) collectively serve the rhetorical function of depreciation.

In addition to the contextual suitability of ἀγάπαις, it is possible to show that the meaning which Spicq ascribes to ἀγάπαις could have existed as early as my chronology for the authorship of Jude. It has already been mentioned in my discussion of Jude's inscriptio that the letter of Jude was written before the 'early Catholic' period of the second-century. Robinson has argued that Jude must have been written before the martyrdom of James in 62 AD.[192] Bauckham is more flexible and suggests that Jude must have been written not earlier than 50 AD, and not later than the end of the first century AD.[193] The opponents, at whom Jude's polemic is directed, cannot be associated with second-century Gnosticism but should rather be linked with the kind of anti-nomianism which existed at Corinth in the 50s and in Asia in the 90s.[194] The earliest usage of the word ἀγάπη to denote a love-feast (other than in Jude) is c. 115 AD in Ignatius *Smyrn.* 8.3.[195] It is, therefore, possible that only 30 years separate the writing activities of Jude and Ignatius and that the use of ἀγάπη to describe a love-feast was established at the time of Jude's authorship. That this use of ἀγάπη could have predated the 'early Catholic' period is illuminated by Bauer, who writes that in the classical period, 'the common meals of the Lacedaemonians καλεῖται φιλίτια', and that this connotation of φιλία could have been transferred to ἀγάπη during or before Jude's lifetime.[196]

Another argument which favours ἀγάπαις (but not ἀπάταις or εὐωχίαις) is that ἀγάπαις has been included in one of the writer's

---

191. Green, *General Epistle of Jude*, p. 189.

192. J.A.T. Robinson, *Redating the New Testament* (London: SCM Press, 1976), p. 197.

193. Bauckham, *Jude, 2 Peter*, p. 13.

194. Bauckham, *Jude, 2 Peter*, p. 13; Eybers, 'Aspects', pp. 118-19.

195. Kilpatrick, 'ΑΓΑΠΗ', p. 180; Eybers, 'Aspects', p. 123, n. 31.

196. BAGD, *Introduction*, pp. xxvi-xxvii.

networks of catchwords.[197] This particular network is reproduced from Charles:

ἀγάπη / ἀγαπητοί: vv. 1, 2, 3, 12, 17, 20, 21.

Catchwords do not have to be exact synonyms: they merely need to possess morphological similarity which might be strengthened by a semantic connection. The link here is probably between ἀγάπαις at v. 12 and ἀγαπητοί at vv. 3, 17, and 20, especially since there is antithesis in v. 12 between οὗτοι and ὑμῶν. The word ἀγάπαις juxtaposed with ὑμῶν equates to ἀγαπητοί in vv. 3, 17 and 20, and ἀγάπαις with ὑμῶν is also part of the antithetical balance in v. 12.

A final argument in favour of ἀγάπαις is its apparent status as a *hapax legomenon*. As I noted at variation unit 7.3, Jude uses *hapax legomena* at vv. 3, 4, 7 (×3), 10, 12 (×2), 13 (×2), 16 (×2) and 19. It should, therefore, not be surprising that the meaning conveyed by ἀγάπαις at this unit is unique in New Testament Greek.

The reading εὐωχίαις is explicable as a deliberate change, a response to the contextual unsuitability of ἀπάταις, or to the possible immoral connotations which ἀγάπαις may have held for some scribes. The need for Whallon's conjecture rests mainly on the assumption that οἱ at Jude 12 is problematic and cannot be original. Less convincing is his unhappiness with ἀγάπαις. Against the assumption concerning οἱ, I have already explained at my second unit why οἱ need not be seen as problematic at v. 12. Although Whallon's conjecture is scholarly, plausible and imaginative, it is also unnecessary, since there is a perfectly good reading in ἀγάπαις among the extant MSS.

Variation Unit 12.4

συνευωχουμενοι ℵ A B L Ψ 049
συνευχομενοι 𝔓72
συνευοχουμενοι K 314 330
συνευωχουμενοι υμιν C 88 323

The reading συνευοχουμενοι [*sic*] appears to be an accidentally transmitted spelling mistake. According to LSJ, there is such a verb as συνεύχομαι (= join in prayer) from which the reading συνεύχομενοι could be derived, but this case is almost certainly an itacism in 𝔓72. Meanwhile, Bauckham's translation of v. 12 suggests that

197. Charles, 'Literary Artifice', p. 112.

συνευωχούμενοι is a reference to 'people who feast with you'.[198] This accurate translation understands an implicit ὑμῖν with συνευωχούμενοι even if ὑμῖν is not printed. The explicit ὑμῖν in C 88 323 is explicable through harmony with 2 Pet. 2.13, where there is an explicit ὑμῖν firm in the MS tradition with συνευωχούμενοι. At this unit συνευωχούμενοι should be printed.

Variation Unit 12.5

εαυτους   𝔓72ᶜ ℵ A B C K L Ψ 049
αυτους   𝔓72*

This unit is more significant than would appear to be the case at first glance since variation involving reflexive pronouns becomes an issue at vv. 16, 18 and 19. The activity of the corrector 𝔓72ᶜ at this unit suggests strongly that the reading αὐτούς resulted from the accidental omission of the epsilon in 𝔓72*. To put the matter beyond doubt, I may note the writer's preference for the reflexive pronoun ἑαυτόν rather than ordinary pronouns with participles.[199] This preference is evident at vv. 12, 13, 16, 20, 21 and possibly at v. 19 if ἑαυτούς preserved in C 323 378 is regarded as original. At this unit the presence of the reflexive ἑαυτούς with the participle ποιμαίνοντες accords with the writer's stylistic preference.[200] The evidence favours ἑαυτούς at this unit.

Variation Unit 12.6

υπο ανεμων   𝔓72 A B C K L Ψ 049
υπ ανεμων   467 1175
παντι ανεμω   ℵ 104 459

Elision in New Testament Greek is unlikely to occur before nouns (such as ἀνέμων here) or verbs.[201] In view of these factors and of the tendency of Atticizing scribes to introduce elision wherever possible,[202] it would seem safe to reject the reading ὑπ' ἀνέμων as a deliberate change to the text resulting from Atticism. This leaves me with two options: ὑπὸ ἀνέμων and παντὶ ἀνέμῳ. Since παντὶ ἀνέμῳ is explicable through harmony with Eph. 4.14 where the same phrase occurs, my verdict at this unit is in favour of ὑπὸ ἀνέμων.

198.   Bauckham, *Jude, 2 Peter*, p. 77.
199.   Kubo, *𝔓72 and the Codex Vaticanus*, p. 88.
200.   Further discussion on this aspect of style is provided at variation unit 16.1.
201.   BDF §17; MHT, II, p. 61.
202.   Elliott, *Timothy and Titus*, p. 26.

Variation Unit 12.7

παραφερομεναι 𝔓72ᶜ ℵ A C K L 049
παραφερομενοι 𝔓72* B Ψ

Since παραφερόμεναι agrees with the feminine noun νεφέλαι, I must reject the alternative variant παραφερόμενοι, the latter being explicable as an accidental error, AI being misheard as OI by a copyist during dictation.

Variation Unit 13.1

κυματα αγρια 𝔓72 A B C K L Ψ 049
αγρια κυματα ℵ

The inclination of the writer to conform to adjectival word order tendencies which exist in New Testament Greek generally has been demonstrated in my discussion of variation unit 6.5. If the agreeing noun is anarthrous, and if the adjective describes a quality (rather than a quantity), then the adjective is positioned after the agreeing noun.[203] At this unit, the noun κῦμα is anarthrous, and the adjective ἄγριος describes quality. In view of this, the most acceptable reading at this unit is κύματα ἄγρια since it preserves the position of ἄγρια after κύματα. Without a decisive argument in favour of ἄγρια κύματα, I must reject this singular reading.

Variation Unit 13.2

επαφριζοντα ℵ A B K L Ψ 049
απαφριζουτα 𝔓72 C
μεταφριζουτα 429

The verb ἐπαφρίζω means 'cause to splash up like foam', while the verb ἀπαφρίζω conveys the meaning 'cast off like foam'.[204] According to Kubo, the variation at this unit is deliberate, and I should print the reading in 𝔓72 'unless good reasons can be given for its rejection'.[205]

The main factor here is the context of the verse. Admittedly, the semantic difference between ἀπαφρίζοντα and ἐπαφρίζοντα is slender, but, as I can show, ἐπαφρίζοντα fits the context better. 'Casting off' (ἀπαφρίζοντα) the foam of their deeds of shame suggests that the

---

203. BDF §474.
204. BAGD, s.vv. ἐπαφρίζω, ἀπαφρίζω.
205. Kubo, *𝔓72 and the Codex Vaticanus*, p. 87.

opponents are now free of these deeds and have abandoned them, an image which does not fit into the wider scheme of Jude's polemic. But 'casting up' (ἐπαφρίζοντα) the foam of these deeds suggests that the opponents still practise immorality continually and thus coheres with the wider context of Jude's attack on the opponents. Against the argument that ἐπαφρίζοντα could be a deliberate change introduced precisely in order to improve the context, it should be remembered that the sort of deliberate changes seen so far have been apparent rather than genuine improvements to the text. My suggestion at this unit is that the change from ἐπαφρίζοντα to ἀπαφρίζοντα was deliberate, effected as a reaction to ἐπαφρίζοντα as a *hapax legomenon*. Meanwhile μετα-φρίζοντα is also explicable as a reaction to ἐπαφρίζοντα as a *hapax legomenon*. Print ἐπαφρίζοντα here as the context demands.

Variation Unit 13.3

ο ζοφος   ℵ A C K L Ψ 049
ζοφος   𝔓 72 B

In attempting to decide whether ζόφος is anarthrous or articular here, I must first decline the notion that ὁ ζόφος is the result of harmonization with ὁ ζόφος at 2 Pet. 2.17. Harmonization cannot be permitted as a determinant at this unit because (as Kubo points out) one would normally expect more than two MSS to resist harmonization.

In favour of ὁ ζόφος is the comment that 'the author of 2 Peter [at 2 Pet. 2.17] has accurately followed Jude'.[206] I can expand on Kubo's idea here by looking at both parallels between Jude and 2 Peter involving the word ζόφος. At 2 Pet. 2.4 anarthrous ζόφου is firm in the text, thus following anarthrous ζόφον at Jude 6, which is also firm in the MS tradition. At 2 Pet. 2.17, articular ζόφος is the reading accepted in GNT4, and my deduction is that it follows articular ζόφος at Jude 13. Although it could be argued that 2 Peter often changes the wording in Jude, my rebuttal would be that the author of 2 Peter has not added an article to ζόφου at 2 Pet. 2.4 (the parallel to anarthrous ζόφον at Jude 6) and is not, therefore, likely to have removed an article at 2 Pet. 2.17. Since there is no reason for the author of 2 Peter to have removed the definite article from his source v. 13, my solution must be to accept ὁ ζόφος at this unit.

206.   Kubo, *𝔓72 and the Codex Vaticanus*, p. 142.

Variation Unit 13.4

του σκοτους   𝔓72 ℵ A C K L Ψ 049
σκοτους   B

Firm in the MS tradition at 2 Pet. 2.17 is τοῦ σκότους, and there is no reason to assume that τοῦ σκότους at 2 Pet. 2.17 is not accurately reproduced from Jude 13. The omission of the article from the reading in B may have arisen through hom., due to the morphological proximity of <u>τοῦ</u> and <u>σκότους</u>, so I must reject the singular reading. Accept τοῦ σκότους here.

Variation Unit 13.5

εις τον αιωνα   K 049
εις αιωνα   ℵ A B C L
εις αιωνας   Ψ 206 242
εις εωνα   𝔓72

The reading εις εωνα [*sic*] in 𝔓72 is the result of itacism. The remaining three variants at this unit can each be defended on internal grounds. The reading εἰς αἰῶνα is printed in Tischendorf, von Soden, De Zwaan, WH, BFBS2, Vogels, Merk, GNTMT and GNT4. Against these editions, εἰς τὸν αἰῶνα is accepted in Kilpatrick, *Diglot*. The reading εἰς αἰῶνα could be original if it is argued that it was unfamiliar to scribes and would thus have been changed to εἰς τὸν αἰῶνα, a set expression which crops up elsewhere in the New Testament. However, it is also possible to argue in the opposite direction and see εἰς τὸν αἰῶνα as original, with εἰς αἰῶνα(ς) arising as a result of the accidental omission of the definite article. It would seem precarious to use transcriptional probability as an acceptable solution here, but since one of the variants (εἰς τὸν αἰῶνα) is a New Testament set expression, it might be more fruitful to look at intrinsic evidence.

With set expressions, one needs to determine the inclinations of an individual author, and also whether or not these inclinations conform to the New Testament as a whole.[207] Some set expressions may be unique to an individual author, others may be shared by several New Testament authors. Before I examine tendencies in Jude, I may quickly establish that εἰς τὸν αἰῶνα enjoys wide distribution as a New Testament set expression, as evidenced by its occurrence at Mt. 21.19; Mk 3.29, 11.14;

---

207. See, for example, J.K. Elliott, 'The Text of Acts in the Light of Two Recent Studies', *NTS* 34 (1988), pp. 250-58, esp. pp. 252-55.

Jn 6.51, 58, 8.35, 12.34, 14.16; 1 Pet. 1.25; 1 Jn 2.17; 2 Jn 2; 1 Cor.
8.13; and Heb. 1.8. Despite its brevity, there is quite a liberal sprinkling
of New Testament fixed expressions in the letter of Jude:

v. 1	Ἰησοῦ Χριστοῦ δοῦλος
v. 4	κύριον ἡμῶν Ἰησοῦν Χριστὸν
v. 17	κυρίου ἡμῶν Ἰησοῦ Χριστοῦ
v. 20	ἐν πνεύματι ἁγίῳ
v. 21	εἰς ζωὴν αἰώνιον
v. 21	κυρίου ἡμῶν Ἰησοῦ Χριστοῦ
v. 25	Ἰησοῦ Χριστοῦ τοῦ κύριου ἡμῶν

The expression Ἰησοῦ Χριστοῦ δοῦλος is common to Jude 1 and Jas
1.1. The set expression κύριος ἡμῶν Ἰησοῦς Χριστός which is visible
at Jude 4, 17 and 21 can also be found at Acts 15.26; Rom. 5.1, 11,
15.6, 30; 1 Cor. 1.2, 7, 10, 15.57; 2 Cor. 1.3, 8.9; Gal. 6.14, 18; Eph. 1.3,
1.5, 5.20, 6.24; Col. 1.3; 1 Thess. 1.3, 1.5, 5.9, 23, 28; 2 Thess. 2.1, 14,
16, 3.18; 1 Tim. 6.3, 14; Jas 2.1; 1 Pet. 1.3; and 2 Pet. 1.8, 14, 16. The
set expression ἐν πνεύματι ἁγίῳ at Jude 20 can also be found at
Mt. 3.11; Lk. 3.16; Jn 1.33; Acts 1.5, 11.16; Rom. 9.1, 14.17, 15.16;
1 Cor. 12.3; 2 Cor. 6.6; 1 Thess. 1.5; and 1 Pet. 1.12. The set expression
εἰς ζωὴν αἰώνιον at Jude 21 is also evident at Mt. 25.46 and at
Rom. 5.21, 6.22. The set expression Ἰησοῦς Χριστός ὁ κύριος ἡμῶν
at Jude 25 is also employed at Rom. 1.4, 5.21, 7.25 and at 1 Cor. 1.9.
Since no intrinsic explanation has been forthcoming to explain why Jude
might have refrained from using the New Testament set expression εἰς
τὸν αἰῶνα when there is clear evidence that Jude employs other New
Testament set expressions, the balance of probability favours the variant
εἰς τὸν αἰῶνα as printed in Kilpatrick, *Diglot*.

Variation Unit 14.1

επροφητευσεν	𝔓72 B*
προεφητευσεν	A C K L Ψ 049
προεπροφητευσεν	ℵ
επροεφητευσεν	B²

The readings προεπροφητευσεν and επροεφητευσεν are both orthographical errors, the cause in both cases (according to Albin) being dittography.[208] This leaves a choice between ἐπροφήτευσεν and
προεφήτευσεν. If Moulton is correct in asserting that προεφήτευσα is

---

208. Albin, *Judasbrevet*, p. 611.

the normal Attic aorist form of the verb, then I should reject προεφήτευσεν at v. 14 as an Atticist correction.[209] Elsewhere in the New Testament, variation involving the position of the augment and the aorist of προφητεύω (reproduced below from Tischendorf) can only be explicable as deliberate interference resulting from Atticism:

Mt. 7.22	επροφητευσαμεν	ℵ B* C L Z
	προεφητευσαμεν	B² E G K M S U V X Δ Π
Mt. 11.13	επροφητευσαν	X B* C D Z
	προεφητευσαν	B** E F G K L M S U V X Γ Π
Mt. 15.7	επροφητευσεν	X B* C D L Tᶜ
	προεφητευσεν	B** E F G K M S U V X Γ Θ Π
Mk 7.6	επροφητευσεν	X B* D L Δ
	προεφητευσεν	A B² X Γ Π
Lk. 1.67	επροφητευσεν	ℵ* A B* C L
	προεφητευσεν	ℵᶜ B³ Γ Δ
Jn 11.51	επροφητευσεν	ℵ B D L X
	προεφητευσεν	A I M² Γ Δ Λ Π

The GNT4 editors have printed the non-Attic variant ἐπροφήτευσα and its derivatives at Mt. 7.22, 11.13, 15.7; Mk 7.6; Lk. 1.67, and Jn 11.51. However, they have printed the Attic variant προεφήτευσεν at Jude 14. Unless it can be explained why the deliberate change was in one direction at Mt. 7.22, 11.13, 15.7; Mk 7.6, Lk. 1.67 and Jn 11.51, but in the opposite direction at Jude 14, GNT4 cannot be defended at this unit.[210] Further, if the GNT4 editors have accepted the variant χάριτα at Jude 4 in preference to χάριν on the grounds that χάριν is an Atticism, they ought to have exercised the same judgment at Jude 14 with προφητεύω. The only acceptable variant here is ἐπροφήτευσεν.

209. MHT, II, p. 192.

210. According to Albin, *Judasbrevet*, p. 738, '... für die allgemein bezeugte Form προεφητευσεν spricht die bedeutsame προ-Triade in Jd 4 14 17 (προγεγραμμενοι—προεφητευσεν—προειρημενων)'. This argument in favour of προεφήτευσεν strains credibility when one examines other occurrences of triadic illustration in Jude as shown at variation unit 2.2 where it is clear that most instances of triadic illustration occur within the boundary of a single verse and that the remaining instances span a boundary not exceeding three verses.

Variation Unit 14.2

κυριος   𝔓72 A B C K L Ψ 049
ο κυριος   ℵ 181 378

The variants here are κύριος and ὁ κύριος. There is some doubt as to whether κύριος at v. 14 refers to God or to Jesus. If it can be decisively demonstrated that κύριος is a reference to Jesus Christ, then the variant ὁ κύριος could be original, since elsewhere (with only one exception) Jude uses an article with the word κύριος when referring to Christ, whereas κύριος at 1 Enoch 1.4 is a reference to God. If I accept the view that Jude is re-interpreting 1 Enoch 1.9 to apply it to the Parousia of Jesus, then κύριος at Jude 14 could denote Jesus.[211] However, against this theory, I should note (as Dehandschutter has pointed out) that whenever Jude uses κύριος of Jesus, he uses κύριος in conjunction with Ἰησοῦς Χριστός as at vv. 4, 17, 21 and 25. Since it cannot be proved beyond doubt that κύριος at v. 14 denotes Christ, I cannot argue decisively in favour of the variant ὁ κύριος.

Two arguments can be advanced in favour of κύριος and against ὁ κύριος. Firstly, it may be asserted that the copyist of ℵ may have inserted an article at v. 14 deliberately if we recall that deliberate change was the reason given for variants at v. 3 (τοῦ γράφειν) and at v. 9 (ὁ κύριος). Secondly, as I have explained in detail at v. 5, it is probable that articular κύριος at vv. 5, 9 and 14 is an anti-adoptionist alteration to the text. My verdict is to accept anarthrous κύριος here.

Variation Unit 14.3

εν μυριασιν αγιαις αυτου   C 323 378
εν αγιων αγγελων μυριασιν   𝔓72
εν αγιαις μυριασιν αυτου   A B K L 049

---

211. R.J. Bauckham, 'A Note on a Problem in the Greek Version of 1 Enoch 1.9', *JTS* 32 (1981), p. 136, n. 5; M. Black, 'The Maranatha Invocation and Jude 14, 15 (1 Enoch 1.9)', in B. Lindars (ed.), *Christ and Spirit in the New Testament: Essays in Honour of C.F.D. Moule* (Cambridge: Cambridge University Press, 1973), p. 194; and C.D. Osburn, 'The Christological Use of 1 Enoch 1.9 in Jude 14-15', *NTS* 23 (1977), p. 337, have all argued that κύριος at Jude 14 denotes Christ. Against these three scholars, B. Dehandschutter, 'Pseudo-Cyprian, Jude and Enoch: Some Notes on 1 Enoch 1.9', in J.W. van Henten (ed.), *Tradition and Reinterpretation in Jewish and Early Christian Literature: Essays in Honour of Jurgen C.H. Lebram* (Leiden: Brill, 1968), p. 118, has stated that a christological adaptation is unlikely.

εν μυριασιν αγιων αγγελων ℵ 104 378
εν αγιαις μυριασιν αγγελων Ψ
εν μυριασιν αγιων αγγελων αυτου   1838 1845
εν αγιαις μυριασιν αγγελων αυτου   181 1837
εν μυριασιν αγιαις αγγελων αυτου   88 915
εν αγιαις μυριασιν   1852

Two issues need to be addressed here: (1) word order involving ἀγίαις and μυριάσιν; and (2) whether I should keep or omit ἀγγέλων. Although the possibilities surrounding ἀγίων ἀγγέλων are well discussed by Bauckham,[212] the issue of word order affecting ἀγίαις and μυριάσιν has been neglected in all of the available literature. Osburn's approach to the variation at this unit is disappointingly conservative: he stresses the importance of older and allegedly better MSS but fails to examine whether his preferences for the readings ἐν ἀγίων ἀγγέλων μυριάσιν and ἐν ἀγίαις μυριάσιν αὐτοῦ are justified on intrinsic grounds. In particular he fails properly to consider word order as a factor.

Concerning word order, the main question to be addressed is: Does one accept ἐν μυριάσιν ἀγίαις, or ἐν ἀγίαις μυριάσιν? Since μυριάσιν is an anarthrous substantive, and, since ἀγίαις is an adjective of quality rather than quantity, in New Testament Greek the relevant rule is that the adjective should normally follow its substantive.[213] The writer's careful adherence to the rule can be seen in his word order preferences when using qualitative adjectives with anarthrous substantives:

v. 7	πυρὸς αἰωνίου
v. 12	νεφέλαι ἄνυδροι
v. 12	δένδρα φθινοπωρινὰ ἄκαρπα
v. 13	κύματα ἄγρια
v. 20	ἐν πνεύματι ἀγίῳ
v. 21	εἰς ζωὴν αἰώνιον[214]

The importance of the examples from vv. 20 and 21 is that the presence of a preposition does not cause any change in word order. The preference in Jude is: preposition + substantive + adjective (PR + S + A) with the qualitative adjective always being positioned after the substantive. In

212. Bauckham, 'Note on a Problem', pp. 137-38.
213. BDF §474.
214. We should recall here that the phrase ἀγίων ἀγγέλων which appears among our variants violates this rule in BDF, but that it is an established exception to the rule.

view of the writer's word order preference, variants which do not preserve the order PR + S + A can be eliminated, for example, I can eliminate the reading in 𝔓72, where there is PR + A + QG + S. The only
remaining possibilities are thus:

εν μυριασιν αγιαις αυτου   C 323 378
εν μυριασιν αγιων αγγελων αυτου   1838 1845
εν μυριασιν αγιαις αγγελων αυτου   88 915
εν μυριασιν αγιων αγγελων   ℵ 104 378

Since the reading in C 323 378 is acceptable on grounds of word order,
I still need to assess Osburn's comment that 'the alteration of the
sequence of the words μυριάσιν ἁγίαις in C...is a variation of the AB
text and is a common enough error in the textual tradition of the New
Testament'.[215] Yet it is the reading in the AB text which violates the rule
that the adjective should follow the anarthrous substantive since the
reading ἐν ἁγίαις μυριάσιν places the adjective before the substantive.
It is impossible to defend Osburn's preference for ἐν ἁγίαις μυριάσιν
on intrinsic grounds. The broad reason for the variation involving
ἁγίαις and μυριάσιν appears to be uncertainty among scribes about
correct word order, and the word order violation in the AB reading may
result from such uncertainty.

To choose from among the four variants each beginning with ἐν
μυριάσιν, I need to decide upon whether the word ἀγγέλων should be
retained or omitted. The main consideration here is that the word
ἁγίαις in isolation, as it appears in the reading ἐν μυριάσιν ἁγίαις
αὐτοῦ, is ambiguous, or certainly would have appeared so to scribes,
since οἱ ἅγιοι in the early church could have been understood either as
a reference to angels or Christians, depending on the context.[216] It is
probable that ἀγγέλων was added by the copyists of 𝔓72 and other
MSS as an explanatory gloss to underscore that the reference in this context of ἁγίαις is to angels rather than to Christians.[217] To argue as
Osburn has done that ἀγγέλων could be original because it accurately
renders the text of Enoch 1.9 in 4QHen is unconvincing for two reasons: (1) 4QHen preserves only fragments of Enoch 1.9 and not the
complete text, so one cannot be sure that Jude's rendition of 1 Enoch
1.9 is always closer to 4QHen than to other copies of 1 Enoch 1.9; and

215. Osburn, 'Christological Use', p. 337.
216. Bauckham, 'Note on a Problem', p. 137.
217. Bauckham, 'Note on a Problem', pp. 137-38.

(2) the extant Greek copy of 1 Enoch 1.9 excludes ἀγγέλων and it could be argued that Jude is following the Greek copy by excluding ἀγγέλων. In the light of the evidence discussed, the variant which conforms to P + S + A and which omits ἀγγέλων is the one that should be accepted: ἐν μυριάσιν ἁγίαις αὐτοῦ.

Variation Unit 15.1

παντας τους ασεβεις   A B C Ψ
πασαν ψυχην   𝔓72 ℵ cop^sa syr^ph
παντας τους ασεβεις αυτων   K L 049

Although the GNT4 editors have accepted πᾶσαν ψυχήν, editors such as Vogels have opted for πάντας τοὺς ἀσεβεῖς:

> ποιῆσαι κρίσιν κατὰ πάντων καὶ ἐλέγξαι <u>πάντας τοὺς ἀσεβεῖς</u> περὶ <u>πάντων τῶν ἔργων</u> ἀσεβείας αὐτῶν ὧν ἠσέβησαν καὶ περὶ <u>πάντων τῶν σκληρῶν</u> ὧν ἐλάλησαν κατ' αὐτοῦ ἁμαρτωλοὶ ἀσεβεῖς (Vogels)

The variant πάντας τοὺς ἀσεβεῖς is one of three phrases which I have underlined. These three phrases clearly adhere to a stylistically polished formula: πᾶς + definite article + adjective or substantive (hereafter Π + DA + AS). Taken together, the three phrases (all the ungodly; all the deeds; all the hard utterances) form a distinctive triadic unity, similar to the triadic structures which are evident at vv. 1, 2, 4, 5-7, 8, 9, 11, 12, 13, 16, 19, 20-21, and 25.[218] The triadic unity of these three phrases is further enhanced by the repetition of certain vowels and consonants, notably pi, alpha, nu, tau and omega, conforming to the writer's predilection for paronomasia[219] reproduced here from Charles:[220]

v. 3	Ἀγαπητοί, πᾶσαν σπουδὴν ποιούμενος...περί...γράψαι...παρακαλῶν ἐπαγωνίζεσθαι...ἅπαξ παραδοθείσῃ...πίστει
v. 7	ἐκπορνεύσασαι...ἀπελθοῦσαι...πρόκεινται...ὑπέχουσαι
v. 8	μέντοι...οὗτοι ἐνυπνιαζόμενοι

218. As shown at variation unit 2.2.

219. Charles, 'Literary Artifice', p. 114, defines paronomasia as a form of parallelism 'where resemblance in sound is exploited for literary effect...[and which takes into account] instances of alliteration, assonance, homoioteleuton, rhyme, word- and name-play'. Where paronomasia is mentioned hereafter, this is the definition which is understood.

220. Charles, 'Literary Artifice', p. 114.

v. 8   μιαίνουσιν...ἀθετοῦσιν...βλασφημοῦσιν
v. 10   ἐπίστανται...φθείρονται
v. 11   ἐπορεύθησαν...ἐξεχύθησαν
vv.12-13   δένδρα φθινοπωρινὰ ἄκαρπα...ἀποθανόντα ἐκριζωθέντα, κύματα ἄγρια θαλάσσης ἐπαφρίζοντα
v. 15   περὶ πάντων τῶν ἔργων...αὐτῶν ὧν ἠσέβησαν...περὶ πάντων τῶν σκληρῶν ὧν ἐλάλησαν
v. 16   Οὗτοι...μεμψίμοιροι...πορευόμενοι
v. 19   Οὗτοι...οἱ...ψυχικοί

The use of triadic illustration in v. 15 serves the purpose of rhetorical amplification, which in turn is intended to magnify (by way of allusion) the totality of the ungodliness of the opponents, and the totality of the judgment which they will be required to face.[221]

An obvious objection to my argument in favour of πάντας τοὺς ἀσεβεῖς could be that stylistic polishing is exactly the sort of thing expected in a deliberate scribal alteration. But I can counter such an objection by showing that the threefold repetition of the formula Π + DA + AS is Jude's own creation. Bauckham has argued that Jude 14-15 is essentially a direct quotation from 1 Enoch 1.9 with minor alterations.[222] I would argue that a comparison of the Greek text of 1 Enoch 1.9 (preserved in the Codex Panopolitanus) and the text of v. 15 reveals that Jude derived the formula Π + DA + AS from the phrase πάντας τοὺς ἀσεβεῖς in 1 Enoch 1.9 and that Jude developed this formula himself:

1 Enoch 1.9	*Jude 15*
πάντας τοὺς ἀσεβεῖς...	πάντας τοὺς ἀσεβεῖς...
πάντων ἔργων...	πάντων τῶν ἔργων...
σκληρῶν...	πάντων τῶν σκληρῶν...

The reading πάντας τοὺς ἀσεβεῖς thus serves as the model for the pattern which is developed in the second and third phrases in v. 15, πάντων τῶν ἔργων and πάντων τῶν σκληρῶν, since all three phrases are intrinsically linked in the various respects described. Meanwhile, arguments thus far advanced *in favour* of the reading πάντας τοὺς ἀσεβεῖς are also indirect arguments against the reading πᾶσαν ψυχήν: for example, the latter reading does not conform to the writer's formula Π + DA + AS and does not form part of a closely structured triadic entity.

---

221. See Watson, *Invention*, p. 66.
222. Bauckham, *Jude, 2 Peter*, p. 94.

Although Kubo is vague on intrinsic evidence at this unit, his comments on transcriptional evidence are compelling: (1) scribes objected to πάντας τοὺς ἀσεβεῖς and substituted πᾶσαν Ψυχήν to reduce what they saw as the excessive repetition of ἀσεβής; (2) πᾶσαν ψυχήν is harmonized from Rom. 2.9.[223] For different reasons, Albin is also not convinced of the originality of the reading πᾶσαν ψυχήν.[224] Whether I agree with Albin or Kubo, the weight of transcriptional evidence is against πᾶσαν ψυχήν.

The addition of αὐτῶν as reflected in K L 049 is explicable through internal harmony with αὐτῶν after ἀσεβείας a little later in the verse. The reading in K L 049 is unacceptable simply because, whereas the additional αὐτῶν makes sense only if ἀσεβεῖς is viewed as a reference to ungodly deeds, in fact (as can be inferred from the translation provided in Bauckham's commentary) πάντας τοὺς ἀσεβεῖς at this unit is a reference to ungodly *people*, not to ungodly *deeds*. In view of the intrinsic and transcriptional evidence discussed, against GNT4 πάντας τοὺς ἀσεβεῖς should be printed here.

Variation Unit 15.2

των εργων ασεβειας αυτων   A B K L 049
των ασεβειων αυτων   Ψ* 876 1245
των εργων των ασεβειων αυτων   Ψ^c 630 1611
των εργων αυτων   C 321 442
των εργων   ℵ 322 323
om. των εργων ασεβειας αυτων ων ησεβησαν και περι παντων   𝔓72

The omission of the words τῶν ἔργων ἀσεβείας αὐτῶν ὧν ἠσέβησαν καὶ περὶ πάντων by the copyist of 𝔓72 is a hom. induced error. In this case the error arose when πάντων (the eleventh word in v. 15) was confused with πάντων (the twentieth word in v. 15), thus causing the omission of nine words. Of the remaining readings, it will be seen that τῶν ἔργων ἀσεβείας αὐτῶν is the most plausible.

Two issues need to be settled: (1) whether I should include or exclude ἔργων; and (2) whether ἀσεβείας should be included or excluded. Intrinsic evidence favours the inclusion of both of these words. In view

---

223. Kubo, *𝔓72 and the Codex Vaticanus*, p. 88.
224. According to Albin, *Judasbrevet*, pp. 738-39: 'Die Lesung πασαν ψυχην ist offenbar eine Emendation: zur Vermeidung von Wiederholung und möglicherweise als Konformation zu κατα παντων'.

of the fact that πάντων τῶν ἔργων is part of the threefold formula Π + DA + AS, ἔργων should definitely be included. The inclusion of ἀσεβείας can be defended on intrinsic grounds in view of the author's tendency to use catchwords, since ἀσεβείας here can be linked with ἠσέβησαν and ἀσεβεῖς in the same verse.[225] Only two variants satisfy both of these intrinsic conditions: τῶν ἔργων ἀσεβείας αὐτῶν and τῶν ἔργων τῶν ἀσεβείων αὐτῶν.[226]

The reading τῶν ἔργων τῶν ἀσεβείων αὐτῶν preserved in Ψ^c 630 1611 allows the inference that the omission of τῶν ἔργων from Ψ* 876 1245 was accidental, and that a conflated reading is reflected in Ψ^c 630 1611 which combines τῶν ἔργων from A B C and other MSS, and τῶν ἀσεβείων αὐτῶν from Ψ* 876 1245. Meanwhile, the omission of ἀσεβείας from other MSS in the apparatus appears to be deliberate, if it is recalled that at variation unit 15.1 πᾶσαν ψυχήν is explicable as a deliberate change in reaction to the excessive repetition of ἀσεβής / ἀσέβεια. Accept τῶν ἔργων ἀσεβείας αὐτῶν here.

Variation Unit 15.3

των σκληρων   A B K L Ψ 049
των σκληρω   𝔓72
των σκληρων λογων   ℵ C cop^sa

Firstly, σκληρω [*sic*] is another accidental error in 𝔓72. Secondly, whether I accept τῶν σκληρῶν or τῶν σκληρῶν λόγων at this unit has no adverse bearing on my argument that πάντων τῶν σκληρῶν adheres to Jude's threefold formula Π + DA + AS. There seems no reason here to disagree with Bauckham's view that λόγων here is an explanatory gloss, and so τῶν σκληρῶν should be printed.[227]

Variation Unit 16.1

επιθυμιας εαυτων   𝔓72^c C L P 049
επιθυμιας αυτων   ℵ A B K Ψ
om. κατα τας επιθυμιας εαυτων πορευομενοι   𝔓72*

---

225. The author's predilection for catchwords is explained in greater detail at variation unit 1.3.
226. The reading in Ψ also satisfies Π + DA + AS, but is indefensible on transcriptional grounds.
227. Bauckham, *Jude, 2 Peter*, p. 93.

The words κατὰ τὰς ἐπιθυμίας ἑαυτῶν πορευόμενοι are omitted by the original copyist of 𝔓72 through hom., but have been added by the corrector who noticed the mistake. There is no doubt that the words should be included. The remaining crux is whether I should read ἐπιθυμίας ἑαυτῶν or ἐπιθυμίας αὐτῶν. In favour of the reading ἐπιθυμίας ἑαυτῶν is the argument that the writer has a tendency to use a reflexive pronoun with participles rather than an ordinary pronoun.[228] Examples of this tendency are as follows:

v. 12	<u>ἑαυτοὺς</u> ποιμαίνοντες
v. 13	ἐπαφρίζοντα τὰς <u>ἑαυτῶν</u> αἰσχύνας
v. 18	ἐπιθυμίας <u>ἑαυτῶν</u> πορευόμενοι[229]
v. 19	ἀποδιορίζοντες <u>ἑαυτοὺς</u>[230]
v. 20	ἐποικοδομοῦντες <u>ἑαυτοὺς</u>
v. 21	<u>ἑαυτοὺς</u>...προσδεχόμενοι

A reasonable explanation for αὐτῶν as a variant here must be that the epsilon was omitted by mistake (cf. the accidental αὐτῶν in 𝔓72* at v. 12), so ἑαυτῶν should be accepted at this unit.[231]

Variation Unit 17.1

μνημονευετε 323 1739
μνησθητε 𝔓72 ℵ A B C K L P Ψ 049

There is certainly a case to be made for μνημονεύετε since v. 17 is a midrash commentary, one among several in which the writer would normally use the present tense.[232] The writer only departs from this tense code on one or two occasions specifically when he uses the aorist at the end of a given commentary in order to introduce a new text. Otherwise, the aorist is reserved for the midrash texts, and the present is reserved for the midrash commentaries. In view of this, μνήσθητε is difficult to defend on intrinsic grounds. The reading μνήσθητε is explicable as a deliberate change, generated through internal harmony with

228. Kubo, *𝔓72 and the Codex Vaticanus*, p. 88.
229. Against GNT4.
230. Against GNT4.
231. Albin, *Judasbrevet*, p. 739, comments: 'Die Variante επιθυμιας εαυτων ist nunmehr gut bezeugt, doch besteht der Verdacht, sie könne, mit oder ohne Einfluss von Jd 18, eine absichtliche Verstärkung eines ursprünglichen επιθυμιας αυτων sein. Will man trotzdem auf εαυτων als ursprünglicher Lesung bestehen, so kann man -ε bei den übrigen Textzeugen als Wegfall von ε nach ς erklären'.
232. Ellis, 'Prophecy and Hermeneutic', p. 225.

the aorist imperative τηρήσατε at v. 21. Since v. 17 is undoubtedly a midrash commentary, μνημονεύετε should be printed at this unit.

Variation Unit 17.2

των ρηματων των προειρημενων   𝔓72 ℵ B C K L P Ψ 049
των προειρημενων ρηματων   A 323 378

The order employed in both of these readings is acceptable in New Testament Greek, so, on the face of it, either could be original. There are three arguments in favour of τῶν ῥημάτων τῶν προειρημένων, the first two intrinsic and the third transcriptional. The first argument is one of inference rather than definite proof: firm in the text in the same verse is τῶν ἀποστόλων τοῦ κυρίου, preserving the same order as τῶν ῥημάτων τῶν προειρημένων. The second argument rests upon the presupposition that Semitic word order is a factor at this unit. Faced with the choice between τὸν ἐμὸν λὸγον and τὸν λόγον τὸν ἐμὸν, Elliott at Jn 8.51 would print τὸν λόγον τὸν ἐμὸν as the reading with the more Semitic word order.[233] There is evidence in Jude of Semitic influence at vv. 5, 7, 11, 16, 17, 18, 21 and possibly 24.[234] If Elliott's preference at Jn 8.51 is an appropriate paradigm, at this unit τῶν ῥημάτων τῶν προειρημένων should be printed as the reading which reflects the more Semitic word order.[235] Meanwhile the rival reading τῶν προειρημένων ῥημάτων is explicable through harmony with τῶν προειρημένων ῥημάτων at 2 Pet. 3.2. Accept τῶν ῥημάτων τῶν προειρημένων here.

Variation Unit 18.1

οτι ελεγον υμιν   𝔓72 ℵ A B C L P Ψ 049
οτι ελεγεν ημιν   K 639 641
οτι ελεγον ημιν   226 606

The only reading which coheres with the context of vv. 17-18 is ὅτι ἔλεγον ὑμῖν, translated 'how they said to you' by Bauckham.[236] ἔλεγον should be accepted at this unit because 'they said' must be

---

233. Elliott, *Essays and Studies*, p. 32.
234. MHT, IV, pp. 139-40; Bauckham, *Jude, 2 Peter*, pp. 6, 104.
235.   That Elliott's choice at Jn 8.51 may indeed be an appropriate guide may be argued in view of the adjectival quality of ἐμὸν at Jn 8.51 and of προειρημένων at this unit in Jude.
236. Bauckham, *Jude, 2 Peter*, p. 102.

ascribed to the apostles who make the predictions mentioned in v. 17. The reading ὅτι ἔλεγεν ἡμῖν—'how he said to us'—wrongly attributes the predictions in v. 17 not to the apostles but to Jesus Christ. The copyists of K 639 641 have misconstrued why Ἰησοῦ Χριστοῦ in v. 17 is genitive: it is not the predictions which belong to Christ, but the apostles. The third reading in my apparatus—ὅτι ἔλεγον ἡμῖν—is explicable as a conflation of the first two readings. By contrast, ὑμῖν is a clear echo of ὑμεῖς in v. 17. The reading accepted here is thus ὅτι ἔλεγον ὑμῖν.

Variation Unit 18.2

οτι (*secundum*)   𝔓72 A C K Lᶜ P 049
om. οτι (*secundum*)   ℵ B L* Ψ

Whether I regard the second ὅτι as part of a straightforward indirect statement or a recitative introduction to the 'quotation' which begins ἐπ' ἐσχάτου χρόνου, there is nothing redundant about its presence. The fact that there is λέγων without ὅτι introducing the allusion to Enoch at v. 14, does not necessarily mean that the writer would have excluded ὅτι after an indicative such as ἔλεγον at v. 18. The omission of ὅτι is explicable as an internal harmonization with v. 14, where λέγων appears without ὅτι. With no reason for opposing the inclusion of ὅτι here, against GNT4, it should be printed without brackets.

Variation Unit 18.3

επ εσχατου χρονου   𝔓72 B C Ψ
επ εσχατου του χρονου   ℵ A
επ εσχατων των χρονων   442 610
εν εσχατω χρονω   𝔓74ᵛⁱᵈ K L 049
εν εσχατω τω χρονω   P 2400

Although the writer is fond of New Testament set expressions and uses them at vv. 1, 4, 17, 20, 21, 25 and (so I have argued) at v. 13, the absence of the word ἡμέρα among the variants at this unit rules out any possibility that the writer is using a New Testament set expression to refer to the 'last time(s)'. Outside Jude, the only other canonical occurrence of the word χρόνος (rather than ἡμέρα) to denote the 'last time(s)' is at 1 Pet. 1.20, where ἐπ' ἐσχάτου τῶν χρόνων is printed in GNT4. The precise wording of this expression in 1 Pet. 1.20 is not to be found among the variants at this unit in Jude, so I need to work from the assumption that Jude is here using a unique expression.

The reading ἐπ' ἐσχάτων τῶν χρόνων is not unique enough for a favourable verdict . Kubo has argued that this reading harmonizes with 2 Pet. 3.3. Moreover, the reading ἐπ' ἐσχάτων τῶν χρόνων is very close to the New Testament set expression ἐπ' ἐσχάτου τῶν ἡμερῶν, especially in regard to the genitive plural in the last two words of each expression.

A possible approach to choose from among the remaining rivals might be to look at arguments relating to the two prepositions. Kubo's comment that variants which contain ἐν are not reduplicated at Heb. 1.2, 1 Pet. 1.20 and 2 Pet. 3.3 'where the same situation prevails' ostensibly favours either ἐν ἐσχάτῳ χρόνῳ or ἐν ἐσχάτῳ τῷ χρόνῳ.[237] On the other hand, as Kubo points out, the presence of ἐν in place of ἐπί can be explained as a reaction to the ambiguity of ἐπ' ἐσχάτου χρόνου. As we shall see, there is nothing to fault Kubo's argumentation in favour of the latter variant.

Although Bauckham favours ἐπ' ἐσχάτου τοῦ χρόνου on the grounds that it is an awkward expression which has been made smoother in 𝔓72 and others, this view does not concord with Bauckham's general position that awkward Greek is not what readers should expect in a text whose wording has been 'composed with exquisite care'.[238] The variant ἐπ' ἐσχάτου τοῦ χρόνου should be rejected here primarily because the addition of τοῦ is explicable as the result of an imperative to make ἐπ' ἐσχάτου χρόνου less ambiguous, which can mean either 'in the last time' or 'in the last of time', depending upon whether ἐσχάτου is taken as a substantive or an adjective.[239] To Kubo's reasoning I can add that the deliberate addition of an article in ℵ is not unexpected in view of the same phenomenon in ℵ at v. 3 (τοῦ γράφειν), v. 9 (ὁ κύριος) and v. 14 (ὁ κύριος). The other readings can also be seen as reactions to the ambiguity of ἐπ' ἐσχάτου χρόνου.[240] Against GNT4 ἐπ' ἐσχάτου χρόνου at this unit should be printed.

Variation Unit 18.4

εσονται   𝔓72 ℵ* B C* K L P 049
ελευσονται   ℵ² A C²
αναστησονται   Ψ

237. Kubo, *𝔓72 and the Codex Vaticanus*, p. 144.
238. Bauckham, *Jude, 2 Peter*, pp. 104, 142.
239. Kubo, *𝔓72 and the Codex Vaticanus*, p. 145.
240. Kubo, *𝔓72 and the Codex Vaticanus*, pp. 145-46.

As we saw at vv. 6 and 10, the copyist of Ψ likes to embellish words by adding prepositions to form compounds. In view of this, ἀναστήσονται preserved singularly in Ψ at this unit cannot be accepted. The reading ἐλεύσονται is explicable through harmonization with 2 Pet. 3.3, where the same word occurs. The only remaining option is ἔσονται which is correctly printed in GNT4.

Variation Unit 18.5

κατα τας επιθυμιας εαυτων   ℵᶜ 460 483
κατα τας εαυτων επιθυμιας   𝔓72 A B C K L P 049
κατα τας επιθυμιας αυτων   ℵ* 630 1611
κατα τας αυτων επιθυμιας   Ψ 218 452

Two issues need to be addressed here: (1) whether I should read ἑαυτῶν or αὐτῶν; and (2) the position of ἐπιθυμίας. In view of the writer's strong preference for using reflexive pronouns with participles as evidenced at vv. 12, 13, 16, 20, 21 and (so I will argue) at v. 19, the intrinsic probability at this unit favours ἑαυτῶν over against αὐτῶν. The reading with αὐτῶν in ℵ* 630 1611 probably arose through the accidental omission of the epsilon, the mistake having been noticed by a corrector who has inserted the letter. Accidental omission also accounts for the reading with αὐτῶν in Ψ 218 452. Having ruled out κατὰ τὰς ἐπιθυμίας <u>αὐτῶν</u> and κατὰ τὰς <u>αὐτῶν</u> ἐπιθυμίας, I am left with the first two readings in my apparatus which differ only in word order.

The absence or presence of a preposition affects the position of the pronoun ἑαυτοῦ in Jude as these examples demonstrate:

v. 6   τὴν ἑαυτῶν ἀρχήν
v. 13   τὰς ἑαυτῶν αἰσχύνας
v. 16   κατὰ τὰς ἐπιθυμίας ἑαυτῶν

At vv. 6 and 13, where the preposition is absent, the order is article + pronoun + substantive (DA + PN + S). At v. 16, where a preposition is present, the order is preposition + article + substantive + pronoun (PR + DA + S + PN). Since at this unit there is a preposition present, the reading which I accept should conform to PR + DA + S + PN: such a reading is κατὰ τὰς ἐπιθυμίας ἑαυτῶν. The variant which I should reject here, κατὰ τὰς ἑαυτῶν ἐπιθυμίας, is explicable through internal harmonization to the position of ἑαυτῶν at vv. 6 and 13, where the order is DA + PN + S. The point here is that the absence or presence of a preposition does make a difference in the order of words where PN is involved. Print κατὰ τὰς ἐπιθυμίας ἑαυτῶν here.

Variation Unit 19.1

αποδιοριζοντες εαυτους   C 323 378
αποδιοριζοντες   ℵ A B L P Ψ 049
αποδιωριζοντες   𝔓72 K

Although the text editors all prefer ἀποδιορίζοντες, Kilpatrick does not rule out ἀποδιορίζοντες ἑαυτούς.[241] At the very least Kilpatrick's idea should be explored. Three arguments can be advanced in favour of ἀποδιορίζοντες ἑαυτούς: (1) Jude has a strong preference for the reflexive pronoun ἑαυτοῦ as evidenced at vv. 12, 13, 16, 18, 20 and 21; (2) the context of the verse; and (3) the antithetical parallel between v. 19 and v. 20, to which ἑαυτούς in v. 19 is essential. The second and third of these reasons need to be explained in more detail.

Regarding the context of v. 19, if I exclude ἑαυτούς, the result is: 'These men draw a line between spiritual and unspiritual persons...' (NEB), or 'These men create divisions...' (NEB margin). Whichever of these interpretations is correct, the text without ἑαυτούς seems to leave too much to the reader's imagination. If, on the other hand, I include ἑαυτούς, the result is more explicit: 'These men draw a line between *themselves* [explicit] and *others* [implicit]...' or even 'These men separate themselves...' (my translations). The latter translation coheres with Bauckham's view of the opponents as a self-styled élitist group who claim to possess the spirit.[242]

The use of contrast and antithesis is a characteristically Judan stylistic feature, as attested by these examples cited from Charles:[243]

> δοῦλος (v. 1) vs. κύριος (vv. 4, 5, 9, 14, 17, 21 and 25)
> οὗτοι (vv. 4, 8 10, 11, 12, 16 and 19) vs. ὑμεῖς (vv. 3, 5, 12, 17, 18, 20 and 24)
> ἀσεβεῖς (vv. 4, 15, 18) vs. ἅγιος (vv. 3, 14, 20, 24)
> ἔλεος (vv. 2, 21, 22, 23) vs. κρίσις (vv. 6, 9, and 15)
> οὗτοι (v. 8) vs. Μιχαήλ (v. 9)
> οἶδα and ἐπίσταμαι (v. 10) vs. ἄλογος (v. 10)

---

241. The photostat copy of the text of Jude in Kilpatrick's *Diglot* which was kindly given to me by J.K. Elliott includes a marginal note in Kilpatrick's own handwriting to the effect that one should consider accepting ἀποδιορίζοντες ἑαυτούς preserved in C 323 378 at v. 19; although, Kilpatrick does not provide any reasons for this preference. Since I agree with Kilpatrick's choice here, what follows is an attempt to substantiate it.

242. Bauckham, *Jude, 2 Peter*, p. 105.

243. Charles, 'Literary Artifice', pp. 113-14.

ἀφόβως (v. 12) vs. ἐν φόβῳ (v. 23)
σάρξ and ἐπιθυμία (vv. 7, 16, 18 and 23) vs. ἄμωμος and μισοῦντες τὸν
  ἀπὸ τῆς σαρκὸς ἐσπιλωμένον χιτῶνα (vv. 23 and 24)
χάρις (vv. 4 and 16) vs. ἀσέλγεια (v. 4)
κύριος ἅπαξ... σώσας (v. 5) vs. τὸ δεύτερον... ἀπώλεσεν (v. 5)
νεφέλαι (v. 12) vs. ἄνυδροι (v. 12)
δένδρα (v. 12) vs. ἄκαρπα (v. 12)
σκότος and ζόφος (vv. 6 and 13) vs. δόξα (vv. 24-25)
τὸ στόμα αὐτῶν (v. 16) vs. ῥῆμα ὑπὸ ἀποστόλων (v. 17)
ἀποδιορίζομαι (v. 19) vs. ἐποικοδομεῖν (v. 20)
ἐλεεῖν (v. 22) vs. διακρίνειν (v. 22)
πῦρ αἰώνιον (v. 7) vs. δόξα... κράτος... ἐξουσία... αἰῶνας (v. 25)

Watson discusses Jude's use of antithesis at vv. 9-10 and at vv. 19-20 in
some detail.[244] Whereas the opponents described in v. 19 are deprived of
the Spirit, the addressees identified in v. 20 are urged to pray in the
Holy Spirit.[245] Also noted by Watson (and included in Charles's list
above) is the antithesis between ἀποδιορίζοντες at v. 19 and
ἐποικοδομοῦντες at v. 20. The antithetical parallel is more balanced
and complete if ἀποδιορίζοντες ἑαυτούς at v. 19 is accepted, because
ἐποικοδομῦντες ἑαυτούς is at v. 20.

Since ἀποδιορίζοντες ἑαυτούς has meagre MS support, I am
obliged to explain how its rival variant ἀποδιορίζοντες came about
and why ἀποδιορίζοντες is preserved in most MSS. We know from
Elliott that pronouns were used in Hellenistic Greek more frequently
than in Attic Greek and that stylistically conscious scribes would remove
pronouns which they considered to be redundant.[246] At this unit the
influence of Atticism explains the removal of ἑαυτούς. Accept
ἐποικοδομοῦντες ἑαυτούς at this unit.

Variation Unit 20.1

υμεις   ℵ A B K L P Ψ 049
υμις   𝔓72
ημεις   C 1829 1852

Again in 𝔓72 we have itacism: in this case, as Michel Testuz puts
it: '...le copiste écrit volontiers ει pour ι, ou ι pour ει'.[247] Jude's

244. Watson, *Invention*, pp. 55, 73-74.
245. Watson, *Invention*, p. 74.
246. J.K. Elliott, 'A Second Look at the United Bible Societies' *Greek New
Testament*', *BT* 26 (1975), pp. 325-32; esp. p. 331.
247. M. Testuz, *Papyrus Bodmer VII-IX. VII: L'épître de Jude; VIII: Les deux*

addressees are invoked with the personal pronoun ὑμεῖς at vv. 2, 3, 5, 12, 17 and 18. Of particular significance is the expression ὑμεῖς δέ ἀγαπητοί which is firmly in the MS tradition at v. 17: the word ἀγαπητοί confirms the direct address to ὑμεῖς (and not ἡμεῖς). The presence of the word ἀγαπητοί at v. 20 confirms that again the direct address of the writer is to ὑμεῖς. Additionally, my decision at variation unit 21.2 in favour of τηρήσατε compels me to accept ὑμεῖς here. There is no reason not to accept ὑμεῖς at this unit.

Variation Unit 20.2

εποικοδομουντες εαυτους τη αγιωτατη υμων πιστει	ℵ A B Ψ
εποικοδομουντες εαυτους τη αγιωτατη ημων πιστει	C 322 323
τη αγιωτατη υμων πιστει εποικοδομουντες εαυτους	K L P 049
τη εαυτων αγιοτητι πειστι ανοικοδομεισθαι	𝔓72

Two problems need to be solved here: (1) whether I should read ἐποικοδομοῦντες or ἀνοικοδομεῖσθαι; and (2) whether I should accept the order of words in ℵ A B C Ψ or the order in 𝔓72 K L P 049.

Verses 20-21 comprise a single complete sentence, the main verb being τηρήσατε in v. 21. The participles ἐποικοδομοῦντες and προσευχόμενοι in v. 20 are usually translated as imperatives by commentators and editors, for example, 'But you, beloved, build yourselves up on your most holy faith; pray in the Holy Spirit...' (RSV). As Jerome Neyrey and others have pointed out, the idea behind ἐποικοδομοῦντες is a Pauline metaphor (for example, 1 Cor. 3.10-13) whereby the addressees can be 'built up' by their faith like a building.[248] Thus there is no difficulty in accepting the reading ἐποικοδομοῦντες, preserved in all MSS except 𝔓72. However, the reading ἀνοικοδομεῖσθαι (from the verb ἀνοικοδομέω) does not cohere with the context of the verse, since there is no sense (either metaphorical or literal) in which Jude's addressees have been 'destroyed' and then 'rebuilt'. Meanwhile, the unacceptability of ἡμεῖς at variation unit 20.1 renders ἡμῶν unacceptable at this unit.

Although ἀνοικοδομεῖσθαι should be rejected in favour of ἐποικοδομοῦντες, it is less easy to be decisive about the order of words which the writer is likely to have used. On the one hand the order

épîtres de Pierre; IX: Les Psaumes 33 et 34. (Geneva: Bibliotheca Bodmeriana, 1959), p. 16, cited in Massaux, 'Papyrus Bodmer VII (𝔓72)', p. 109.

248. J.H. Neyrey, *2 Peter, Jude: A New Translation with Introduction and Commentary* (New York: Doubleday, 1993), p. 89.

in ℵ A B Ψ is attractive because it has ἐποικοδομοῦντες as near as possible to the beginning of the sentence, which is the order I would more often than not expect in New Testament Greek. On the other hand, the order in 𝔓72 K L P 049 could be original as a 'difficult' reading.[249] I cannot entirely rule out either of these word order options, although, for the time being, I will accept the reading in ℵ A B Ψ.

Variation Unit 20.3

om. εαυτοις ℵ A B C K L P 049
εαυτοις 𝔓72

Because I have rejected ἀνοικοδομεῖσθαι in 𝔓72, a question mark is placed over the reading as a whole in this MS at unit 20.2. In all probability, ἑαυτοῖς here has been added to compensate for the omission of ἑαυτούς with the participle.[250] At this unit I should therefore reject ἑαυτοῖς. This does not mean that I am discounting the possibility that at unit 20.2 the reading in K L P 049—which reflects the word order in 𝔓72—could be original.

Variation Unit 21.1

εαυτους 𝔓72 ℵ A B C L P Ψ
εαυτοις K 049

It is probable that the change from ἑαυτούς to ἑαυτοῖς in K and 049 resulted from an awareness of the phrase δεσμοῖς ἀϊδίοις ὑπὸ ζόφον τετήρηκεν at v. 6, where it is possible to misconstrue that τετήρηκεν takes an object (δεσμοῖς) in the dative. However the real direct object in v. 6 is accusative (ἀγγέλους). Likewise here at v. 21, ἑαυτούς is the direct object and should be accusative, with ἀγάπῃ as the indirect object in the dative. It is also possible that ἑαυτοῖς was substituted under the influence of προσευχόμενοι at the end of v. 20—'praying for themselves'. Print ἑαυτούς here.

Variation Unit 21.2

τηρησατε ℵ A K L P 049
τηρησωμεν 𝔓72 B C* Ψ
τηρησητε C²
τηρησαντες 431 621

249. Kubo, *𝔓72 and the Codex Vaticanus*, pp. 145-46.
250. Kubo, *𝔓72 and the Codex Vaticanus*, pp. 145-46.

The reading τηρήσαντες leaves the text without a main verb and so cannot be accepted. This leaves me with three possibilities as displayed in the apparatus.

The problem with τηρήσητε is that if it is intended to be a hortatory subjunctive, I would expect it to have a first person plural ending rather than a second person plural ending.[251] The reading τηρήσητε appears to be a conflation of τηρήσωμεν and τηρήσατε, since τηρήσητε combines both the subjunctive from τηρήσωμεν and the second person plural ending from τηρήσατε. To Kubo's analysis of this unit (wherein it is not properly explained why τηρήσητε is unacceptable), I can add that τηρήσητε should be rejected both because it transgresses grammatical convention and because it is a conflated reading.

Either of the two remaining rival variants could be original. The reading τηρήσωμεν could be acceptable as a hortatory subjunctive, thus rendering part of the verse: 'Let us keep ourselves in the love of God'. My judgment must be directed by what I know of the writer's preference when conveying an imperative or hortatory message to the ἀγαπητοί: is he more likely to have used the subjunctive here, or the imperative? Kubo rightly suggests that we should be guided by v. 17, which has ὑμεῖς δέ ἀγαπητοί, the same opening as that for vv. 20-21. Since Jude uses the imperative μνημονεύετε at v. 17, there is no reason to suppose that he would not have used the imperative τηρήσατε at v. 21.[252] My solution is therefore to accept τηρήσατε.

Variation Unit 21.3

ημων ιησου χριστου εις ζωην αιωνιον   ℵ A B C K L P Ψ 049
εις ζοην ημων ιησου χριστου αιωνιον   𝔓72

At this unit I am concerned with word order variation involving two New Testament set expressions: τοῦ κυρίου ἡμῶν Ἰησοῦ Χριστοῦ and εἰς ζωὴν αἰώνιον. Whereas the reading preserved in ℵ and others retains these two set expressions as separate entities: the singular reading in 𝔓72 intermingles the set expressions by altering the word order,

251. We can infer this from BDF §364.

252. Kubo, *𝔓72 and the Codex Vaticanus*, p. 147. See also variation unit 17.1 where I have accepted μνημονεύετε over against μνήσθητε. It is also worth noting that whereas v. 17 is within the midrash structure, v. 21 is outside the same structure, a state of affairs which accounts for the difference in tense between μνημονεύετε at v. 17, and τηρήσατε at v. 21.

splitting εἰς ζωὴν αἰώνιον into two parts. As we saw at variation unit 13.5, Jude uses set expressions at vv. 1, 4, 17, 20 and 25. Without exception, all of these set expressions preserve the New Testament word order that is normal for such expressions. Even at v. 25 where there is variation involving the set expression Ἰησοῦ Χριστοῦ τοῦ κυρίου ἡμῶν, the alternative reading in 𝔓72 still preserves the order of words in the set expression intact. Since there is no evidence that Jude ever tampers with word order in set expressions, ἡμῶν Ἰησοῦ Χριστοῦ εἰς ζωὴν αἰώνιον should be printed at this unit.

Variation Unit 22-23.1

ους μεν εκ πυρος αρπασατε
διακρινομενους δε ελεειτε εν φοβω   𝔓72 it^t cop^{sa} syr^{ph}

και ους μεν ελεατε διακρινομενους
ους δε σωζετε εκ πυρος αρπαζοντες (א* αρπαζετε)
ους δε ελεατε εν φοβω   א^c Ψ

και ους μεν ελεγχετε διακρινομενους
ους δε σωζετε εκ πυρος αρπαζοντες
ους δε ελεατε εν φοβω   A 33 81

και ους μεν ελεατε διακρινομενους
σωζετε εκ πυρος αρπαζοντες
ους δε ελεατε εν φοβω   B

και ους μεν ελεατε (C* ελεγχετε) διακρινομενους
ους δε σωζετε εκ πυρος αρπαζοντες εν φοβω   C^2 syr^h

και ους μεν ελεειτε διακρινομενοι
ους δε εν φοβω σωζετε (049 σωζεται) εκ πυρος αρπαζοντες   K L P 049

There is not much to write about this unit which has not already been written, but I can attempt to strengthen the case of those who have argued in favour of the two-clause text preserved in 𝔓72 and other MSS by showing that the argument concerning triadic illustration which has been used to defend the three-clause text is not watertight.

The two main rivals at this unit are the two-clause text in 𝔓72 and other MSS which is defended by Bauckham, and the three-clause text in א^c Ψ which is printed in GNT4.[253] In the conclusion to his chapter in the

253. Those who have defended the two-clause reading include J.N. Birdsall, 'The Text of Jude in 𝔓72', *JTS* 14 (1963), pp. 394-99; Kubo, *𝔓72 and the Codex Vaticanus*, pp. 89-92; C.D. Osburn, 'The Text of Jude 22-23', *ZNW* 63 (1972),

first Metzger Festschrift, Kubo opts for a hypothetical reading based on the three-clause text in ℵ having defended the latter as a *lectio difficilior*: 'Thus the reading of ℵ with its three divisions but with double ἐλεεῖτε (instead of ἐλεᾶτε), with διακρινομένους, and with ἐν φόβῳ following the second ἐλεεῖτε is to be accepted as the original reading'.[254] It is quite an irony that Kubo should (only a few paragraphs earlier) have reprimanded Hauck and Schrage for proposing conjectures based on B, when Kubo's own preference is for a reading which is not to be found in any extant MS.[255] Perhaps I should begin where Kubo ends, and ask: is ἐλεεῖτε preferable to ἐλεᾶτε? If the answer is affirmative, my search for a solution should surely be restricted to real readings in real MSS which do indeed preserve the form ἐλεεῖτε.

The first factor in favour of ἐλεεῖτε and against ἐλεᾶτε is the overwhelming predominance of the form ἐλεέω in New Testament Greek. Whereas the form ἐλεάω can be found at Rom. 9.16 and 12.8: the form ἐλεέω occurs firmly in the MS tradition at Mt. 5.7, 9.27, 15.22, 17.15, 18.33, 20.30, 20.31; Mk 5.19, 10.47, 48; Lk. 16.24, 17.13, 18.38; Rom. 9.15, 11.31, 12.8, 1 Cor. 7.25, and with minor variation at Rom. 11.30, 32; 2 Cor. 4.1; Phil. 2.27 and 1 Pet. 2.10. The second factor in favour of ἐλεεῖτε and against ἐλεᾶτε is that the latter is a deliberate alteration to the text, 'in view of the tendency of Alexandrian scribes to write -εω verbs with -αω.[256] If I choose ἐλεεῖτε over against ἐλεᾶτε, then I can eliminate all of the readings in the apparatus which preserve ἐλεᾶτε.

---

pp. 139-44; Neyrey, *2 Peter, Jude*, pp. 85-86; and Bauckham, *Jude, 2 Peter*, pp. 108-11. Arguing in favour of the three-clause reading are Green, *General Epistle of Jude*, pp. 202-204; Metzger, *Textual Commentary*, pp. 658-661; Watson, *Invention*, pp. 74-75; and (against his earlier judgment) Kubo, 'Jude 22-3', pp. 239-53. Meanwhile Fuchs, *Saint Jude*, pp. 187-88, prefers the two-clause reading, but with ἐλέγχετε in place of ἐλεεῖτε. If we accept Elliott's view, *Essays and Studies*, p. 38, that the original reading at any given variation unit in the New Testament 'lies somewhere in our extant manuscripts', then we are obliged to find a solution at this unit which is not based upon conjectural emendation.

254. Kubo, 'Jude 22-3', p. 253.

255. F. Hauck, *Die Briefe des Jakobus, Petrus, Judas und Johannes* (Göttingen: Vandenhoeck & Ruprecht, 1957), p. 112; W. Schrage, *Die katholischen Briefe* (Göttingen: Vandenhoeck & Ruprecht, 1973), p. 231, both cited in Kubo, 'Jude 22-3', p. 242, and both reprimanded in *idem*, p. 248.

256. Osburn, 'Text of Jude 22-23', p. 140, n. 5. In support of this, Osburn cites MHT, II, p. 196.

Most of the critics and commentators who prefer the three-clause text advance the argument that it is in keeping with the writer's style, 'in view of the author's predilection for arranging his material in groups of three'.[257] Although there can be no doubt that Jude often does use triadic illustration, there are two reasons for doubting the validity of the triadic argument as a defence of the three-clause text. First of all, the sort of triadic illustration observed thus far in Jude falls into two specific categories: (1) the grouping of three completely different elements (such as the three paradigms of judgment at vv. 5-7); and (2) the threefold repetition of exactly the same element (such as the threefold repetition of πάντων at v. 15). At vv. 22-23 even if I accept the three-clause text I am dealing neither with a grouping of three different elements nor with a threefold repetition of the same element: irrespective of the reading accepted at vv. 22-23, I still have only two elements (those upon whom we should have mercy, and those whom we should snatch from the fire).[258] The second major problem with the defence of the three-clause text by style, is the absence of a similar three-clause text at v. 10 where I would expect one. Indeed I should press this point and ask why, if there is a three-clause text at vv. 22-23 involving the relative ὅς, is there not also a three-clause text at v. 10 involving the relative ὅσος? Since there is a two-clause text at v. 10, it is certainly not necessary for me to argue stylistically for a three-clause text at vv. 22-23.

The case in favour of the three-clause text is further weakened by the probability that the word σῴζετε was added to the text by scribes as an assimilation to 1 Cor. 3.15 where there is αὐτὸς δὲ σωθήσεται οὕτως δὲ ὡς διὰ πυρός ('though he has saved himself, it will be as one who has gone through the fire' [JB]). The wording at 1 Cor. 3.15 is not exactly duplicated in the three-clause text in vv. 22-23, but the obvious parallel is in the link between the verb σῴζω and the noun πῦρ. As Grosheide suggests, the idea at 1 Cor. 3.15 is of people being narrowly saved, just as an object which passes through fire can avoid being totally

257. Metzger, *Textual Commentary*, p. 726.

258. The point about there only being two elements in vv. 22-23 has been made by Sidebottom, *James, Jude, 2 Peter*, pp. 92-93. Although we have the threefold repetition of οὓς in the three-clause text, this does not diminish the validity of Sidebottom's observation: there are still only two groups of people. Bauckham deduces correctly from this that Jude would not have used triadic illustration where it would not have been required. Meanwhile according to Birdsall, 'Text of Jude in 𝔓72', p. 398, the second οὓς in the three-clause text arose through dittography of the last three letters of διακρινομένους.

destroyed.[259] The same idea is present in vv. 22-23, where σῴζετε in the three-clause text provides the sort of clarification I might expect in a deliberate scribal interpolation.[260]

Bauckham enumerates four reasons for supporting the two-clause text at vv. 22-23 in 𝔓72: (1) 𝔓72 does not include the interpretative gloss σῴζετε; (2) that the participle διακρινομένους should take the place of the second οὓς is good Greek style; (3) διακρινομένους is acceptable in the context if it is taken to mean 'disputing'; (4) the longer readings can be regarded as expansions and adaptations of the two-clause text in 𝔓72.[261] In support of Bauckham I can add: (5) ἐλεεῖτε in 𝔓72 is the form of ἐλεέω which I would expect in New Testament Greek; and (6) the argument concerning triadic illustration is inconclusive as a defence of the three-clause text.

Meanwhile the following considerations are against alternatives to the two-clause text in 𝔓72: (1) ἐλεᾶτε is not the form of ἐλεέω which we would expect in New Testament Greek; (2) σῴζετε is a scribal gloss; (3) ἐλέγχετε in A and C* is explicable as a reaction to the ambiguity of διακρινομένους and is therefore unlikely to be original.[262] In view of the evidence discussed, my verdict is in favour of οὓς μὲν ἐκ πυρὸς ἁρπάσατε, διακρινομένους δὲ ἐλεεῖτε ἐν φόβῳ.

Variation Unit 24.1

στηριξαι ασπιλους αμωμους αγνευομενους   𝔓72
φυλαξαι υμας απταιστους και στησαι   ℵ B L Ψ
φυλαξαι ημας απταιστους και στησαι   A 4*
φυλαξαι αυτους απταιστους και στησαι   K P 049
φυλαξαι υμας απταιστους και ασπιλους στησαι   C

Assumptions about impressive MSS have in the present work been replaced by arguments for impressive readings. Just such a reading is στηρίξαι ἀσπίλους ἀμώμους ἀγνευομένους at this unit.[263] In this

259. F.W. Grosheide, *Commentary on the First Epistle to the Corinthians* (Grand Rapids: Eerdmans, 1953), p. 89.

260. Osburn, 'Text of Jude 22-23', p. 141 argues convincingly that σῴζετε is a scribal gloss provided to explain ἐκ πυρὸς ἁρπάσατε, though he does not examine the point that σῴζετε in the three-clause text could be an assimilation to 1 Cor. 3.15.

261. Bauckham, *Jude, 2 Peter*, p. 110.

262. Osburn, 'Text of Jude 22-23', pp. 141-43.

263. Although στηρίξαι does not have an explicitly expressed direct object, the reading in 𝔓72 still makes good sense if the word ὑμᾶς is understood.

reading there is a striking example of triadic illustration in the juxta-position of ἀσπίλους, ἀμώμους and ἀγνευομένους, roughly trans-lated: 'spotless, without blemish, purified'. The use of triadic illustration reflected in 𝔓72 has the same rhetorical purpose of amplification by accumulation which we saw at variation unit 2.2, and which is evident on the many occasions when the writer uses triadic illustration. This reading in 𝔓72 also contains vowel and diphthong repetition (α + ους is repeated thrice), and it can be recalled that paronomasia is a device which is also evident at vv. 3, 7, 8, 10, 11, 12-13, 15, 16 and 19.[264] By contrast, there is nothing strikingly Judan about φυλάξαι ὑμᾶς ἀπταίστους καὶ στῆσαι which is printed in GNT4. Jude uses the verb τηρεῖν to convey the sense of keeping or guarding at vv. 1, 6 (×2), 13 and 21, and it is odd that he should switch to φυλάσσειν just for a single verse at v. 24.

The argument that φυλάξαι ὑμᾶς ἀπταίστους καὶ στῆσαι has no special Judan characteristics is also true of the readings in K P 049 and in C. The reading φυλάξαι ὑμᾶς ἀπταίστους καὶ ἀσπίλους στῆσαι combines ἀπταίστους from ℵ B L Ψ and ἀσπίλους from 𝔓72, and so should be rejected as a conflated reading. My verdict is to print στηρίξαι ἀσπίλους ἀμώμους ἀγνευομένους primarily on the basis of intrinsic evidence in its favour.

Variation Unit 24.2

απεναντι   𝔓72
κατενωπιον   ℵ A B K L P Ψ 049
ενωπιον   C 254 630
κατεναντι   88 915

It is difficult to agree with the choice of the GNT4 editors at this unit, since their chosen reading κατενώπιον is explicable as an assimilation to Eph. 1.4, where there is ἀμώμους κατενώπιον αὐτοῦ. The reading ἐνώπιον may have predated κατενώπιον, but not ἀπέναντι, the latter being an unfamiliar word. The reading κατέναντι preserved in 88 915 is an obvious conflation of κατενώπιον and ἀπέναντι and can there-fore be eliminated. On the basis of transcriptional evidence cited against the other readings, I should accept ἀπέναντι at this unit.

---

264. As pointed out by Charles, 'Literary Artifice', p. 114.

Variation Unit 24.3

om. αμωμους   𝔓72
αμωμους   ℵ B C K L P Ψ 049
αμεμπτους   A

The choice here is between ἀμώμους occupying a position between αὐτοῦ and ἐν as reflected in ℵ B C K L P Ψ 049, and ἀμώμους being omitted here but being included at variation unit 24.1 as witnessed in 𝔓72. Since I have accepted the reading στηρίξαι ἀσπίλους ἀμώμους ἀγνευομένους at variation unit 24.1, my logical preference here must be for the omission of ἀμώμους. Meanwhile, it is possible that the word ἀμέμπτους for ἀμώμους was more familiar to the copyist of A, hence the substitution. Omit ἀμώμους here.

Variation Unit 25.1

μονω σοφω θεω   K L P 049 *Lect*
μονω θεω   𝔓72 ℵ A B C Ψ

According to the UBS committee records, σοφῷ at this unit is an interpolation derived from Rom. 16.27.[265] This claim about harmonization is impossible to prove: one could equally well posit that μόνῳ σοφῷ θεῷ was original in Jude, and that Rom. 16.25-27 as a scribal addition to Romans included the words μόνῳ σοφῷ θεῷ through harmony with Jude 25. Although μόνῳ θεῷ could be original, there are no intrinsic reasons which can be cited to defend it. Meanwhile the reading μόνῳ σοφῷ θεῷ is consistent with the author's inclination to employ paronomasia (as at vv. 3, 7, 8, 10, 11, 12-13, 15, 16, 19, and [so I have argued] at v. 24) in particular with the threefold repetition of a consonant or vowel such as the triple omega here. Transcriptional evidence also favours μόνῳ σοφῷ θεῷ, since hom. accounts for the omission of σοφῷ from 𝔓72 and other MSS. Print μόνῳ σοφῷ θεῷ here.

Variation Unit 25.2

σωτηρι   ℵ A B C K L P Ψ 049
om. σωτηρι   𝔓72

Ehrman has noted that the phrase 'God our saviour and Jesus Christ our hope' at 1 Tim. 1.1 is problematic for some scribes, who have removed καὶ to emphasise the divinity of Christ.[266] The word σωτήρ applicable to God alone was regarded by some scribes as an implied denial of Christ's divinity. A reasonable assumption at this unit is that the word σωτήρ at v. 25 was removed by the copyist of 𝔓72 because it is linked to God alone, implying a denial of Christ's divinity. Not for the first time am I dealing with a probable anti-adoptionist change in 𝔓72. An alternative transcriptional argument can also be cited against 𝔓72 at this unit. Bauckham has noted the awkwardness of διὰ Ἰησοῦ Χριστοῦ τοῦ κυρίον ἡμῶν at v. 25 if this set expression is attached to σωτῆρι.[267] The removal of σωτῆρι by the copyist of 𝔓72 could be a reaction to this awkwardness. Accept σωτῆρι here.

Variation Unit 25.3

αυτω δοξα κρατος τιμη   𝔓72
om. αυτω δοξα κρατος τιμη   ℵ A B C K L P Ψ 049

There are two intrinsic reasons for accepting αὐτῷ δόξα κράτος τιμή at this unit: (1) if 2 Peter was modelled on Jude, as Bauckham has plausibly suggested, then the presence of αὐτῷ ἡ δόξα in the doxology at 2 Pet. 3.18 could be sourced from an original αὐτῷ δόξα at Jude 25 as witnessed by 𝔓72 here; and (2) the triadic juxtaposition of δόξα, κράτος and τιμή in 𝔓72 is consistent with Jude's stylistic and rhetorical inclinations. The rhetorical purpose behind the triadic grouping δόξα κράτος τιμή is that of amplification by accumulation, the same rhetorical technique which is explained in greater depth at variation units 2.2 and 24.1. It is not clear why such an obviously Judan example of triadic illustration should have been excluded by all MSS except 𝔓72, unless possibly the phrase was removed to avoid the twofold repetition of the word δόξα which results if I accept the reading in 𝔓72. Print αὐτῷ δόξα κράτος τιμή here.

Variation Unit 25.4

δια ιησου χριστου του κυριου ημων   𝔓72 ℵ A B C L Ψ
om. δια ιησου χριστου του κυριου ημων   K P 049

Jude is liberal in his use of set expressions and the inclusion of the set expression διὰ Ἰησοῦ Χριστοῦ τοῦ κυρίον ἡμῶν is in keeping

---

266. Ehrman, *Orthodox Corruption*, p. 87.
267. Bauckham, *Jude, 2 Peter*, p. 123.

with his stylistic preference. The exclusion of this set expression by the copyists of K P 049 is explicable as a deliberate omission caused by grammatical awkwardness which results if it is attached to the noun σωτῆρι.[268] This awkwardness is apparent rather than real when it is realised that διὰ Ἰησοῦ Χριστοῦ τοῦ κυρίον ἡμῶν 'should be taken with the attributes which follow...i.e. [that Christ] mediates the glory and authority of God to him'.[269] Accept διὰ Ἰησοῦ Χριστοῦ τοῦ κυρίον ἡμῶν here.

Variation Unit 25.5

δοξα μεγαλωσυνη   ℵ A B C Ψ
αυτω δοξα και μεγαλωσυνη   𝔓72 cop^sa,bo
δοξα και μεγαλωσυνη   K L P 049

The phrase αὐτῷ ἡ δόξα does not appear twice in the doxology at 2 Pet. 3.18, and the second αὐτῷ δόξα in 𝔓72 here seems to be redundant, perhaps the result of dittography. At variation unit 25.6 I will argue that κράτος should be included, so the variant δόξα μεγαλωσύνη here forms part of a triadic expression: δόξα μεγαλωσύνη κράτος. As with the earlier triadic expression δόξα κράτος τιμή which I accepted at variation unit 25.3, the unity of the triadic grouping is not disturbed by the presence of conjunctions. In view of this, the reading δόξα καὶ μεγαλωσύνη preserved in 𝔓72 K L P 049 is unacceptable because the presence of καὶ disrupts the balance of the triadic expression δόξα μεγαλωσύνη κράτος. The addition of καὶ is an apparent improvement introduced because of the predominance of καὶ elsewhere in the verse. If I omit καὶ here, I am left with καὶ (×3) in the verse as a whole, and thus with a characteristically Judan example of threefold repetition. The GNT4 editors should be followed and δόξα μεγαλωσύνη should be printed here.

Variation Unit 25.6

κρατος και εξουσια   ℵ A B C K L P 049
κρατος εξουσια   Ψ
om. κρατος και εξουσια   𝔓72

268. Bauckham, *Jude, 2 Peter*, p. 123.
269. Bauckham, *Jude, 2 Peter*, p. 123.

As part of the triadic expression δόξα μεγαλωσύνη κράτος, the word κράτος coheres with the author's strong preference for triadic illustration, a preference which serves the rhetorical purpose of amplification by accumulation. Intrinsic probability therefore compels me to doubt the originality of 𝔓72 here in omitting κράτος. It is also unlikely that κράτος ἐξουσία is original, since ἐξουσία is not part of the triad mentioned earlier, so καὶ should remain to demarcate the boundary between δόξα μεγαλωσύνη κράτος on the one hand, and ἐξουσία on the other. The copyist of Ψ appears to have removed καὶ *outside* of the triadic structure to harmonize with the absence of καὶ *within* the triadic structure, so the improvement is apparent rather than real.

Another intrinsic argument in favour of the inclusion of κράτος καὶ ἐξουσία is that if I accept αὐτῷ δόξα κράτος τιμή at variation unit 25.3 as I have advocated, then κράτος appears twice in the verse, and therefore functions as a catchword similar to other such catchwords as listed at variation unit 1.3. Accept κράτος καὶ ἐξουσία here.

Variation Unit 25.7

προ παντος του αιωνος ℵ A B C L Ψ
om. προ παντος του αιωνος 𝔓72 K P 049

Intrinsic evidence favours πρὸ παντὸς τοῦ αἰῶνος since this phrase is part of a triadic structure the components of which are: (1) πρὸ παντὸς τοῦ αἰῶνος; (2) καὶ νῦν; and (3) καὶ εἰς πάντας τοὺς αἰῶνας.[270] The omission of the phrase πρὸ παντὸς τοῦ αἰῶνος by the copyists of 𝔓72 and other MSS is explicable through harmony with 2 Pet. 3.18.[271] A combination of intrinsic and transcriptional evidence would appear to undermine Kubo's conviction that the phrase πρὸ παντὸς τοῦ αἰῶνος was originally absent. Print πρὸ παντὸς τοῦ αἰῶνος at this unit.

Variation Unit 25.8

παντας τους αιωνας A B C K P Ψ 049
τους παντας εωνας 𝔓72
τους αιωνας ℵ 36 1836
παντας τους αιωνας των αιωνων L 33 88

---

270. Charles, 'Literary Artifice', p. 123, explains that the function of this instance of triadic illustration is to emphasize the author's view of time.
271. Kubo, *𝔓72 and the Codex Vaticanus*, p. 59.

The two main rivals at this unit are τοὺς πάντας εωνας where the copyist intends αἰῶνας, and πάντας τοὺς αἰῶνας. The latter of these two readings has better intrinsic credentials. As I explained at variation unit 15.1, the writer's word order preference with πᾶς is for πᾶς + definite article + adjective or substantive (Π + DA + AS). In view of this tendency, the variant which conforms most closely to the writer's stylistic preference is πάντας τοὺς αἰῶνας. The singular reading is unacceptable because it violates Π + DA + AS. Faced with this variation involving the position of πάντας and being unable to decide on the correct reading, the copyists of ℵ 36 1836 omit πάντας altogether. The additional τῶν αἰῶνων in L 33 88 appears to be a scribal embellishment (cf. τοῦ ἁγίου ἀπόστολου Ἰούδα ἐπιστολή preserved in L at variation unit 26.1). Print πάντας τοὺς αἰῶνας here.

Variation Unit 26.1

ιουδα   ℵ B
ιουδα επιστολη   𝔓72 A Ψ
επιστολη ιουδα   452 605
επιστολη ιουδα αποστολου   P syrʰ
ιουδα επιστολη καθολικη   C 90 623
του αγιου αποστολου ιουδα επιστολη   L 049
επιστολη του αγιου αποστολου ιουδα   131 330
του αγιου αποστολου ιουδα καθολικη επιστολη   462
τελος της ιουδα καθολικης επιστολης   103
τελος γραφης ενθαδε της εξ ιουδα   205 209
ετελειωθη συν θεω και η του ιουδα καθολικη επιστολη   K

The readings Ἰούδα ἐπιστολὴ καθολική, τοῦ ἁγίου ἀπόστολου Ἰούδα καθολικὴ ἐπιστολή, τέλος τῆς Ἰούδα καθολικῆς ἐπιστολῆς, and ἐτελειώθη σὺν θεῷ καὶ ἡ τοῦ Ἰούδα καθολικὴ ἐπιστολή all include the word καθολική, and are all therefore unacceptable on theological grounds as explained at variation unit 0.1. The readings ἐπιστολὴ Ἰούδα ἀπόστολου, τοῦ ἁγίου ἀπόστολου Ἰούδα ἐπιστολὴ and ἐπιστολὴ τοῦ ἁγίου ἀπόστολου Ἰούδα can be eliminated because the word ἀπόστολος is explicable as a scribal addition written to underscore Jude's canonical status.[272] Readings such as Ἰούδα ἐπιστολή and ἐπιστολὴ Ἰούδα are to be rejected because the word ἐπιστολή was added by scribes to eliminate the doubt about

272. Cf. variation unit 0.1.

Jude's epistolary status.[273] By a process of elimination, I am left with Ἰούδα as the only reading which is unblemished by scribal additions. If I accept that I am dealing here with the phenomenon of a 'growing text',[274] then Ἰούδα as the shortest reading is the one which should be accepted at this unit.

273. Cf. variation unit 0.1.
274. Cf. variation unit 0.1, and Metzger, *Text*, pp. 198-99.

Chapter 3

CONCLUSION

1. *Eclecticism and Internal Evidence*

My eclectic approach has enabled me to reject the notion that any single MS or group of MSS has a special claim to superiority over against others and to sift the evidence at points of variation in Jude mainly on the basis of internal evidence. My approach is corroborated by the results recorded in appendix B below, where the inference is clear that the New Testament MSS cited consistently in my study cannot be adjudged superior or inferior on grounds of antiquity or text type.

By far the most frequently invoked criterion in my study has been the style criterion. There are four reasons for this: (1) the presupposition that an author should have a consistent style for eclecticism to be effective as a text-critical method is met in Jude; (2) the factors which render the style canon problematic for the Pauline epistles and for Luke–Acts are not applicable to Jude; (3) criteria such as style, theology and context are deemed preferable in an eclectic approach to criteria such as the shortest reading or the hardest reading since I consider the latter two to be inadequate substitutes for a nuanced discussion of the evidence; and (4) my study is in the tradition of C.H. Turner, G.D. Kilpatrick and J.K. Elliott, all of whom place emphasis upon style in their approach to the New Testament text. It may be fruitful to review briefly the main respects in which Jude can be said to have a consistent style.

There are at least 11 groups of catchwords in Jude, 19 occurrences of triadic illustration, 24 instances of synonymous parallelism, and 18 instances of contrast or antithesis. The predominance of such stylistic features and of a carefully designed midrashic rhetorical structure make Jude one of the most stylistically distinctive books in the New Testament. These and other considerations such as the writer's word order tendencies and use of vocabulary and set expressions have been the strongest influences on my judgment at points of variation in Jude.

Wherever possible, transcriptional reasons have been provided for the existence of readings deemed invalid on stylistic or other grounds.

None of this is to deny that my eclectic approach has limitations. Intrinsic evidence conflicts with transcriptional evidence on occasion; style conflicts with context on occasion; transcriptional evidence can sometimes appear to point in opposite directions; and intrinsic evidence can sometimes appear to divide. These limitations are perhaps most strongly evident in my analysis of variation units 25.3, 25.5 and 25.6, where there is not much to choose between two apparently rival instances of triadic illustration (δόξα κράτος τιμή and δόξα μεγαλωσύνη κράτος) neither of which I can confidently reject. At variation unit 2.2, on the other hand, I was able to look beyond apparent internal contradictions towards an acceptable and plausible solution. If a lesson can be learnt about the handling of internal evidence at a variation unit such as 2.2, then the time I devoted to arguing a case against a reading preserved in two minuscules was worthwhile. The extent to which I have succeeded in making informed choices in the face of the difficulties posed by conflicting internal evidence is for the reader to judge. What is clear, however, is that my results (as shown in appendix A) differ with GNT4 at 21 variation units, a state of affairs which poses a challenge to the status of the text of Jude in GNT4 as a truly eclectic text.

2. *The Greek Text of Jude in the Greek New Testament,*
Fourth Edition

There are those who would argue that GNT4 is largely the product of decisions made by eclectic generalists, and that as such, it attempts to satisfy two mutually incompatible ideals: the ideal of a text reconstructed from the presupposition of the superiority of Alexandrian MSS [local genealogy], and the ideal of a text reconstructed on the basis of internal and external evidence [moderate or reasoned eclecticism]. There are those who would argue further that in attempting to satisfy both of these ideals, GNT4 satisfies neither.

What is beyond doubt is that GNT4 does not always satisfy the ideal of thoroughgoing eclecticism. Where I have differed with GNT4 it has usually been over intrinsic evidence in general, and often over stylistic considerations in particular. And yet I have often accepted readings printed in GNT4 on intrinsic grounds. From my analysis it can be adduced that GNT4 is an eclectic text at some points of variation, but not at others. Expressed differently, it could be said that GNT4 is eclectic to the extent that it reflects the Greek text of Jude which I have printed in Appendix C.

Appendix A

A Summary of Variant Readings Accepted

What follows is a summary of all of the results obtained in my analysis. Each variation unit is identified in the left-hand column, with the reading accepted and its apparatus shown in the right-hand column. In the tradition of NA26, a MS within parentheses indicates a minor deviation such as itacism. An asterisk and a bracketed comment are provided for each reading accepted against GNT4. Altogether 95 variation units were analysed. A total of 21 readings were accepted against GNT4, a figure which includes the removal of brackets from ὅτι at v. 18. The decisions against GNT4 are reflected in the text printed in Appendix C.

0.1	ιουδα	ℵ B
1.1	ιησου χριστου	𝔓72 ℵ A B L
1.2	τοις εν θεω πατρι	𝔓72 ℵ A B K L P Ψ 049
1.3	ηγαπημενοις	𝔓72 ℵ A B Ψ
1.4	ιησου χριστω	𝔓72 ℵ A B L P 049
2.1	και ειρηνη	𝔓72 ℵ A B L P Ψ 049
2.2	και αγαπη	𝔓72 ℵ A B K L P Ψ 049
3.1	ποιουμενος	ℵ A B C K L P 049
3.2	γραφειν	A B C K L P 049
3.3	ημων	𝔓72 𝔓74 ℵ A B C^vid Ψ
3.4	σωτηριας	𝔓72 A B C K L P 049
3.5	γραψαι	𝔓72 𝔓74 A B C K L P 049
4.1	παρεισεδυσαν	𝔓72 ℵ A K L P Ψ 049
4.2	κριμα	𝔓72 ℵ A B C K L P 049
4.3	χαριτα	(𝔓72) A B
4.4*	δεσποτην θεον	K L P Ψ 049 syr^ph,h [against GNT4]
4.5	om. ημων	𝔓78 ℵ A B C K L P Ψ 049
4.6	και	𝔓72 ℵ A B C K L P Ψ 049
4.7	κυριον ημων ιησουν χριστον	𝔓78 ℵ A B C K L P 049
5.1	δε	𝔓72 𝔓78 ℵ A B K L 049
5.2*	βουλομαι ειδοτας	𝔓72 A C Ψ [against GNT4]
5.3*	παντα οτι κυριος απαξ	ℵ Ψ [against GNT4]
5.4	γης αιγυπτου	(𝔓72) ℵ A B C K L 049

6.1*   δε   A 625 638 [against GNT4]
6.2   αλλα   𝔓72 ℵ A B K L 049
6.3   απολιποντας   ℵ A B C K Ψ
6.4   οικητηριον   𝔓72 ℵ A B C K L 049
6.5   δεσμοις αιδιοις   (𝔓72) ℵ A B C K L 049
6.6*   υπο ζοφον αγιων αγγελων conjecture from Lucifer Speculum
         [against GNT4]

7.1   ως σοδομα και γομορρα   (𝔓72) ℵ A B K L Ψ 049
7.2   τροπον τουτοις   𝔓72 ℵ A B C
7.3   υπεχουσαι   𝔓72 B C K L Ψ 049

8.1   ομοιως   𝔓72 𝔓78 ℵ B C K L Ψ 049
8.2   ουτοι   𝔓72 ℵ A B C K L Ψ 049
8.3   σαρκα μεν   𝔓78 ℵ A B C K L Ψ 049
8.4   κυριοτητα   𝔓72 A B C K L 049
8.5   δοξας   𝔓72 ℵ A B C K L Ψ 049

9.1   ο δε μιχαηλ ο αρχαγγελος οτε   (𝔓72) ℵ A C K L Ψ 049
9.2*   σωματος μωυσεως   378 632 [against GNT4]
9.3   επενεγκειν   𝔓72 ℵ A B C K L 049
9.4   αλλα   𝔓72 A B Ψ
9.5*   εν σοι   B* Ψ Origen [against GNT4]
9.6   κυριος   𝔓72 A B C K L Ψ 049

10.1   δε   𝔓72 ℵ A B C K L Ψ 049
10.2   τα αλογα ζωα   𝔓72 ℵ A B C K L Ψ 049
10.3   φθειρονται   (𝔓72) ℵ A B C K L 049

11.1   τη οδω   𝔓72 ℵ A B C K L Ψ 049
11.2   βαλααμ   ℵ A B C K L Ψ 049
11.3   τη αντιλογια   (𝔓72) 𝔓74 ℵ A B C K L Ψ 049

12.1   ουτοι εισιν   𝔓72 ℵc A B K L Ψ 049
12.2   οι   𝔓72 ℵc A B L Ψ
12.3   αγαπαις υμων   𝔓72 ℵ B K L 049
12.4   συνευωχουμενοι   ℵ A B (K) L Ψ 049 (314) (330)
12.5   εαυτους   𝔓72c ℵ A B C K L Ψ 049
12.6   υπο ανεμων   𝔓72 A B C K L Ψ 049
12.7   παραφερομεναι   𝔓72c ℵ A C K L 049

13.1   κυματα αγρια   𝔓72 A B C K L Ψ 049
13.2   επαφριζοντα   ℵ A B K L Ψ 049
13.3   ο ζοφος   ℵ A C K L Ψ 049
13.4   του σκοτους   𝔓72 ℵ A C K L Ψ 049
13.5*   εις τον αιωνα   K 049 [against GNT4]

14.1*   επροφητευσεν   𝔓72 B* [against GNT4]
14.2   κυριος   𝔓72 A B C K L Ψ 049
14.3   εν μυριασιν αγιαις αυτου   C 323 378

15.1*   παντας τους ασεβεις   A B C Ψ [against GNT4]
15.2   των εργων ασεβειας αυτων   A B K L 049
15.3   των σκληρων   (𝔓72) A B K L Ψ 049

16.1   επιθυμιας εαυτων   𝔓72ᶜ C L P 049

17.1*   μνημονευετε   323 1739 [against GNT4]
17.2   των ρηματων των προειρημενων   𝔓72 ℵ B C K L P Ψ 049

18.1   οτι ελεγον υμιν   𝔓72 ℵ A B C L P Ψ 049
18.2*   οτι   𝔓72 A C K Lᶜ P 049 [without brackets against GNT4]
18.3*   επ εσχατου χρονου   𝔓72 B C Ψ [against GNT4]
18.4   εσονται   𝔓72 ℵ* B C* K L P 049
18.5*   κατα τας επιθυμιας εαυτων   ℵᶜ 460 483 [against GNT4]

19.1*   αποδιοριζοντες εαυτους   C 323 378 [against GNT4]

20.1   υμεις   (𝔓72) ℵ A B K L P Ψ 049
20.2   εποικοδομουντες εαυτους τη αγιωτατη υμων πιστει   ℵ A B Ψ
20.3   *om.* εαυτοις   ℵ A B C K L P 049

21.1   εαυτους   𝔓72 ℵ A B C L P Ψ
21.2   τηρησατε   ℵ A K L P 049
21.3   ημων ιησου χριστου εις ζωην αιωνιον   ℵ A B C K L P Ψ 049

22-23.1*   ους μεν εκ πυρος αρπασατε
           διακρινομενους δε ελεειτε εν φοβω   𝔓72 itᵗ copˢᵃ syrᵖʰ
           [against GNT4]

24.1*   στηριξαι ασπιλους αμωμους αγνευομενους   𝔓72
        [against GNT4]
24.2*   απεναντι   𝔓72 [against GNT4]
24.3*   *om.* αμωμους   𝔓72 [against GNT4]

25.1*   μονω σοφω θεω   K L P 049 *Lect* [against GNT4]
25.2   σωτηρι   ℵ A B C K L P Ψ 049
25.3*   αυτω δοξα κρατος τιμη   𝔓72 [against GNT4]
25.4   δια ιησου χριστου του κυριου ημων   𝔓72 ℵ A B C L Ψ
25.5   δοξα μεγαλωσυνη   ℵ A B C Ψ
25.6   κρατος και εξουσια   ℵ A B C K L P 049
25.7   προ παντος του αιωνος   ℵ A B C L Ψ
25.8   παντας τους αιωνας   A B C K P Ψ 049

26.1   ιουδα

Appendix B

INTERNAL EVALUATION OF MANUSCRIPTS CITED CONSISTENTLY

In the table of results shown below, individual MSS are shown in the left-hand column, with the number of correct and incorrect readings found in each MS in the right-hand column. A correct reading is understood as a reading which appears in Appendix A. A reading supported by a MS in parentheses—e.g. των σκληρων (𝔓72) in Appendix A—counts as a correct reading for such a MS. A *corrected* reading which appears in Appendix A—e.g. παραφερομεναι 𝔓72ᶜ—does not count as a correct reading for the MS which contains it. Incorrect readings are understood as occurrences of omission, addition, substitution or transposition, all four of which were found in all MSS evaluated. Only MSS which contain the entire text of Jude appear below. It can be inferred from the results shown below that no MS has a monopoly of the truth. MSS belonging to different text types and of differing antiquity both yield remarkably similar results: two striking examples are the results for B and L (in different text types), and the results for 𝔓72 and K (of differing antiquity) respectively.

𝔓72	correct readings	57
	incorrect readings	38
ℵ	correct readings	57
	incorrect readings	38
A	correct readings	69
	incorrect readings	26
B	correct readings	70
	incorrect readings	25
K	correct readings	59
	incorrect readings	36
L	correct readings	64
	incorrect readings	31
Ψ	correct readings	51
	incorrect readings	44
049	correct readings	62
	incorrect readings	33

Appendix C

THE GREEK TEXT OF JUDE

ΙΟΥΔΑ

1 Ἰούδας Ἰησοῦ Χριστοῦ δοῦλος, ἀδελφὸς δὲ Ἰακώβου, τοῖς ἐν θεῷ πατρὶ ἠγαπημένοις καὶ Ἰησοῦ Χριστῷ τετηρημένοις κλητοῖς· **2** ἔλεος ὑμῖν καὶ εἰρήνη καὶ ἀγάπη πληθυνθείη.

3 Ἀγαπητοί, πᾶσαν σπουδὴν ποιούμενος γράφειν ὑμῖν περὶ τῆς κοινῆς ἡμῶν σωτηρίας, ἀνάγκην ἔσχον γράψαι ὑμῖν παρακαλῶν ἐπαγωνίζεσθαι τῇ ἅπαξ παραδοθείσῃ τοῖς ἁγίοις πίστει. **4** παρεισέδυσαν γάρ τινες ἄνθρωποι, οἱ πάλαι προγεγραμμένοι εἰς τοῦτο τὸ κρίμα, ἀσεβεῖς, τὴν τοῦ θεοῦ ἡμῶν χάριτα μετατιθέντες εἰς ἀσέλγειαν καὶ τὸν μόνον δεσπότην θεὸν καὶ κύριον ἡμῶν Ἰησοῦν Χριστὸν ἀρνούμενοι.

5 Ὑπομνῆσαι δὲ ὑμᾶς βούλομαι, εἰδότας πάντα, ὅτι κύριος ἅπαξ λαὸν ἐκ γῆς Αἰγύπτου σώσας τὸ δεύτερον τοὺς μὴ πιστεύσαντας ἀπώλεσεν, **6** ἀγγέλους δὲ τοὺς μὴ τηρήσαντας τὴν ἑαυτῶν ἀρχὴν ἀλλὰ ἀπολιπόντας τὸ ἴδιον οἰκητήριον εἰς κρίσιν μεγάλης ἡμέρας δεσμοῖς ἀϊδίοις ὑπὸ ζόφον ἁγίων ἀγγέλων τετήρηκεν, **7** ὡς Σόδομα καὶ Γόμορρα καὶ αἱ περὶ αὐτὰς πόλεις τὸν ὅμοιον τρόπον τούτοις ἐκπορνεύσασαι καὶ ἀπελθοῦσαι ὀπίσω σαρκὸς ἑτέρας, πρόκεινται δεῖγμα πυρὸς αἰωνίου δίκην ὑπέχουσαι.

8 Ὁμοίως μέντοι καὶ οὗτοι ἐνυπνιαζόμενοι σάρκα μὲν μιαίνουσιν κυριότητα δὲ ἀθετοῦσιν δόξας δὲ βλασφημοῦσιν. **9** ὁ δὲ Μιχαὴλ ὁ ἀρχάγγελος, ὅτε τῷ διαβόλῳ διακρινόμενος διελέγετο περὶ τοῦ σώματος Μωϋσέως, οὐκ ἐτόλμησεν κρίσιν ἐπενεγκεῖν βλασφημίας ἀλλὰ εἶπεν, Ἐπιτιμήσαι ἐν σοι κύριος. **10** οὗτοι δὲ ὅσα μὲν οὐκ οἴδασιν βλασφημοῦσιν, ὅσα δὲ φυσικῶς ὡς τὰ ἄλογα ζῷα ἐπίστανται, ἐν τούτοις φθείρονται. **11** οὐαὶ αὐτοῖς, ὅτι τῇ ὁδῷ τοῦ Κάϊν ἐπορεύθησαν καὶ τῇ πλάνῃ τοῦ Βαλαὰμ μισθοῦ ἐξεχύθησαν καὶ τῇ ἀντιλογίᾳ τοῦ Κόρε ἀπώλοντο. **12** οὗτοί εἰσιν οἱ ἐν ταῖς ἀγάπαις ὑμῶν σπιλάδες συνευωχούμενοι ἀφόβως, ἑαυτοὺς ποιμαίνοντες, νεφέλαι ἄνυδροι ὑπὸ ἀνέμων παραφερόμεναι, δένδρα φθινοπωρινὰ ἄκαρπα δὶς ἀποθανόντα ἐκριζωθέντα, **13** κύματα ἄγρια θαλάσσης ἐπαφρίζοντα τὰς ἑαυτῶν αἰσχύνας, ἀστέρες πλανῆται οἷς ὁ ζόφος τοῦ σκότους εἰς τὸν αἰῶνα τετήρηται.

14 Ἐπροφήτευσεν δὲ καὶ τούτοις ἕβδομος ἀπὸ Ἀδὰμ Ἐνὼχ λέγων, Ἰδοὺ ἦλθεν κύριος ἐν μυριάσιν ἁγίαις αὐτοῦ **15** ποιῆσαι κρίσιν κατὰ πάντων καὶ ἐλέγξαι πάντας τοὺς ἀσεβεῖς περὶ πάντων τῶν ἔργων ἀσεβείας αὐτῶν ὧν ἠσέβησαν καὶ περὶ πάντων τῶν σκληρῶν ὧν ἐλάλησαν κατ' αὐτοῦ ἁμαρτωλοὶ ἀσεβεῖς. **16** Οὗτοί εἰσιν γογγυσταὶ μεμψίμοιροι κατὰ τὰς ἐπιθυμίας ἑαυτῶν πορευόμενοι, καὶ τὸ στόμα αὐτῶν λαλεῖ ὑπέρογκα, θαυμάζοντες πρόσωπα ὠφελείας χάριν.

17 Ὑμεῖς δέ, ἀγαπητοί, μνημονεύετε τῶν ῥημάτων τῶν προειρημένων ὑπὸ τῶν ἀποστόλων τοῦ κυρίου ἡμῶν Ιησοῦ χριστοῦ **18** ὅτι ἔλεγον ὑμῖν ὅτι Ἐπ' ἐσχάτου χρόνου ἔσονται ἐμπαῖκται κατὰ τὰς ἐπιθυμίας ἑαυτῶν πορευόμενοι τῶν ἀσεβειῶν. **19** Οὗτοί εἰσιν οἱ ἀποδιορίζοντες ἑαυτούς, ψυχικοί, πνεῦμα μὴ ἔχοντες. **20** ὑμεῖς δέ, ἀγαπητοί, ἐποικοδομοῦντες ἑαυτοὺς τῇ ἁγιωτάτῃ ὑμῶν πίστει, ἐν πνεύματι ἁγίῳ προσευχόμενοι, **21** ἑαυτοὺς ἐν ἀγάπῃ θεοῦ τηρήσατε προσδεχόμενοι τὸ ἔλεος τοῦ κυρίου ἡμῶν Ἰησοῦ Χριστοῦ εἰς ζωὴν αἰώνιον. **22** οὓς μὲν ἐκ πυρὸς ἁρπάσατε, **23** διακρινομένους δὲ ἐλεεῖτε ἐν φόβῳ μισοῦντες καὶ τὸν ἀπὸ τῆς σαρκὸς ἐσπιλωμένον χιτῶνα.

24 Τῷ δὲ δυναμένῳ στηρίξαι ἀσπίλους ἀμώμους ἁγνευομένους ἀπέναντι τῆς δόξης αὐτοῦ ἐν ἀγαλλιάσει, **25** μόνῳ σοφῷ θεῷ σωτῆρι ἡμῶν, αὐτῷ δόξα κράτος τιμή διὰ Ἰησοῦ Χριστοῦ τοῦ κυρίου ἡμῶν, δόξα μεγαλωσύνη κράτος καὶ ἐξουσία πρὸ παντὸς τοῦ αἰῶνος καὶ νῦν καὶ εἰς πάντας τοὺς αἰῶνας, ἀμήν.

ΙΟΥΔΑ

BIBLIOGRAPHY

Aland, B., 'Die Münsteraner Arbeit am Text des Neuen Testaments und ihr Beitrag für die frühe Überlieferung des 2. Jahrhunderts: Eine methodologische Betrachtung', in W.L. Petersen (ed.), *Gospel Traditions in the Second Century: Origins, Recensions, Text, and Transmission* (Notre Dame: Notre Dame University Press, 1989), pp. 55-70.

Aland, B. and K. Aland, *The Text of the New Testament: An Introduction to the Critical Editions and to the Theory and Practice of Modern Textual Criticism* (Grand Rapids: Eerdmans, 2nd edn, 1989).

Aland, B., K. Aland, J. Karavidopoulos, C.M. Martini, and B.M. Metzger (eds.), *The Greek New Testament* (Stuttgart: Deutsche Bibelgesellschaft, 4th edn, 1993).

Aland, K., *Kurzgefasste Liste der griechischen Handschriften des Neuen Testaments. Band 1. Gesamtübersicht* (ANTF, 1; Berlin: De Gruyter, 1963).

—'The Significance of the Papyri for Progress in New Testament Research', in J.P. Hyatt (ed.), *The Bible in Modern Scholarship* (London: Carey Kingsgate, 1966), pp. 325-46.

—*Computer-Konkordanz zum Novum Testamentum Graece* (Berlin: De Gruyter, 1980).

—*Supplementa zu den Neutestamentlichen und den kirchengeschichtlichen Entwürfen* (Berlin: De Gruyter, 1990).

Aland, K., M. Black, C.M. Martini, B.M. Metzger, and A. Wikgren (eds.), *Novum Testamentum Graece* (Stuttgart: Deutsche Bibelgesellschaft, 26th edn, 1979).

Albin, C.A., *Judasbrevet: Traditionen, Texten, Tolkningen* (Stockholm: Natur och Kultur, 1962).

Alford, H., *The Greek Testament* (4 vols.; Chicago: Moody, 1968 [1875]).

Baarda, T., 'ΔΙΑΦΩΝΙΑ—ΣΥΜΦΩΝΙΑ: Factors in the Harmonisation of the Gospels, Especially in the Diatessaron of Tatian', in W.L. Petersen (ed.), *Gospel Traditions in the Second Century: Origins, Recensions, Text, and Transmission* (Notre Dame: Notre Dame University Press, 1989), pp. 133-54.

Bauckham, R.J., 'A Note on a Problem in the Greek Version of 1 Enoch 1.9', *JTS* 32 (1981), pp. 136-38.

—*Jude, 2 Peter* (Waco: Word, 1983).

—'The Letter of Jude: An Account of Research', ANRW II.25.5 (1988), pp. 3791-826.

—'James, 1 & 2 Peter, Jude', in D.A. Carson and H.M.G. Williamson (eds.), *It Is Written: Scripture Citing Scripture. Essays in Honour of Barnabas Lindars* (Cambridge: Cambridge University Press, 1988), pp. 303-17.

—*Jude and the Relatives of Jesus in the Early Church* (Edinburgh: T. & T. Clark, 1990).

Bauer, W., *A Greek-English Lexicon of the New Testament and Other Early Christian Literature* (trans., rev. and augmented by W.F. Arndt, F.W. Gingrich and F.W. Danker; Chicago: Chicago University Press, 2nd edn, 1979).

Bigg, C., *A Critical and Exegetical Commentary on the Epistles of St. Peter and St. Jude* (Edinburgh: T. & T. Clark, 2nd edn, 1902).

Birdsall, J.N., *The Bodmer Papyrus of the Gospel of John* (London: Tyndale, 1960).

—'The Text of Jude in $\mathfrak{P}$72'. *JTS* 14 (1963), pp. 394-99.

—'Rational Eclecticism and the Oldest Manuscripts: A Comparative Study of the Bodmer and Chester Beatty Papyri of the Gospel of Luke', in J.K. Elliott (ed.), *Studies in New Testament Language and Text: Essays in Honour of George D. Kilpatrick on the Occasion of His Sixty-Fifth Birthday* (Leiden: Brill, 1976), pp. 39-51.

—'The Recent History of New Testament Textual Criticism (from Westcott and Hort, 1881, to the Present)'. ANRW II.26.1. (1992), pp. 100-97.

Black, M., 'Critical and Exegetical Notes on Three New Testament Texts: Hebrews 11.11, Jude 5, and James 1.27', in W. Eltester (ed.), *Apophoreta: Festschrift für Ernst Haenchen zu seinem siebzigsten Geburtstag* (Berlin: Töpelmann, 1964), pp. 39-45.

—'The Maranatha Invocation and Jude 14-15 (1 Enoch 1.9)', in B. Lindars (ed.), *Christ and Spirit in the New Testament: Essays in Honour of C.F.D. Moule* (Cambridge: Cambridge University Press, 1973), pp. 189-96.

Black, M., and A.-M. Denis, (eds.), *Apocalypsis Henochi Graece: Fragmenta Pseudepigraphorum Quae Supersunt Graeca* (Leiden: Brill, 1970).

Blass, F., and A. Debrunner, *A Greek Grammar of the New Testament and Other Early Christian Literature* (trans. and rev. from the 9th and 10th German edition by R. Funk; Chicago: Chicago University Press, 1961).

Boismard, M.-E., and A. Lamouille, *Le texte occidental des Actes des Apotres: Reconstitution et réhabilitation. Tome I: Introduction et textes; Tome II: Apparat critique* (Paris: Editions Recherche sur les Civilisations, 1984).

Bolkestein, M.H., *De Brieven van Petrus en Judas* (Nijkerk: Callenbach, 1963).

Boobyer, G.H., 'The Verbs in Jude 11', *NTS* 5 (1958), pp. 45-47.

Botha, J.E., 'A Study in Johannine Style: History, Theory and Practice' (DTh dissertation; Pretoria: University of South Africa, 1989).

Bover, J.M., *Novi Testamenti biblia graeca et latina* (Madrid: Consejo superior de investigaciones científicas, 5th edn, 1968).

Bratcher, R.G., *A Translator's Guide to the Letters from James, Peter and Jude* (New York: UBS, 1984).

Burton, E.D., *Syntax of the Moods and Tenses in New Testament Greek* (Edinburgh: T. & T. Clark, 2nd edn, 1894).

Carson, D.A., *Greek Accents: A Student's Manual* (Grand Rapids: Baker, 1985).

Charles, J.D., '"Those" and "These": The Use of the Old Testament in the Epistle of Jude', *JSNT* 38 (1990), pp. 109-24.

—'Literary Artifice in the Epistle of Jude', *ZNW* 82 (1991), pp. 106-24.

—'Jude's Use of Pseudepigraphical Source-Material as Part of a Literary Strategy', *NTS* 37 (1991), pp. 130-45.

—*Literary Strategy in the Epistle of Jude* (Scranton: University of Scranton Press, 1993).

Charlesworth, J.H. (ed.), *The Old Testament Pseudepigrapha* (2 vols; New York: Doubleday, 1983–1985).

Clark, A.C., *The Descent of Manuscripts* (Oxford: Clarendon Press, 1918).

—*The Acts of the Apostles: A Critical Edition with Introduction and Notes on Selected Passages* (Oxford: Clarendon Press, 1933).

Clark, K.W., 'The Effect of Recent Textual Criticism upon New Testament Studies', in W.D. Davies and D. Daube (eds.), *The Background of the New Testament and its Eschatology* (Cambridge: Cambridge University Press, 1956), pp. 27-51.

Colwell, E.C., *Studies in Methodology in Textual Criticism of the New Testament* (NTTS, 9; Leiden: Brill, 1969).

Combrink, H.J.B., 'Die Griekse teks van die Nuwe Testament: teksuitgawes, projekte en teorieë', *Nederduits Gereformeerde Teologiese Tydskrif* 18 (1977), pp. 230-42.

Cranfield, C.E.B., *I and II Peter and Jude* (London: SCM Press, 1960).

Dana, H.E., and J.R. Mantey, *A Manual Grammar of the Greek New Testament* (New York: Macmillan, 1967).

De Boer, M.C., 'Jesus the Baptizer: 1 John 5.5-8 and the Gospel of John', *JBL* 107 (1988), pp. 87-106.

De Zwaan, J., *II Petrus en Judas* (Leiden: Van Doesburgh, 1909).

Dehandschutter, B., 'Pseudo-Cyprian, Jude and Enoch. Some Notes on 1 Enoch 1.9', in J.W. Van Henten (ed.), *Tradition and Re-interpretation in Jewish and Early Christian Literature: Essays in Honour of Jurgen C.H. Lebram* (Leiden: Brill, 1986), pp. 114-120.

Delobel, J., 'Jean Duplacy: Sa contribution à la critique textuelle du Nouveau Testament', *ETL* 60 (1984), pp. 98-108.

Desjardins, M., 'The Portrayal of the Dissidents in 2 Peter and Jude: Does It Tell Us More About the "Godly" than the "Ungodly"?', *JSNT* 30 (1987), pp. 89-102.

Dover, K.J., *Greek Word Order* (Cambridge: Cambridge University Press, 1960).

Duplacy, J., *Où en est la critique textuelle du Nouveau Testament?* (Paris: Gabalda, 1959).

—*Etudes de critique textuelle du Nouveau Testament* (ed. J. Delobel; BETL, 78; Leuven: Leuven University Press, 1987).

Du Plessis, P.J., 'The Authorship of the Epistle of Jude' (paper presented at The New Testament Society of South Africa congress; Stellenbosch University, 1966).

Dunn, J.D.G., *Unity and Diversity in the New Testament* (London: SCM Press, 1977).

Ehrman, B.D., '1 John 4.3 and the Orthodox Corruption of Scripture', *ZNW* 79 (1988), pp. 221-43.

—'The Cup, the Bread, and the Salvic Effect of Jesus' Death in Luke–Acts', SBLSP (Atlanta: Scholars Press, 1991), pp. 576-91.

—*The Orthodox Corruption of Scripture: The Effect of Early Christological Controversies on the Text of the New Testament* (New York: Oxford University Press, 1993).

Ehrman, B.D., and M.A. Plunkett, 'The Angel and the Agony: The Textual Problem of Luke 22.43-44', *CBQ* 45 (1983), pp. 401-16.

Elliott, J.K., *The Greek Text of the Epistles to Timothy and Titus* (SD, 36; Salt Lake City: Utah University Press, 1968).

—'ΔΙΔΩΜΙ in 2 Timothy', *JTS* 19 (1968), pp. 621-23.

—'The Use of ἕτερος in the New Testament', *ZNW* 60 (1969), pp. 140-41.

—'Nouns with Diminutive Endings in the New Testament', *NovT* 12 (1970), pp. 391-98.

—'In Favour of καυθήσομαι at 1 Cor. 13.3', *ZNW* 62 (1971), pp. 297-98.

—'The Conclusion of the Pericope of the Healing of the Leper and Mark 1.45', *JTS* 22 (1971), pp. 153-57.

—'The Text and Language of the Endings to Mark's Gospel', *TZ* 27 (1971), pp. 255-62.

—'Phrynichus' Influence on the Textual Tradition of the New Testament', *ZNW* 63 (1972), pp. 133-38.

—'Κηφᾶς: Σίμων Πέτρος: ὁ Πέτρος: An Examination of New Testament Usage', *NovT* 14 (1972), pp. 241-56.

—'Rational Criticism and the Text of the New Testament', *Theology* 75 (1972), pp. 338-43.

—'When Jesus Was Apart from God: An Examination of Hebrews 2.9', *ExpTim* 83 (1972), pp. 339-41.

—'The United Bible Societies' Greek New Testament: An Evaluation', *NovT* 15 (1973), pp. 278-300.

—'Can We Recover the Original New Testament?', *Theology* 77 (1974), pp. 338-53.

—'A Second Look at the United Bible Societies' Greek New Testament', *BT* 26 (1975), pp. 325-32.

—'The United Bible Societies' Textual Commentary Evaluated', *NovT* 17 (1975), pp. 130-50.

—'Ho baptizon and Mark 1.4', *TZ* 31 (1975), pp. 14-15.

—'Moeris and the Textual Tradition of the Greek New Testament', in J.K. Elliott (ed.), *Studies in New Testament Language and Text: Essays in Honour of George D. Kilpatrick on the Occasion of His Sixty-Fifth Birthday* (Leiden: Brill, 1976), pp. 144-52.

—'Is λόγος a Title for Jesus in Mark 1.45?', *JTS* 27 (1976), pp. 402-405.

—'The Two Forms of the Third Declension Comparative Adjectives in the New Testament', *NovT* 19 (1977), pp. 234-39.

—'Jerusalem in Acts and the Gospels', *NTS* 23 (1977), pp. 462-69.

—'Plaidoyer pour un éclectisme intégral appliqué à la critique textuelle du Nouveau Testament', *RB* 84 (1977), pp. 5-25.

—'John 1.14 and the New Testament's Use of πλήρης', *BT* 28 (1977), pp. 151-53.

—'Textual Variation Involving the Augment in the Greek New Testament', *ZNW* 69 (1978), pp. 247-52.

—'In Defence of Thoroughgoing Eclecticism in New Testament Textual Criticism', *ResQ* 21 (1978), pp. 95-115.

—'The Healing of the Leper in the Synoptic Parallels', *TZ* 34 (1978), pp. 175-76.

—'Μαθητής with a Possessive in the New Testament', *TZ* 35 (1979), pp. 300-304.

—'The United Bible Societies' Greek New Testament: A Short Examination of the Third Edition', *BT* 30 (1979), pp. 135-38.

—'The Use of Brackets in the Text of the United Bible Societies' Greek New Testament', *Bib* 60 (1979), pp. 575-77.

—'Temporal Augment in Verbs with Initial Diphthong in the Greek New Testament', *NovT* 22 (1980), pp. 1-11.

—'Textual Criticism, Assimilation and the Synoptic Gospels', *NTS* 26 (1980), pp. 231-42.

—'The Language and Style of the Concluding Doxology to the Epistle to the Romans', *ZNW* 72 (1981), pp. 124-30.

—'An Eclectic Textual Commentary on the Greek Text of Mark's Gospel', in E.J. Epp and G.D. Fee (eds.), *New Testament Textual Criticism, Its Significance for Exegesis: Essays in Honour of Bruce M. Metzger* (Oxford: Clarendon Press, 1981), pp. 47-60.

—'An Examination of the Twenty-Sixth Edition of Nestle-Aland *Novum Testamentum Graece*', *JTS* 32 (1981), pp. 19-49.

—'Comparing Greek New Testament Texts', *Bib* 62 (1981), pp. 401-405.

—*Codex Sinaiticus and the Simonides Affair: An Examination of the Nineteenth Century Claim That the Codex Sinaiticus Was Not an Ancient Manuscript* (Thessaloniki: Patriarchal Institute for Patristic Studies, 1982).

—'The Citation of Manuscripts in Recent Printed Editions of the Greek New Testament', *NovT* 25 (1983), pp. 97-132.

—'The International Project to Establish a Critical Apparatus to Luke's Gospel', *NTS* 29 (1983), pp. 531-38.

—Review of *The Greek New Testament According to the Majority Text*, by Z.C. Hodges and A.L. Farstad, *BT* 34 (1983), pp. 342-44.

—'Old Latin Manuscripts in Printed Editions of the Greek New Testament', *NovT* 26 (1984), pp. 225-48.

—'The Citation of Greek Manuscripts in Six Printed Texts of the New Testament', *RB* 92 (1985), pp. 539-56.

—'The Purpose and Construction of a Critical Apparatus to a Greek New Testament', in W. Schrage (ed.), *Studien zum Text und zur Ethik des Neuen Testaments* (Berlin: Töpelmann, 1986), pp. 125-143.

—'An Examination of the Text and Apparatus of Three Recent Greek Synopses', *NTS* 32 (1986), pp. 557-82.

—Review of *The Byzantine Text-Type and New Testament Textual Criticism*, by H. Sturz, *NovT* 28 (1986), pp. 282-84.

—*A Survey of Manuscripts Used in Editions of the Greek New Testament* (NovTSup, 57; Leiden: Brill, 1987).

—'Keeping up with Recent Studies: 15, New Testament Textual Criticism', *ExpTim* 99 (1987), pp. 40-45.

—'The Original Text of the Greek New Testament', *Fax Theologica* 8 (1988), pp. 1-22.

—'The Text of Acts in the Light of Two Recent Studies', *NTS* 34 (1988), pp. 250-58.

—'Anna's Age (Luke 2.36-37)', *NovT* 30 (1988), pp. 100-103.

—'Why the International Greek New Testament Project is Necessary', *ResQ* 30 (1988), pp. 195-206.

—*A Bibliography of Greek New Testament Manuscripts* (SNTSMS, 62; Cambridge: Cambridge University Press, 1989).

—''Ερωτᾶν and ἐπερωτᾶν in the New Testament', *Filología Neotestamentaria* 2 (1989), pp. 205-206.

—'L'Importance de la critique textuelle pour le problème synoptique', *RB* 96 (1989), pp. 56-70.

—'The Position of Causal ὅτι Clauses in the New Testament', *Filología Neotestamentaria* 6 (1990), pp. 155-57.

—'καθώς and ὥσπερ in the New Testament', *Filología Neotestamentaria* 7 (1991), pp. 55-58.

—'The Relevance of Textual Criticism to the Synoptic Problem', in D.L. Dungan (ed.), *The Interrelations of the Gospels* (Leuven: Leuven University Press, 1990), pp. 348-59.

—Review of *The Text of the New Testament: An Introduction to the Critical Editions and to the Theory and Practice of Modern Textual Criticism*, by B. Aland and K. Aland, *NovT* 32 (1990), pp. 374-79.

—'Textkritik heute', *ZNW* 82 (1991), pp. 34-41.

—Review of *Supplementa zu den Neutestamentlichen und den Kirchengeschichtlichen Entwürfen*, by K. Aland, *NovT* 33 (1991), pp. 188-89.

—*Essays and Studies in New Testament Textual Criticism* (Estudios de *Filología Neotestamentaria*, 3; Cordoba: Ediciones el Almendro, 1992).

—'The Translations of the New Testament into Latin: The Old Latin and the Vulgate', *ANRW* II.26.1. (1992), pp. 198-245.

—Review of *The Earliest Gospel Manuscript?*, by C.P. Thiede, *NovT* 36 (1994), pp. 98-100.

—Review of *The Text of the New Testament: Its Transmission, Corruption and Restoration*, by B. M. Metzger, *NovT* 36 (1994), pp. 97-98.

—Review of *The Greek New Testament* (ed. B. Aland *et al.*; 4th edn), *JTS* 45 (1994), pp. 280-82.

—Review of *The Quest for the Original Text of the New Testament*, by P.W. Comfort, *NovT* 36 (1994), pp. 284-87.

Elliott, J.K. (ed.), *Studies in New Testament Language and Text: Essays in Honour of George D. Kilpatrick on the Occasion of His Sixty-Fifth Birthday* (NovTSup, 44; Leiden: Brill, 1976).

—*The Principles and Practice of New Testament Textual Criticism: Collected Essays of G.D. Kilpatrick* (BETL, 96; Leuven: Leuven University Press, 1990).

—*The Language and Style of the Gospel of Mark: An Edition of C.H. Turner's 'Notes on Marcan Usage' Together with Other Comparable Studies* (NovTSup, 71; Leiden: Brill, 1993).

Elliott, W.J., 'The Need for an Accurate and Comprehensive Collation of All Known Greek New Testament Manuscripts with Their Individual Variants Noted in pleno', in J.K. Elliott (ed.), *Studies in the New Testament Language and Text: Essays in Honour of George D. Kilpatrick on the Occasion of His Sixty-Fifth Birthday* (Leiden: Brill, 1976), pp. 137-43.

Ellis, E.E., 'Prophecy and Hermeneutic in Jude', in E.E. Ellis (ed.), *Prophecy and Hermeneutic in Early Christianity: New Testament Essays* (WUNT, 18; Tübingen: Mohr & Siebeck, 1978), pp. 221-36.

—'The Silenced Wives of Corinth (1 Cor. 14.34-35)', in E.J. Epp and G.D. Fee (eds.), *New Testament Textual Criticism, Its Significance for Exegesis: Essays in Honour of Bruce M. Metzger* (Oxford: Clarendon Press, 1981), pp. 213-20.

Epp, E.J., *The Theological Tendency of Codex Bezae Cantabrigiensis in Acts* (SNTSMS, 3; Cambridge: Cambridge University Press, 1966).

—'The Eclectic Method in New Testament Textual Criticism: Solution or Symptom?' *HTR* 69 (1976), pp. 211-57.

—'Toward the Clarification of the Term "Textual Variant"', in J.K. Elliott (ed.), *Studies in New Testament Language and Text: Essays in Honour of George D. Kilpatrick on the Occasion of His Sixty-Fifth Birthday* (Leiden: Brill, 1976), pp. 153-73.

—'A Continuing Interlude in New Testament Textual Criticism?', *HTR* 73 (1980), pp. 131-51.

—'The Ascension in the Textual Tradition of Luke-Acts', in E.J. Epp and G.D. Fee (eds.), *New Testament Textual Criticism, Its Significance for Exegesis: Essays in Honour of Bruce M. Metzger* (Oxford: Clarendon Press, 1981), pp. 131-45.

—'New Testament Textual Criticism Past, Present and Future: Reflections on the Alands' Text of the New Testament', *HTR* 82 (1989), pp. 213-29.

Epp, E.J., and G.D. Fee, *Studies in the Theory and Method of New Testament Textual Criticism* (SD, 45; Grand Rapids: Eerdmans, 1993).

Eybers, I.H., 'Aspects of the Background of the Letter of Jude', *Neot* 9 (1975), pp. 113-23.

Fee, G.D., *Papyrus Bodmer II (𝔓66): Its Textual Relationships and Scribal Characteristics* (SD, 34; Salt Lake City: Utah University Press, 1968).

—'𝔓75, 𝔓66, and Origen: The Myth of Early Textual Recension in Alexandria', in R.N. Longenecker and M.C. Tenney (eds.), *New Dimensions in New Testament Study* (Grand Rapids: Zondervan, 1974), pp. 19-45.

—'Rigorous or Reasoned Eclecticism: Which?', in J.K. Elliott (ed.), *Studies in New Testament Language and Text: Essays in Honour of George D. Kilpatrick on the Occasion of His Sixty-Fifth Birthday* (Leiden: Brill, 1976), pp. 174-97.

—'Modern Textual Criticism and the Revival of the Textus Receptus', *JETS* 21 (1978), pp. 19-33.

—'Modern Textual Criticism and the Majority Text: A Rejoinder', *JETS* 21 (1978), pp. 157-60.

—'A Critique of W.N. Pickering's The Identity of the New Testament Text: A Review Article', *WTJ* 41 (1978/79), pp. 397-423.

—'The Majority Text and the Original Text of the New Testament', *BT* 31 (1980), pp. 107-18.

—Review of *The Byzantine Text-Type and New Testament Textual Criticism*, by H. Sturz, *JETS* 28 (1985), pp. 239-42.

—*The First Epistle to the Corinthians* (Grand Rapids: Eerdmans, 1987).

Ferguson, S.B., D.F. Wright, and J.I. Packer, *New Dictionary of Theology* (Leicester: Inter-Varsity Press, 1988).

Filson, F.V., 'More Bodmer Papyri', *BA* (1962), pp. 50-57.

Flatt, D., 'Thoroughgoing Eclecticism as a Method of Textual Criticism', *ResQ* 18 (1975), pp. 102-14.

Fossum, J., 'Kyrios Jesus as the Angel of the Lord in Jude 5-7', *NTS* 33 (1987), pp. 226-43.

Fuchs, E., and P. Reymond, *La deuxième épître de Saint Pierre. L'épître de Saint Jude* (Geneva: Labor et Fides, 2nd edn, 1988).

Fuller, R.H., *The Foundations of New Testament Christology* (New York: Scribners Press, 1965).

Glatzer, N.N. (ed.), *The Passover Haggadah* (New York: Schocken, 1953).

Goldin, J., 'Not By Means of an Angel and Not By Means of a Messenger', in J. Neusner, *Religions in Antiquity: Essays in Memory of Erwin Ramsdell Goodenough* (Leiden: Brill, 1968), pp. 412-24.

—*Good News For Modern Man: The New Testament in Today's English Version* (New York: American Bible Society, 4th edn, 1976).

Grant, R.M., 'Charges of "Immorality" against Various Religious Groups in Antiquity', in R. Van Den Broek and M.J. Vermasen (eds.), *Studies in Gnosticism and Hellenistic Religions Presented to Gilles Quispel on the Occasion of His Sixty-Fifth Birthday* (Leiden: Brill, 1981), pp. 161-70.

Green, M., *The Second Epistle General of Peter and the General Epistle of Jude: An Introduction and Commentary* (Leicester: Inter-Varsity Press, 2nd edn, 1987).

Greeven, H., (ed.), *Synopse der drei ersten Evangelien mit Beigabe der johanneischen Parallelstellen* (Tübingen: Mohr & Siebeck, 1981).

Gregory, C.R., *Die griechischen Handschriften des Neuen Testaments* (Leipzig: Hinrichs, 1908).

Greijdanus, S., *De Brieven van de Apostelen Petrus en Johannes, en de Brief van Judas* (Amsterdam: Van Bottenburg, 1929).

Grosheide, F. W., *Commentary on the First Epistle to the Corinthians.* (Grand Rapids: Eerdmans, 1953).

Grundmann, W., *Der Brief des Judas und der zweite Brief des Petrus* (Berlin: Evangelische Verlagsanstalt, 1974).

Gunther, J.J., 'The Alexandrian Epistle of Jude', *NTS* 30 (1984), pp. 549-62.

Hanson, A.T., *Jesus Christ in the Old Testament* (London: SPCK, 1965).

Harm, H., 'Logic Line in Jude: The Search for Syllogisms in a Hortatory Text', *Occasional Papers in Translation and Text Linguistics* 3-4 (1987), pp. 147-72.

Hatch, E., and M.A. Redpath, *A Concordance to the Septuagint and the Other Greek Versions of the Old Testament (Including the Apocryphal Books)* (3 vols.; Graz: Akademische Druk, 1975 [1897]).

Hauck, F., *Die Briefe des Jakobus, Petrus, Judas und Johannes* (Göttingen: Vandenhoeck & Ruprecht, 1957).

Hiebert, D.E., 'An Exposition of Jude 12-16', *BSac* 142 (1985), pp. 238-49.

Hill, D., *Greek Words and Hebrew Meanings: Studies in the Semantics of Soteriological Terms* (Cambridge: Cambridge University Press, 1967).

Hodges, Z.C., and A.L. Farstad, *The Greek New Testament According to the Majority Text* (New York: Nelson, 1982).

Holsten, C., *Das Evangelium des Paulus. Teil I* (Berlin: Reimer, 1880).

Horsley, G.H.R., *New Documents Illustrating Early Christianity: Vol. 5, Linguistic Essays* (Macquarie: Macquarie University Press, 1989).

Housman, A.E., 'The Application of Thought to Textual Criticism', in J. Diggle and F.R.D. Goodyear (eds.), *The Classical Papers of A.E. Housman* (Cambridge: Cambridge University Press, 1972), pp. 1058-69.

Howard, G., 'The Tetragram and the New Testament', *JBL* 96 (1977), pp. 63-83.

Hurtado, L., Review of *The Byzantine Text-Type and New Testament Textual Criticism*, by H. Sturz, *CBQ* 48 (1986), pp. 149-50.

Jordaan, G.J.C., *Die beoordeling van woordorde-variante in die manuskripte van die Griekse Nuwe Testament met besondere aandag aan die Evangelie van Lukas: 'n metodologiese studie* (Potchefstroom: Westvalia, 1980).

—'Intrinsieke oorwegings met betrekking tot woordorde-variante', *Humanitas* 8 (1982), pp. 141-50.

Joubert, S.J., 'Language, Ideology and the Social Context of the Letter of Jude', *Neot* 24 (1990), pp. 335-49.

Junack, K., and W. Grunewald, *Das Neue Testament auf Papyrus: 1. Die katholischen Briefe* (ANTF, 6; Berlin: De Gruyter, 1986).

Kelly, J.N.D., *A Commentary on the Epistles of Peter and of Jude* (London: A. & C. Black, 1969).

Kennedy, G., *The Art of Persuasion in Greece* (Princeton: Princeton University Press, 1972).

—*The Art of Rhetoric in the Roman World: 300 BC–AD 300* (Princeton: Princeton University Press, 1972).

Kilpatrick, G.D., 'The Transmission of the New Testament and Its Reliability', *BT* 9 (1958), pp. 127-36.

—'Some Notes on Johannine Usage', *BT* 11 (1960), pp. 173-77.

—*The General Letters: A Greek-English Diglot for the Use of Translators* (London: British & Foreign Bible Societies, 1961).

—'Atticism and the Text of the Greek New Testament', in J. Blinzler, O. Kuss and F. Mussner (eds.), *Neutestamentliche Aufsätze: Festschrift für Professor Josef Schmid zum 70. Geburtstag* (Regensburg: Pustet, 1963), pp. 125-37.

—'An Eclectic Study of the Text of Acts', in J.N. Birdsall and R.W. Thompson (eds.), *Biblical and Patristic Studies in Memory of Robert Pierce Casey* (Freiburg: Herder, 1963), pp. 64-77.

—'The Greek New Testament Text of Today and the Textus Receptus', in H. Anderson and W. Barclay (eds.), *The New Testament in Historical and Contemporary Perspective: Essays in Memory of G.H.C. MacGregor* (Oxford: Blackwell, 1965), pp. 189-206.

—'Style and Text in the Greek New Testament', in B.L. Daniels and M.J. Suggs (eds.), *Studies in the History and Text of the New Testament in Honour of Kenneth Willis Clark* (Salt Lake City: Utah University Press, 1967), pp. 153-60.

—'Κύριος Again', in P. Hoffman, N. Bronx and W. Pesch (eds.), *Orientierung an Jesus: zur Theologie der Synoptikern. Für Josef Schmid* (Freiburg: Herder, 1973), pp. 214-19.

—'Conjectural Emendation in the New Testament', in J.K. Elliott (ed.), *The Principles and Practice of New Testament Textual Criticism: Collected Essays of G.D. Kilpatrick* (Leuven: Leuven University Press, 1990), pp. 98-109.

—'Atticism and the Future of ζῆν', *NovT* 25 (1983), pp. 146-51.

—'KYRIOS in the Gospels', in J.K. Elliott (ed.), *The Principles and Practice of New Testament Textual Criticism: Collected Essays of G.D. Kilpatrick* (BETL, 96; Leuven: Leuven University Press, 1990), pp. 213-15.

—'ΑΓΑΠΗ as Love Feast in the New Testament', in J.K. Elliott (ed.), *The Principles and Practice of New Testament Textual Criticism: Collected Essays of G.D. Kilpatrick* (Leuven: Leuven University Press, 1990), pp. 177-81.

—'Eclecticism and Atticism', in J.K. Elliott (ed.), *The Principles and Practice of New Testament Textual Criticism: Collected Essays of G.D. Kilpatrick* (Leuven: Leuven University Press, 1990), pp. 73-79.

—'Recitative λέγων', in J.K. Elliott (ed.), *The Language and Style of the Gospel of Mark: An Edition of C.H. Turner's 'Notes on Marcan Usage', Together with Other Comparable Studies* (Leiden: Brill, 1993), pp. 175-77.

—'Verbs of Seeing', in J.K. Elliott (ed.), *The Language and Style of the Gospel of Mark: An Edition of C.H. Turner's 'Notes on Marcan Usage', Together with Other Comparable Studies* (Leiden: Brill, 1993), pp. 179-80.

—'Particles', in J.K. Elliott (ed.), *The Language and Style of the Gospels of Mark: An Edition of C.H. Turner's 'Notes on Marcan Usage', Together with Other Comparable Studies* (Leiden: Brill, 1993), pp. 181-84.

Kilpatrick, G.D. (ed.), Η ΚΑΙΝΗ ΔΙΑΘΗΚΗ (London: British & Foreign Bible Societies, 2nd edn, 1958).

King, M.A., 'Notes on the Bodmer Manuscripts', *BSac* 121 (1964), pp. 54-57.

Kistemaker, S.J., *Exposition of the Epistles of Peter and of the Epistle of Jude* (Grand Rapids: Baker, 1987).

Klijn, A.F.J., *A Survey of the Researches into the Western Text of the Gospels and Acts* (Utrecht: Kemink, 1949).

—'Jude 5 to 7', in W.C. Weinrich (ed.), *The New Testament Age: Essays in Honour of Bo Reicke* (Macon: Mercer, 1984), pp. 237-244.

Knopf, R., *Die Briefe Petri und Juda* (Göttingen: Vandenhoeck & Ruprecht, 7th edn, 1912).

Koester, H., 'The Text of the Synoptic Gospels in the Second Century', in W.L. Petersen (ed.), *Gospel Traditions in the Second Century: Origins, Recensions, Text, and Transmission* (Notre Dame: Notre Dame University Press, 1989), pp. 19-37.

Kruger, G. van W., *Die skrywers van die Nuwe Testament* (Stellenbosch: Universiteits-Uitgewers, 1981).

Kruger, M.A., 'ΤΟΥΤΟΙΣ in Jude 7', *Neot* 27 (1993), pp. 119-32.

Kubo, S., 𝔓72 *and the Codex Vaticanus* (SD, 27; Salt Lake City: Utah University Press, 1965).

—'Textual Relationships in Jude', in J.K. Elliott (ed.), *Studies in New Testament Language and Text: Essays in Honour of George D. Kilpatrick on the Occasion of His Sixty-Fifth Birthday* (Leiden: Brill, 1976), pp. 276-82.

—'Jude 22-23: Two Division Form or Three?', in E.J. Epp and G.D. Fee (eds.), *New Testament Textual Criticism, Its Significance for Exegesis: Essays in Honour of Bruce M. Metzger* (Oxford: Clarendon Press, 1981), pp. 239-53.

Lagrange, M.-J., *Etudes Bibliques. Introduction à l'étude du Nouveau Testament: Deuxième Partie. Critique Textuelle. II. La Critique Rationelle* (Paris: Gabalda, 1935).

Lee, J.A.L., 'The Future of ζῆν in Late Greek', *NovT* 22 (1980), pp. 289-98.

Liddell, H.G., and R. Scott, *A Greek-English Lexicon* (rev. and augmented by H.S. Jones; Oxford: Clarendon Press, 9th edn, 1940).

Louw, J.P., *Semantics of New Testament Greek* (Philadelphia: Fortress Press, 1982).

Louw, J.P., and E.A., Nida, *Greek-English Lexicon of the New Testament Based on Semantic Domains* (2 vols.; Cape Town: Bible Society of South Africa, 1989).

Louw, J.P., and E.A. Nida, *Lexical Semantics of the Greek New Testament* (Atlanta: Scholars Press, 1992).

Marshall, H., *New Testament Interpretation: Essays on Principles and Methods* (Exeter: Paternoster, 1977).

Martini, C.M., *Il problema della recensionalità del codice B alla luca del papiro Bodmer XIV* (AnBib, 26; Rome: Editrice Pontificio Istituto Biblico, 1966).

—'Eclecticism and Atticism in the Textual Criticism of the Greek New Testament', in M. Black and W.A. Smalley (eds.), *On Language, Culture and Religion in Honour of Eugene A. Nida* (The Hague: Mouton, 1974), pp. 149-56.

Massaux, E., 'Le Texte de l'épître de Jude du Papyrus Bodmer VII (𝔓72)', in *Scrinium Lovaniense: Mélanges historiques Etienne Van Cauwenberg*, pp. 108-125.

Université de Louvain: Receuil de travaux d'histoire et de philologie, 4ᵉ Série, fasc. 24. (Louvain: Duculot & Gembloux, 1961).

Mayor, J.B., *The General Epistle of Jude* (London: Hodder & Stoughton, 1910).

Mees, M., 'Papyrus Bodmer VII (𝔓72) und die Zitate aus dem Judasbrief bei Clemens von Alexandrien', *Ciudad de Dios* 181 (1968), pp. 551-59.

—'𝔓78 ein neuer Textzeuge für den Judasbrief', *Orient-Press* 1 (1970), pp. 7-9.

Merk, A., *Novum Testamentum graece et latine* (Rome: Editrice Pontificio Istituto Biblico, 9th edn, 1964).

Metzger, B.M., *Chapters in the History of New Testament Textual Criticism* (NTTS, 4; Leiden: Brill, 1963).

—*The Text of the New Testament: Its Transmission, Corruption and Restoration* (Oxford: Clarendon Press, 2nd edn, 1968).

—*A Textual Commentary on the Greek New Testament: A Companion Volume to the United Bible Societies' Greek New Testament (Third Edition)* (New York: UBS, 1st edn, 1971).

—*A Textual Commentary on the Greek New Testament: A Companion Volume to the United Bible Societies' Greek New Testament (Fourth Revised Edition)* (Stuttgart: Deutsche Bibelgesellschaft, 2nd edn, 1994).

—*The Early Versions of the New Testament: Their Origin, Transmission and Limitations* (Oxford: Clarendon Press, 1977).

Milik, J.T. (ed.), *The Books of Enoch: Aramaic Fragments of Qumran Cave 4* (Oxford: Clarendon Press, 1976).

Moir, I., 'Orthography and Theology: The Omicron-Omega Interchange in Romans 5.1 and Elsewhere', in E.J. Epp and G.D. Fee (eds.), *New Testament Textual Criticism, Its Significance for Exegesis: Essays in Honour of Bruce M. Metzger* (Oxford: Clarendon Press, 1981), pp. 179-83.

Moule, C.F.D., *An Idiom Book of New Testament Greek* (Cambridge: Cambridge University Press, 1959).

Moulton, J.H., *A Grammar of New Testament Greek*. I. *Prolegomena* (Edinburgh: T. & T. Clark, 3rd edn, 1908).

Moulton, J.H., and W.F. Howard, *A Grammar of New Testament Greek: II, Accidence and Word Formation. 3 parts* (Edinburgh: T. & T. Clark, 1919-1929).

Murphy-O'Connor, J., 'The Non-Pauline Character of 1 Corinthians 11.2-16?', *JBL* 95 (1976), pp. 615-21.

Neyrey, J.H., *2 Peter, Jude: A New Translation with Introduction and Commentary* (New York: Doubleday, 1993).

Nida, E.A., 'The "Harder Reading" in New Testament Textual Criticism: An Application of the Second Law of Thermodynamics', *BT* 33 (1981), pp. 430-35.

Nolland, J., *Luke 18.35-24.53* (Dallas: Word, 1993).

Novum Testamentum cum Parallelis S. Scripturae Locis Vetere Capitulorum Notatione Canonibus Eusebii (A corrected reprint of Lloyd's 1828 edition of the Stephanus 1550 'Textus Receptus') (Oxford: Clarendon Press, 1889).

Oleson, J.P., 'An Echo of Hesiod's Theogony vv. 190-192 in Jude 13', *NTS* 25 (1979), pp. 492-503.

Omanson, R.L., 'A Perspective on the Study of the New Testament Text', *BT* 34 (1983), pp. 107-22.

Osburn, C.D., 'The Text of Jude 22-23', *ZNW* 63 (1972), pp. 139-44.

—'The Christological Use of 1 Enoch 1.9 in Jude 14-15', *NTS* 23 (1977), pp. 334-41.

—'The Text of Jude 5', *Bib* 62 (1981), pp. 107-15.

—'1 Enoch 80.2-8 (67.5-7) and Jude 12-13', *CBQ* 47 (1985), pp. 296-303.

—'Discourse Analysis and Jewish Apocalyptic in the Epistle of Jude', in D.A. Black, K. Barnwell and S. Levinsohn (eds.), *Linguistics and New Testament Interpretation: Essays on Discourse Analysis* (Nashville: Broadman, 1992), pp. 287-319.

Paap, A.H.R.E., *Nomina Sacra in the Greek Papyri of the First Five Centuries AD: The Sources and Some Deductions* (Leiden: Brill, 1959).

Parker, D.C., 'The Development of Textual Criticism Since B.H. Streeter', *NTS* 24 (1978), pp. 149-62.

—*Codex Bezae: An Early Christian Manuscript and its Text* (Cambridge: Cambridge University Press, 1992).

Parsons, M.C., 'A Christological Tendency in 𝔓75', *JBL* 105 (1986), pp. 463-79.

Petersen, W.L. (ed.), *Gospel Traditions in the Second Century: Origins, Recensions, Text, and Transmission* (Notre Dame: Notre Dame University Press, 1989).

Petzer, J. H., 'The Papyri and New Testament Textual Criticism: Clarity or Confusion?', in J.H. Petzer and P.J. Hartin (eds.), *A South African Perspective on the New Testament: Essays by South African New Testament Scholars Presented to Bruce Manning Metzger During His Visit to South Africa in 1985* (Leiden: Brill, 1986), pp. 18-32.

—'Nuwe-Testamentiese tekskritiek sedert 1881: 'n kritiese evaluering van die belangrikste metoderigtings, met besondere verwysing na die laaste gedeelte van die twintigste eeu' (D Litt dissertation; Potchefstroom: Potchefstroom University for Christian Higher Education, 1987).

—'Shifting Sands: The Changing Paradigm in New Testament Textual Criticism', in J. Mouton, A.G. van Aarde and W.S. Vorster (eds.), *Paradigms and Progress in Theology* (Pretoria: HSRC, 1988), pp. 394-408.

—'Contextual Evidence in Favour of ΚΑΥΧΗΣΩΜΑΙ in 1 Corinthians 13.3', *NTS* 35 (1989), pp. 229-53.

—*Die teks van die Nuwe Testament: 'n inleiding in die basiese aspekte van die teorie en praktyk van die tekskritiek van die Nuwe Testament* (Hervormde Teologiese Studies Supplement Series, 2; Pretoria: Tydskrifafdeling van die Nederduitsch Hervormde Kerk, 1990).

—'Author's Style and the Textual Criticism of the New Testament', *Neot* 24 (1990), pp. 185-97.

—'Eclecticism and the Text of the New Testament', in J.H. Petzer and P.J. Hartin (eds.), *Text and Interpretation: New Approaches in the Criticism of the New Testament* (NTTS, 15; Leiden: Brill, 1991), pp. 47-62.

—'Style and Text in the Lucan Narrative of the Institution of the Lord's Supper (Luke 22.19b-20)', *NTS* 37 (1991), pp. 113-29.

—'Westerse teks, Alexandrynse teks en die oorspronklike teks van die Nuwe Testament: Is daar 'n oplossing vir die probleem?', *Hervormde Teologiese Studies* 47 (1991), pp. 950-67.

—'The Lystre Healing in the Codex Bezae (Acts 14.7-20)', in J.H. Barkhuizen, H.F. Stander and G.J. Swart (eds.), *Hupomnema: feesbundel opgedra aan Professor J.P. Louw* (Pretoria: Pretoria University Press, 1992), pp. 175-187.

—'Reconsidering the Silent Women of Corinth: A Note on 1 Corinthians 14.34-35', *Theologia Evangelica* 26.2 (1993), pp. 132-38.

—'The History of the New Testament Text: Its Reconstruction, Significance and Use in New Testament Textual Criticism', in B. Aland and J. Delobel (eds.), *New Testament Textual Criticism, Exegesis and Church History: A Discussion of Methods* (Contributions to Biblical Exegesis & Theology, 7; Kampen: Kok Pharos, 1994), pp. 11-36.

—Review of *An Introduction to New Testament Textual Criticism*, by L. Vaganay and C.-B. Amphoux, *NovT* 36 (2nd edn, 1994), pp. 287-91.

Plummer, A., *The General Epistles of St. James and St. Jude* (London: Hodder & Stoughton, 1891).

Porter, S.E., *Verbal Aspect in the Greek of the New Testament, with Reference to Tense and Mood* (New York: Lang, 1989).

—*Idioms of the Greek New Testament* (Sheffield: Sheffield Academic Press, 1992).

Porter, S.E. (ed.), *The Language of the New Testament: Classic Essays* (JSNTSup, 60; Sheffield: Sheffield Academic Press, 1991).

Quinn, J.D. 'Notes on the Text of $\mathfrak{P}$72', *CBQ* 27 (1965), pp. 241-49.

Quintilian, *Institutio Oratoria* (trans. H. E. Butler; 4 vols.; LCL; London: Heinemann, 1920–1922).

Rahlfs, A. (ed.), *Septuaginta: Id est Vetus Testamentum graece iuxta LXX interpretes* (2 vols.; Stuttgart: Württembergische Bibelanstalt, 8th edn, 1965).

Reicke, B., *The Epistles of James, Peter and Jude* (New York: Doubleday, 1964).

Robertson, J.A.T., *Studies in the Text of the New Testament* (London: Hodder & Stoughton, 1926).

—*A Grammar of the Greek New Testament in the Light of Historical Research* (Nashville: Broadman, 1934).

Robinson, J.A.T., *Redating the New Testament* (London: SCM Press, 1976).

Rowston, D.J., 'The Most Neglected Book in the New Testament', *NTS* 21 (1975), pp. 554-63.

Schneider, J., *Die Briefe des Jakobus, Petrus, Judas und Johannes: Die katholischen Briefe* (Göttingen: Vandenhoeck & Ruprecht, 1961).

Schrage, W., *Die katholischen Briefe* (Göttingen: Vandenhoeck & Ruprecht, 1973).

Sellin, G., 'Die Häretiker des Judasbriefes', *ZNW* 77 (1986), pp. 206-25.

Sidebottom, E.M., *James, Jude, 2 Peter* (London: Marshall, Morgan & Scott, 1971 [1967]).

Simpson, J.A. and E.S.C. Weiner, *The Oxford English Dictionary* (20 vols.; Oxford: Clarendon Press, 2nd edn, 1989).

Soden, H. von, *Die Schriften des Neuen Testaments in ihrer ältesten erreichbaren Textgestalt* (4 vols.; Göttingen: Vandenhoeck & Ruprecht, 2nd edn, 1911-1913).

Spicq, C., *Agapè dans le Nouveau Testament: analyse des textes* (3 vols.; Paris: Gabalda, 3rd edn, 1966).

Strugnell, J., 'A Plea for Conjectural Emendation in the New Testament, with a Coda on 1 Cor. 4.6', *CBQ* 36 (1974), pp. 543-58.

Sturz, H., *The Byzantine Text-Type and New Testament Textual Criticism* (Nashville: Nelson, 1984).

Testuz, M., *Papyrus Bodmer VII-IX. VII: L'épître de Jude; VIII: Les deux épîtres de Pierre; IX: Les Psaumes 33 et 34* (Geneva: Bibliotheca Bodmeriana, 1959).

Thiele, W. (ed.), *Vetus Latina. Die Reste Der Altlateinischen Bibel: Epistulae Catholicae.* Vol. 26.1, fasc. 6. (Freiburg: Herder, 1967).

Thrall, M.E., *Greek Particles in the New Testament: Linguistic and Exegetical Studies* (Leiden: Brill, 1962).

Tischendorf, C. and C.R. Gregory, *Novum Testamentum Graece* (3 vols.; Leipzig: Hinrichs, 8th edn, 1869-1894).

Traube, L., *Nomina Sacra: Versuch einer Geschichte der christlichen Kürzung* (Munich: Beck, 1907).

Turner, C.H., 'Marcan Usage: Notes, Critical and Exegetical on the Second Gospel', *JTS* 25 (1924), pp. 377-86.

—'A Textual Commentary on Mark 1', *JTS* 28 (1927), pp. 145-58.

—'The Textual Criticism of the New Testament', in C. Gore, H.L. Goudge, and A. Guillaume (eds.), *A New Commentary on Holy Scripture Including the Apocrypha* (London: SPCK, 1928).

Turner, N., *A Grammar of New Testament Greek. III, Syntax; IV, Style* (Edinburgh: T. & T. Clark, 1963-1976).

—'The Literary Character of New Testament Greek', *NTS* 20 (1974), pp. 107-14.

—'The Quality of the Greek of Luke-Acts', in J.K. Elliott (ed.), *Studies in New Testament Language and Text: Essays in Honour of George D. Kilpatrick on the Occasion of His Sixty-Fifth Birthday* (Leiden: Brill, 1976), pp. 387-400.

Vaganay, L., and C.-B. Amphoux, *An Introduction to New Testament Textual Criticism* (trans. from French into English by J. Heimerdinger; Cambridge: Cambridge University Press, 2nd edn, 1986).

Voelz, J. W., 'The Problem of Meaning in Texts', *Neot* 23 (1989), pp. 33-43.

—'Present and Aorist Verbal Aspect: A New Proposal', *Neot* 27 (1993), pp. 153-64.

Vogels, H.J., *Novum Testamentum graece et latine* (2 vols.; Freiburg: Herder, 4th edn, 1949).

—*Handbuch der Textkritik des Neuen Testaments* (Bonn: Hanstein, 2nd edn, 1955).

Walker, W.O., '1 Corinthians 11.2-16 and Paul's Views Regarding Women', *JBL* 94 (1975), pp. 94-110.

Wallace, D.B., 'The Majority Text and the Original Text: Are They Identical?', *BSac* 148 (1991), pp. 150-69.

Wand, J.W.C., *The General Epistles of St. Peter and St. Jude* (London: Westminster Press, 1934).

Watson, D.F., *Invention, Arrangement and Style: Rhetorical Criticism of Jude and 2 Peter* (SBLDS, 104; Atlanta: Scholars Press, 1988).

Weiss, J., *Der erste Korintherbrief* (Göttingen: Vandenhoeck & Ruprecht, 1970 [1910]).

Wendland, E.R., 'A Comparative Study of "Rhetorical Criticism", Ancient and Modern: With Special Reference to the Larger Structure and Function of the Epistle of Jude', *Neot* 28 (1994), pp. 193-228.

Westcott, B.F., and F.J.A. Hort, *The New Testament in the Original Greek. I, Text; II, Introduction and Appendix* (London: Macmillan, 1881-1882).

Whallon, W., 'Should We Keep, Omit or Alter the οἱ in Jude 12?', *NTS* 34 (1988), pp. 156-59.

Wikgren, A., 'Some Problems in Jude 5', in B.L. Daniels and M.J. Suggs (eds.), *Studies in the History and Text of the New Testament in Honour of K.W. Clark* (SD, 29; Salt Lake City: Utah University Press, 1967), pp. 147-52.

Williams, C.S.C., *Alterations to the Text of the Synoptic Gospels and Acts* (Oxford: Blackwell, 1951).

Windisch, H., *Die katholischen Briefe* (Tübingen: Mohr & Siebeck, 1951).

Wisse, F., 'The Epistle of Jude in the History of Heresiology', in M. Krause (ed.), *Essays on the Nag Hammadi Texts in Honour of Alexander Böhlig* (Leiden: Brill, 1972), pp. 133-43.

—'The Nature and Purpose of Redactional Changes in Early Christian Texts: The Canonical Gospels', in W.L. Petersen (ed.), *Gospel Traditions in the Second Century: Origins, Recensions, Text, and Transmission* (Notre Dame: Notre Dame University Press, 1989), pp. 39-53.

Wohlenberg, G., *Der erste und zweite Petrusbrief und der Judasbrief* (Leipzig: Erlangen, 1923).

Zerwick, M., and J. Smith, *Biblical Greek* (Rome: Editrice Pontificio Istituto Biblico, 1990).

Zerwick, M., and M. Grosvenor, *A Grammatical Analysis of the Greek New Testament* (Rome: Editrice Pontificio Istituto Biblico, 4th edn, 1993).

Zuntz, G., *The Text of the Epistles: A Disquisition upon the Corpus Paulinum* (London: Oxford University, 1953).

INDEXES

INDEX OF REFERENCES

OLD TESTAMENT

NEW TESTAMENT

INDEX OF AUTHORS

JOURNAL FOR THE STUDY OF THE NEW TESTAMENT
SUPPLEMENT SERIES

DATE DUE

Printed
in USA

HIGHSMITH #45230